SAINT

SINNER

SINGER

AN UNEXPECTED, REDIRECTED,

RESURRECTED LIFE

BILL NASH

WITH KIM NASH

SAINT SINNER SINGER
Bill Nash with Kim Nash
Edited by Jimmy Nash
Copyright © 2020
William Dowen & Kimberlee Nash

This is a memoir, a work of non-fiction. The authors strive to be objective, but in some cases the author may remember the exact words said by certain people, and exact descriptions of certain effects, events and timeline differently than other people, and for that we apologize and did not intend to cause any ill feeling.

Published by Building Bridges of Hope
For information contact:
info@bbofhope.org
http://www.bbofhope.org

Cover Photo Shot by Rex Kramer
Author Photos by Sebastian Vikkelsoe
Cover Artwork by Cloverdale Productions

ISBN 13:
978-1-7361334-2-2

First Edition 2020

10 9 8 7 6 5 4 3 2 1

DEDICATED TO
MY WIFE AND PARTNER
KIMBERLEE NASH

CONTENTS

Foreword by Hank Moore

MUSIC IS LIFE. MUSIC PROVIDES PURPOSE. Music brings you up, and it makes you reflect. Music is a major part of people's being.

Purveyors of music are important beacons to the public. They tap their talents and energies, thus inspiring audiences of one and many.

One of the great beacons of the Music of Life is Bill Nash. I discovered him in 1974 and remain enthralled by his versatility and understanding of the creative art.

I've known many people in the entertainment world. Some have talent but lack direction. Some have fallen victim to life matters. Others have risen and came back.

What strikes me about Bill Nash is his immense talent, his humble nature and the way in which he genuinely connects with people. His ministry of the best in all of us is done through music and is reinforced by the magnitude of community stewardship.

This book is about widening the scope much further. Whenever we review what made relationships and lives successful, we see that Big Picture thinking occurred. The potentiality of people and organizations is a progressive journey from information to insight to knowledge.

Bill Nash has impacted me because of his warmth, sincerity, know-how, determination and the ability to make you seem to be the most important person in the room, the society and the world.

That's the essence of this humanity-focused book. It had its genesis with making music. It has been articulated by the involvement with Champions Kids Camp and its impact on others.

Much of the wisdom to succeed lies within. People under-perform because they are not given sufficient direction, nurturing, standards of accountability, recognition and encouragement to out-distance themselves. Societies start to crumble when their people quit on each other.

Happy people absorb all the knowledge and insight they can, embracing change, continuous quality improvement and purpose in life.

This book and its author, Bill Nash, embrace the heart and soul of the music of life. Chapters are written in such a way as to be interpreted on several levels. Part common sense and part deep wisdom, they are intended to widen your focus and inspire the visionary that exists within you, the reader.

Bill Nash says that he is an average person who is trying to make a difference. I say that he is an exemplary role model, with advice and insights well worth hearing and taking to heart. I say that he brings out the greatness in us.

- Hank Moore
Futurist--Corporate Strategist™
Author of 13 books.
Nominated four times for the Pulitzer Prize.
Member of seven halls of fame.
Community steward and humanitarian.
Big fan of Bill, Kim, and Jimmy Nash.

Preface

AS I THINK OF THE WORDS I've written down in this book to share my life story, I feel like I should quote the words to Kris Kristofferson's song, "Why Me Lord." In his song he said, "Maybe Lord, I can show someone else, what I've been through myself, on my way back to You."

When my dad was fired from the church he pastored, I was bound and determined to get as far away from "The church" as I possibly could, and I did exactly that! I used this as an excuse for way too long to live a life of debauchery and wild living, just like the Prodigal Son, which you will read more about in the story.

After several failed major label deals, and being consumed only by my desire to be a "star," one day, I met this beautiful gal who totally changed my life. I had never known a love like the one she and I shared almost from the very start of our relationship, and still do now. That led me back to the God of my roots and to the forgiveness I know we are all bound to extend to those who do us wrong. We must forgive in order to be forgiven. Meeting her, my beautiful, talented wife, Kim, was the beginning of my return to God and what He had in the way of plans for me and her and the rest of our lives together. I was thirty-five, and she was nineteen, and her dad wasn't happy, but her mom liked me (moms rule).

Maybe some chapters of our life will ring a bell with you, and you can see what we did, and how God brought us through some really tough times, from dealing with the loss of both our dads, to my son, Billy, having to deal with the dreaded disease, Leukemia, that had invaded his body and threatened his life which occurred while our second son, Jimmy, was still on the way.

Hang on through the wild ride of building a business and then losing it, to pulling up stakes and moving to Nashville to start a new life, and then going through the ups and downs of the music business (the downer lawsuit that threatened our very existence), and the ins and outs of raising two sons, hoping for the dream of a lifetime of writing hit songs for the stars. Then finding a calling beyond music in helping our children at Champions Kids Camp who have survived more trauma than most of us could imagine.

It's all here, the intrigue, the chances we took, and losses and victories that we achieved. This is truly a story you can't make up. I've heard that real life stories are sometimes more bizarre and strange than any fictional stories, with more twists and turns than one can even imagine. Given my story, I totally agree.

P.S. I've included fun facts called "Nash Notes" throughout the book, and "Casting A Light" sections, which are spiritual reflections on my life at my age now looking back.

SAINT
"So then you are no longer strangers and aliens, but you are fellow citizens with the Saints, and are of God's household."
Ephesians 2:19 NASB

SINNER
"But God demonstrates his own love for us in this: While we were still sinners, Christ died for us." Romans 5:8 NIV

SINGER
"Sing to the LORD a new song; sing to the LORD, all the earth." Psalm 96:1 NIV

Chapter One

Where I Come From

I WAS BORN IN SPRINGFIELD, MISSOURI ON September 25, 1944 to Reverend Leslie L. Nash and Clara Augusta Johnson Nash, pastors of an Assembly of God Church there in Springfield.

Dad, Reverend Leslie L. Nash:

My dad was raised on a farm and hails from Lasara, Texas. There were eight kids in dad's family, seven brothers and one sister. Most everyone in those days did have large families and they all started out milking the cows, gathering the eggs and helping plow the fields. As a young boy, Dad rode his pony to the one-room schoolhouse every day. However, one day a lady evangelist came through town and dad was so taken with the

Gospel she preached that, at her encouragement, he decided to go to Bible school at the ripe old age of 13.

Mom, Clara Augusta Johnson:

Mom was born in Fairfield, Texas, located about halfway between Houston and Dallas. Mom and dad married in 1935 in Humble, Texas. My older brother, Dave, came along in 1940, four years ahead of me. Dad moved us to Chariton, Iowa after Springfield to pastor a church there, but a couple years later we moved to a church in Robstown, Texas, just a few miles from Corpus Christi.

As a young girl, my momma was made to practice the piano one hour a day. Her dad, my grandfather (PePaw Johnson), who was a barber by trade, set an old Big Ben Clock on top of the piano and set the alarm for one hour. He could hear her playing in his barbershop up in the front of that old shotgun style building in Galena Park. She didn't dare stop playing because there was the old familiar "switch" that would be employed to motivate her to continue to practice.

Momma told me that, at first, she hated having to sit there and practice, so she offered a prayer up to God asking Him to help her. She said He gave her a love for the piano that she hadn't experienced before her prayer. Thank God for her incredible ability to play piano which served her so well all of her life. PePaw knew what it took to play an instrument because, in addition to being a barber, he himself had learned to play fiddle when he was a young boy around the dining room table in the backwoods of Keechi, Texas, where his siblings all played an instrument. Don't know how my MeMaw learned to play, but she did, and the two of them used to fiddle for dances in the backwoods of East Texas. After a meaningful revival meeting at the Raymond T. Richie Temple in Houston, my Mom's parents both became Christians and decided that they would no longer play for dances, but would only play for church.

One of the ministry things mom and MeMaw did was to hold street services on the town square of the small, East Texas towns like Keechi and Buffalo and on over to Baytown (at this time Goose Creek and Pelli were part of Baytown).

On Saturdays, they would load up the old Model T Ford

and start out at one place in the morning, another at noon, and maybe a couple more by the end of day. Momma would play accordion and sing, and MeMaw would play guitar. Momma somehow learned to play guitar, accordion, and saxophone; she could play just about anything she picked up. Unbelievable!

They both preached about Jesus at the top of their lungs. You must remember that in those days, which is to say the late 1920s, a girl evangelist was a phenomenon. Women were supposed to just be in the background in support of the husband; not mom and MeMaw, though.

Here's a story that I've never forgotten that speaks of mom's intestinal fortitude, or guts in country talk, and determination to preach and sing about Jesus.

They were holding a revival in the backwoods of Fairfield, just out of town under a make-shift edifice they called a brush arbor. The men that supported these meetings would cut down trees and use the branches for the covering, and the sawdust of the trees for the floor.

Even the bootlegger that lived close by helped out and made several good donations in the offering and supplied the coal oil lanterns that they hung up on the makeshift poles to provide light for the evening services; he just liked mom's preaching and singing. One evening on the way to the meeting as mom drove that buggy, and MeMaw rode along in this one-horse carriage, some big guy who didn't approve of women like mom and MeMaw jumped out of the woods from behind a tree and tried to stop them. He said they were evil

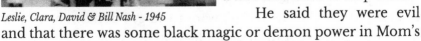

Leslie, Clara, David & Bill Nash - 1945

and that there was some black magic or demon power in Mom's

guitar pick (how ignorant). As he tried to grab the reins of the horse, mom took the buggy whip out of its holder and lashed him a good one and told him to get out of their way in Jesus' name. She said she wasn't going to let anyone stop her from preaching the "Good News" to anyone and everyone who would listen. It so shocked him that it scared him off, and he ran back into the woods, and they drove on to the meeting.

MEMORIES OF ROBSTOWN

Robstown is where my parents first discovered that I could sing. I was between 3 and 4 years old, so I don't remember all the specifics, but I remember singing at my dad's church and watching the folks react with big smiles and laughter. I thought they were laughing at me. Momma said they weren't laughing at me, they were just expressing how much they liked hearing me sing, and it was a laughter of joy, but I just hated to sing in front of the church because of how I perceived their reactions.

The culmination of my "earliest" singing career came about around this time at a small recording studio in Corpus Christi where dad and mom took me to make an acetate record.

They stuck me up there in front of that big old mike and said, "Sing." Since it wasn't in front of the church and it was just them plus the engineer that were the only people around, I suppose they figured I wouldn't mind singing. Well, I balked. They did their best to bribe me like you do a little kid. Nothing. Then after a while my dad decided he must be more firm about it and he gave me a small whack on my backside and said, "Sing Billy."

Well, that started my flood gates opening, and soon in full flow here came the tears and my exclamation, "I don't want to." They turned the recorder on anyway and I did try to sing through my tears, "The B-I-B-L-E, yes that's the Book for me, I stand alone on the cornerstone, the B-I-B-L- E." You should've heard it, but there's no way to put in words the sound of a kid singing and blubbering at the same time.

They stopped the recorder, and Momma then stepped in and said to dad, "If he doesn't want to sing, I don't want you to spank him to make him sing, just let him be." I thought, "Thanks

Momma. What a relief! I don't have to sing anymore," and I didn't sing again in front of the church or anybody until 7th grade.

In order to make enough money to support us and augment the small church offerings, dad and my Uncle Joe bought old used cars and fixed them up and re-sold them. It was their business on the side. You must take into consideration that it was just after World War II when you couldn't buy a new car due to all the materiel (military materials) going into the vehicles necessary for the war effort. So, starting in about 1946, the new cars started coming off the line, and used cars were being traded in by the thousands. Dad and Uncle Joe would buy these used cars sometimes for as little as $10 and fix them up and sell them for $100.

My Uncle Joe was a musician, and he was my inspiration for wanting to play guitar. I remember going to his church in Corpus Christi on Sunday night and watching him play with his church band and listening to him and his wife, my Aunt Ellen, sing. That's where I started to develop my love for the music. The music of those Pentecostal song services was highly inspirational. At the end of the service, I'd step up on the platform and take Uncle Joe's guitar and try to strum it.

Bill & David Nash - 1945

At my dad's church, my earliest remembrances of my love for singing started to develop as I sat and sang along in song service on the front pew of the church on Sunday morning and evening. I remember thinking that whoever was the loudest singer was the best, so I sang as loudly as I could and found myself really enjoying it. I sang songs like, "I'll Fly Away," "Power in The Blood," "Old Time Religion" and on and on. I sincerely enjoyed song service, and there was no pressure of being up in front of the congregation or having to endure the people laughing. It's where what I call the "thread" of what I would be doing the rest of my life began weaving its way into the tapestry of my life.

One day, the Reverend Calvin Cook and his wife came down

from Perryton, Texas (the Panhandle area of Texas) and made an arrangement with my dad.

We would travel to Perryton to pastor his church for the summer months, and he and his wife would in turn pastor ours and do missionary work on the border of Mexico in a small village called La Paloma.

This little village was synonymous with poverty. It all worked out well though, because the Perryton church had a wheat farmer, Mr. George, who had discovered oil on his land by driving out into one of his fields one day and getting this awful, black tar-looking stuff on his wheels. At first, he was extremely annoyed because he wasn't sure how he was going to get that "junk" off of his car. However, it was this "junk" that made him wealthy overnight and allowed him to support the church heavily.

His support ensured dad a really good salary for the summer months. We all got new clothes, shoes and school supplies for the up-coming year. When it was time for school to start again, we would head back to the Rio Grande Valley and resume pastoring in San Benito. This only lasted for two years, but we then continued our missionary work on the border simultaneously while pastoring.

Those were the days we would go to La Paloma on Sunday afternoons to distribute food and clothing sent to us by the Northern churches which we deemed "rummage." In these boxes of used clothing is where we found our own clothes too, so we Nash kids had something to wear to school: never fitting jeans, shirts and sometimes if we were lucky, we would maybe find some shoes. Shoes were the hardest to deal with because if they didn't fit, it was really a pain to keep them on your feet and walk or run.

My first true experience with God came at this time when I was only 5 years old. We were living in the parsonage in San Benito where Dad pastored. There were 2 bedrooms and a screened-in porch where I slept. I was in my bed, and somewhere in the night I had a dream. In this dream, three beings I can only describe as angelic appeared before me, and the one in the middle began to rub my right arm. I remember being confused in the dream and brushing this angel's arm away. Each time I did, the angel would start rubbing my arm again, and the third time, I reached out and pinched the angel, and then all three began to drift off into the distance. The dream was so vivid, and it felt more like real life. I can see it just as clearly today as I did then. I told my mom the next morning about the dream, and she told me it meant that God had set me apart for His purpose, and that I was meant to do something great with that right arm. That was a lot for me to take in at 5 years old, but I've never stopped thinking about that dream, and perhaps momma was right in her interpretation. I went on after all to use that arm to write songs and play guitar. I didn't understand it all then, or even now, but something like that, an experience with the spiritual world, with God, impacted me greatly.

Another vivid memory that is still burned in my mind is the little red garage where dad held services in La Paloma, which was located very close to the Rio Grande River, the dividing line between the United States and Mexico. On those hot, Sunday afternoons we would sing and mama played the accordion and different evangelists would join us from time to time.

I remember seeing a woman with a "goiter." That's what they called this particular growth that she had developed around her neck. Dad prayed for her according to the Bible and Jesus' instructions and it fell off; she was instantly healed.

The news spread fast, and soon you couldn't even get in that little red, unair-conditioned garage. The doors were left open, the side-windows were propped open with two by fours so people could stand outside and see the proceedings, the crowd got bigger and bigger, and the food and clothing from the rummage boxes went fast.

Leslie & Clara Nash with children, Alice, Ellen, Bill, and David

My most "broke" story comes from that time in my life. One night we only had a dozen corn tortillas to eat for dinner for my parents and three of us kids; the baby, Ellen, thankfully, was still taking a bottle. At this particular time, we had just come through a church "split" at the A.G. Church that dad had built with his own hands along with help from church members.

At church on that particular Sunday morning, all we heard was, "We love you, we love you." That night we were voted out thanks to a deacon and his wife who were disgruntled with who knows what. We were told to vacate the parsonage right away, not even a two-week notice, and with no severance pay for dad. BRUTAL, especially for my mom with two babies under the age of five and then there was Dave and me.

The only accommodation near San Benito that were available to us was a shack just out of town near a small body of water known as a resaca. My Grandpa Nash leased this farm land and had a crop in that field and a field hand's shack for living quarters. We moved into it immediately.

LIVING IN POVERTY

I honestly don't know how my mom dealt with this poverty living. She did a good job making this all seem like a game, and we even thought that digging a hole and building a fire in it to bake our potatoes was just a lot of fun. We couldn't even afford tin foil for them. We just took newspaper, several layers worth, soaked them in water, and then wrapped the potato in them (where we got the potatoes, I don't even know). There were mesquite trees all around, so we used their branches to make the fire. Since we couldn't afford to buy anything from the store, we could only use whatever was within reach, literally.

Can you imagine? We had an outhouse for a bathroom (spiders galore) and a Sears catalog for toilet paper. We had no electricity and no running water, just a well we had to hand pump. We had a garden hose connected to the well on a make-shift contraption with no hot water, and that was our "shower." That kind of poverty weighs on a parent, but I had no idea at the time how deep that heartbreak must have been for momma.

In the meantime, dad got a job driving a San Benito school bus in order to carry us over until another church would hopefully turn up. We were so looking forward to moving to a church with a parsonage so we could get out of the shack. Dad did soon get that call and we were moving to Pharr, Texas, about 30 miles west of San Benito.

But one last thing: I'd like to give you some perspective on how small this shack was that we were moving out of. As we were finished loading up our meager possessions to move to Pharr, Grandpa Nash drove up. Right behind him came a big cotton truck driven by a foreman who had his crew of migrant workers with him from Mexico that the government called Braceros. The foreman paid grandpa $5 for the shack, and those men then gathered on all four sides around that shack, picked it up by hand and loaded it on the back of that cotton truck and drove away. What a picture! To this day, it is still vivid in my memory.

SCHOOL DAYS 1954-55
CARNAHAN

Bill Nash 1954 School Photo

We moved to Pharr in the middle of my second-grade year, and along with us we took a Mexican woman named Bertha. One Sunday after service in the little red garage as we all loaded in the car to leave, we noticed a Mexican lady just standing by dad's car door. He said, "Good-bye, see you next Sunday, have a safe journey home." She in turn replied that she had no home and wasn't sure where to go. My dad glanced at my mother and looked back toward Bertha and said, "Get in." So, she climbed in that green '49 model Oldsmobile with no air conditioning and went home with us. She lived with us for many years and was the key to my passable accent in Spanish.

One of my favorite memories was when dad would bring home corn masa, and Bertha would shape this masa into a perfectly round circle and cook it on a hot plate on the stove.

It was a perfect tortilla and boy, was it great tasting. Dave and I would slather a "gob" of butter on it, roll it up and gobble it down, one right after the other. Man, it makes my mouth water to think about her tortillas even now. They were so delicious!

So, one day as I was waiting for my tortilla to come off the stove, I said something about, "el toro," in what I call Gringo

Spanish. In Spanish "el toro" means the bull. Well, she promptly stopped me and said (and I can't write with her accent, but here's my best effort) "No, Beelay, deesay torrrro (meaning roll my r's)."

Well, I did it and spoke it right back to her just like she said it to me. Oh, she was so pleased, and that was the beginning of my speaking Spanish and the training that has served me so well in singing my Spanish music. I carry it with me everywhere I perform. No more Gringo Spanish for me (ha ha).

REVIVAL CENTER CHURCH

Revival Center Church was located between McAllen and Pharr. This is where two of my most meaningful life experiences occurred.

The first took place during a revival meeting at our church where a movie actor, Redd Harper, had come to hold a two-week revival. Redd was the star of one of the first ever Christian movies produced by Billy Graham.

In those days, it was quite a novelty to have a movie play at church. Redd set up the projector and placed the screen on the platform. The movie would play first and Redd would subsequently take the platform and tell the story of his own salvation. At the end of his presentation, he would offer an invitation to anyone who would like to come down front to the altar and give their heart to Jesus Christ.

This particular evening, I was sitting on the back pew of the church. When Redd asked for a show of hands of people who were interested in salvation, I raised my hand. However, when he asked for those that raised their hands to come on down front, I didn't go. I just bowed my head and kept my eyes closed. In a minute or two I felt a tap on my shoulder, and it was Redd. He had walked back where I was seated and asked if I would like for him to walk with me down to the altar. I nodded my head yes and got up, and we walked together. I knelt and prayed the sinner's prayer, "Jesus, I repent of my sins and ask you to be my Lord and Savior." I know I was only 10 years old, but I felt like a huge weight had just been lifted off my shoulders, and I stayed on my knees and cried and prayed for a good long while.

It's one of those spiritual experiences that words cannot describe. It made such an impact on my life, and I'll never forget it.

The second thing that happened at Revival Center Church was the founding of our family singing group, The Nash Family Trio. Momma had decided to start a choir at the church. She made the announcement and several people showed up on that Tuesday evening. Naturally, Dave and I both went along with mom to the church. Ironically, this came about in my tenth year as well, right after my spiritual experience at Redd's revival. Coincidence? I don't think so, but only God knows.

The Nash Family Trio - 1956

I still had my "little boy" voice, which was in the female range. I could sing almost as high as my mom. On the other hand, my brother, Dave, had already experienced his voice change and his range was down in the lower part of the scale; he was a bass.

That night, Momma found out we could both sing, and she then purposed in her heart to experiment with the two of us in a group situation of our own. She had us sing with her at home on a couple of old familiar Gospel songs and it sounded real good. She kind of took her focus off the church choir and began to work up a song or so every week for us to sing as special songs aside from the choir at church.

I was actually just beginning to learn to sing harmony, and I used to sit by the organ player, Mrs. Jeannette Snowden, at choir rehearsal. She taught me to sing the alto part by patiently singing it with me and playing my notes on the organ over and over. So now on Sunday morning, the choir would sing a couple of songs, and then the new Nash Trio would sing a song.

We were really well received by the congregation who began to request that we sing more. So, we started practicing at home each week and learning new songs with our vocal blend. It was kind of amazing, and Dave and I really enjoyed singing together at church. I didn't mind now being up front on the platform because my big brother was right beside me, and momma was seated there closely on the piano bench.

As our repertoire grew and we sang more and more, it required more rehearsal. That's the only part of it that Dave and I used to have a bit of a challenge with. Here we have a momma who is so excited that we sound that good as a vocal group, but on the other hand, we have two teen-age boys who still want to play football and baseball out in the yard and play with our school friends on Saturdays and Sunday afternoons. But my momma knew how much I loved her and that if she said we were going to rehearse, then I would be there to do just that. She and I were kind of pals as well as mother and son. I enjoyed that relationship with her all our lives. I still miss her now. I got my music from her.

So really, when we talk about the Nash Family Trio, we're not talking about a family group that just sat around the house at family reunions and sang for the enjoyment of it. We were the hope of my mother's dreams of getting us up to a higher level in life and out of being a poverty-line family like we had been thus far.

Mom rehearsed us for hours and hours and prayed over us and then started getting us out to civic clubs like the Kiwanis and Lions and Rotary Clubs. This helped us hone our talent in our quest to climb a bit higher on the ladder of success. Those civic clubs were the only ones that were near us there in the Valley. Just about each town had its own club and somehow mom would get us booked to sing in every town up and down the Valley for their weekly luncheons.

Dave and I really enjoyed the good food we got when we did luncheons; that's the only time we ever got full. Most people can't sing on a full stomach, but I could because I learned how to at those wonderful luncheons.

The other perk to that was that Dave and I got to leave school at lunch and go sing. Our teachers at the Pharr-San Juan-Alamo school district were so very supportive of our efforts and were great to help make sure we got our assignments beforehand so we could be out at those times.

Chapter Two

Nash Family Trio Success

A S THE TRIO GAINED MOMENTUM IN the community, we were asked to sing at many more functions and events. We took our Gospel music to lots of different situations, wherever anyone would listen. The music and performances kept coming. We sang for the Winter Texans groups all over the Valley and we sang on a noon-time television talk show on the ABC affiliate in Weslaco hosted by a really interesting character named Ty Cobb (not the baseball player).

We also sang at the CBS TV affiliate in Harlingen for a lady named Jane Raybel who had a noontime show. She herself was a professional clown, and we did several live appearances with her in the Harlingen area.

The most embarrassing moment for us on live TV was the time she waited until the last few minutes of the show to dedicate our last song to a friend of hers who was in the hospital and very close to dying.

She had not previously talked with us about this situation, so after she made the dedication, she then turned to us over on the music set and asked us what we were going to sing. Mom hesitated for what seemed like an eternity in TV time, but finally had to go ahead and announce the name of the song. The song was entitled, "Goodbye World Goodbye." Oh my, what a moment for all of us. But what can you do? There's really nothing you can do at that point on live television but go on and do the song you rehearsed as best you can.

We learned a lot in those early days of TV about performing with TV cameras in your face, and the fact that the camera operator would constantly be moving all around you as he was directed over his head-set by the director in the control room. The Klieg lights were so bright, and all these goings-on could be so distracting.

Bill, Clara, & David Nash At KRIO Radio

Another very important aspect of TV was wardrobe. Mom did a really amazing job of putting together some kind of ensemble of matching outfits on a very meager, almost non-existent, budget. We soon got it down pretty good, and we got lots of compliments on many of our outfits that friends of mom's would sew for us.

We also traveled from one end of the Valley to the other performing for the National Safety Circus. There was always a clown act, a magician act, an animal act, and then us. One thing we learned in this instance was to try never to follow an animal act or a kid act because those two things usually bring such huge response from the crowd that the act after them doesn't have much of a chance of succeeding.

The head guy for this Safety Circus asked us to go on the road on an extensive tour all over the United States starting in September. We thought it was our big break, and for me it meant giving up my high school education as I was about to enter the ninth grade. But this situation turned from being an exciting adventure into a deeply hurtful thing.

The day this guy departed from our last performance, he said he would be calling us to give us the exact dates and times and cities we would be traveling to. He had always kept his word in the past when it came to our business affairs, but this time he just skipped town.

Mom had already enrolled me into correspondence school with the American School, and we were set and ready to get on the road and travel and live our dream due to the success this guy painted to us. We couldn't believe it when he didn't call or write and September came and went, and so did October.

What a heartbreaker, more for my mom than anyone. She just knew this was the big break we had been praying for. Well, I can't explain show business and why some people will carry on and simply lie to young performers and play the "big shot" card.

If we had just asked even a mediocre attorney about these negotiations, he would have asked to see the contract. Contract? Who needs a contract? Isn't everyone as honest as my dad whose "word" was his bond and my grandparents who had always done business that way?

Unfortunately, they are not. I have learned over the years that some of those sayings about contracts are true, like "the devil's in the details" or "the big print giveth and the small print taketh away."

If you are an aspiring artist, please learn this at the beginning of your career. I was told by one of my record producers, Mr. Dave Burgess, Administrator for Hank Williams Publishing Company, that no contract was better than a bad contract, and man, was he right!

There was also a national talent show in those days called the Ted Mack Amateur Hour. Momma found out that it was coming to Houston and auditions had been scheduled for the live performance that was to take place at the Houston coliseum. The winners would later then perform on the nationally televised show. The show was very successful, and many folks had achieved success by being discovered on the Ted Mack

Amateur Hour. Pat Boone was one of the contestants that had gained national prominence appearing on this show wearing his "white bucks" (white buckskin shoes).

So, we packed our suitcases and headed to Houston. Mom felt like this would pick us back up from such a devastating let-down and get us back on track to continue to pursue our big dreams.

We were invited by mom's cousins, Carl and Dorothy Becker, to stay in their home in Houston since we would need to stay in town for the weekend. We would have to drive back and forth to the auditions for the live coliseum show, which was the precursor to the TV show for the top three winners. We were very thankful to our family for providing us their spare bedroom and couches. Indeed, it was a wonderful blessing due to our budget issues.

We auditioned and got picked to perform on that show on a Saturday night at the old, downtown coliseum. The crowd loved us, and we were a hit with the producers of the show, as well. They immediately cleared us to be on the nationally televised Ted Mack Amateur Hour TV show.

What a great night and what a way to bounce back from the disappointing events that had taken place earlier with the National Safety Circus. Carl and Dorothy, along with their kids, my cousins, Linda, Boo and Carol Becker, had a big and exciting celebration with us that night after the show.

Here's a bit of a twist for you: we never got to do that TV show, but unlike the National Safety Circus that fell through, this time, it was because of the most exciting thing that had ever happened to us!

NEW YORK CITY

We had been going to Corpus Christi on a pretty regular basis to sing for the military bases. We met lots of wonderful people in the services who were stationed there far from home. It was very meaningful for us because our family has always been, and still is, very patriotic. After a performance at the Naval base, we were approached by the president of the Grandmothers of America group. She asked if we would consider going to New York City to sing for their national convention at the Statler Hilton Hotel. Mom was all over that. Who knew what might come from that? We ended up back in Pharr telling my dad what we three wanted to do. However, in order to make that happen, dad would have to borrow the money for us to go.

The plan he laid out put us on the strictest of budgets. It was one dollar per person per meal per day, there and back, or we couldn't go. I admit that a dollar went a lot farther in those days than it does now, but still, we were two growing boys who were always hungry, and this was going to be a great challenge for Dave and me. Mom was just excited about it all.

We all agreed, though, and we were invited to ride with one of the grandmothers from Corpus Christi, Granny Ogden, in her new 1957 Edsel. That was definitely an answer to our prayer, because at that time we didn't have a car that could make it all the way there and back. So, off we went. There were no super highways in those days and very few restaurants and gas stations at which to stop. It seems like there may have been a few places here and there, but the roadside restaurant chain, Stuckey's, is the only one that sticks out in my mind. We would stop and eat, stretch our legs a bit, and hit the road again. It took three long days of driving from early morning until a little past evening. Mom, Dave and I stayed in one motel room, and Granny Ogden stayed in her own room. Since I was the smallest one, I seemed to always get the rollaway bed. That was fine; I was on a big adventure.

We finally arrived at our destination at the Statler Hilton Hotel in Manhattan and got checked in. Wow! We were in New York City!

The first night had its own drama to start our New York City adventure. When it was announced at the beginning of the first night of the Grandmothers Convention that the Nash Trio (name later changed to Nash Family Trio) would be performing, the head waiter immediately came to the president of the Grandmothers and asked if the Nashes were union members or not. We obviously were not. We hadn't even heard of a union in the Rio Grande Valley. The head waiter then informed the president that he was going to pull every waiter off the floor if we performed. For a minute, it didn't look good, and here we had traveled so far to sing for these beautiful, absolutely wonderful grandmas. My mom immediately bowed her head

and began to pray. That was what we were taught to do about everything. After a bit of conversation back and forth with the hotel staff, the verdict came down. The union head waiter was told we were there "gratis." "Oh, well, that's a different story," he said, and since we weren't knocking a union act out of a gig, we were cleared to sing.

The Nash Family Trio at the Grandmothers Convention - 1957

It was the truth. Mom had agreed to accept a "free-will" offering from the grandmothers that would be collected after we sang. We were relying on our faith that we would get a meaningful offering to offset our travel and hotel expenses. I don't even remember how much it was, but it was certainly welcomed, and that technicality got us past the union.

We were really well-received by the crowd that night. I remember the little grandmas coming up to me, and every one of them wanted to hug me. I was just tall enough to get smothered in each one of their bosoms, which almost suffocated me each time I got a hug. I did my best to hide behind my big brother or mom, but it was no use. Oh my, I can still remember dreading the smothering hugs. I did appreciate their accolades, though, and I realized that I reminded each one of them of their grandkids back home.

It was actually kind of funny to my brother who would laugh at me. He was four years older, 17, and was already 6'1". He grew up all at once when he was between 12 & 13, tall and skinny.

Before the night was over, a little grandma came up to us and asked if we would like to have her tickets to the game shows over at NBC-TV there in Manhattan. Since we had no daytime plans, mom said sure. She handed us three tickets that she had written for in advance, and we decided to go the next morning. We got to NBC and were directed to the studio where Gene Rayburn's *Dough-Re-Mi* show was to be televised. We sat down and watched the whole musical show which was NBC's answer to CBS' *Name That Tune.*

After the thirty-minute show ended, we were hurrying out to the next game show just down the corridor when one of the spotters for the *Dough-Re-Mi* show stopped us and asked if we wouldn't mind staying around for Mr. Rayburn to interview mom to be a contestant on the next show.

I've always said that I don't know how they picked us out of that crowd of people because we were dressed like everyone else in New York (lol); Dave and I were in jeans, cowboy boots, red shirts with white flowers embroidered on the front and back, and our little white string ties which totally rounded out our dashing ensemble. Mom was just in a simple

> *Nash Note*
>
> Most of you probably know Gene Rayburn better as the host of the *Match Game* show in the '60's.

dress-up dress with high heels. We found out later that's how NBC got their contestants in those days. They had spotters who would scan the audience for people they thought would make interesting guests.

We reluctantly said OK, but told the spotter we were sort of in a hurry to get to the *Hugh Downes Show.* He said it wouldn't take long. So, we sat back down in the bleacher-type seating they had set up, and in a few minutes, Gene Rayburn came back out along with the music director of NBC, Mr. Paul Taubman.

Since we were sitting in the seats closest to where Mr. Rayburn came out from his dressing room, we were first in line to be interviewed. Dave stood up from his position on the first rung of the bleachers and he sort of towered over Mr. Rayburn. Dave then proceeded to stick his hand out to shake Mr. Rayburn's hand and he said, "Hi, I'm Dave Nash from Pharr, Texas, and this is my mother and my brother. Would you like to hear us saaannnng?" That's South Texas talk for "sing."

Well, Mr. Rayburn was sort of taken aback and stepped back one step to analyze the situation. He pondered my brother's question for a moment, then he shrugged his shoulders and said, "Yeah."

Mom and I had no idea Dave was going to do something like that, but we just followed his lead. They rolled a piano out there where we were. We took our places around it with mom seated

The Nash Family Trio - 1956

on the piano bench. Mom started the intro to the song; I think it was "Looking For A City." That was one of our most popular, up-tempo Gospel songs, and we just sang it like we had sung it a thousand times before at the top of our lungs.

When we finished, Mr. Rayburn just stood there for the longest few seconds, and then asked us to stick around a minute while he and Paul Taubman stepped over to the side to talk privately. They must have talked for 10 minutes, and we were getting antsy to get out of there and get to the *Hugh Downes Show*.

They returned to us at the piano and Mr. Rayburn popped the question, "Would you all sing on our TV show tomorrow morning?"

We couldn't believe it! The Nashes from Pharr, Texas on national television, NBC TV? We were on stun! Naturally, mom said yes as she somehow held back all the pent-up excitement that was now welling up inside her. We couldn't wait to get back to the hotel and call dad to tell him the news. We were going to sing on the *Dough-Re-Mi* show at 9:00 a.m. the next morning.

In those days you had to call the long-distance operator and give her the number, and she dialed it for you. When dad answered the phone, we blurted the news out to him. He was in shock and partial disbelief that such good fortune had come our way, but he finally grasped the moment and celebrated with us over the phone.

After hanging up from us, dad promptly started calling all our friends and neighbors and anyone else he could think of. The folks that got the word all met at our local café on Cage Street in Pharr called the Junction Cafe, which is still there to this day. They put a small TV set up high on a shelf over the counter and the next morning the place was packed to watch us on TV.

Everyone was excited back in Texas, and we were excited in New York. So, the next morning, we showed up at NBC and mom sat on the panel as a contestant on the show with two other participants. During the on-air interview conducted by Mr. Rayburn, it came out that mom played piano and sang with her two sons. Then Mr. Rayburn asked her if she would mind singing right then. Of course, it was all pre-planned, but she acted like it was a spur of the moment thing.

She got up from where she was seated on the panel and came over to the piano where Dave and I were already positioned to sing. She sat down and started the introduction to the song and we just sang like we had for the past three years at all those churches, civic clubs and countless other places.

I must say we have never sung better, never been more inspired. How could you not be inspired when you are now singing on national television to a nationwide audience as opposed to singing in a little, red garage to a small crowd on a hot and muggy Sunday? It was a moment in time never to be forgotten.

When we finished our song, the studio audience erupted in applause and just kept on applauding so loudly as they stood to their feet. We thought they would never stop. Mr. Rayburn was really caught off guard with the audience reaction, and so were we, but it was just a wonderful and memorable experience for me as a 13-year old. If nothing more than that alone had taken place, it would have been worth it all; the long trip, the tight food budget, the one hotel room with two double beds and a roll-away. Plus, everyone back home was so proud of us because mom had said in her interview that we were from the great town of Pharr, Texas. No one else from Pharr had ever been on national television and our hometown was sincerely proud. I don't really know how mom walked back over to the set where the other panel members were sitting or how she kept from just flying away, but she had to play out the contestant part.

Dave and I were hoping that she would give the correct answer to the song question she was asked, but she didn't know a lot about pop music since all she had ever sung was Gospel music. She missed the title to the song, "The Bridge Over the River Kwai," from the big movie of the day.

Too bad, so sad, sorry dad, no dough. It would have been like rain on a desert for us.

So, the show ends and everyone is coming around shaking our hands and giving us accolades when Mr. Rayburn says for us to come with him and Paul Taubman and hurry it up. They whisked us to the elevators and down to the front doors of NBC where a shiny, black Cadillac limousine was waiting for us.

We were off to somewhere, and where that was we didn't have a clue. We sped off, and several city blocks later the driver pulled up in front of a very large, old church, and over the top of the archway at the front door we saw a big sign that read, "Columbia Records."

At the time I had no idea how significant that was, and I also had no idea who the stars were that recorded for that label. All I knew was that we were taken there by the music director of NBC Television and Mr. Gene Rayburn, star of one of the game shows at NBC TV. They obviously had some major clout because they got us in with less than a day's notice and in the middle of a recording session that was in progress.

We walked in and met a man named Ernie Altschuler. He was the producer of several of the world's biggest stars, including Perry Como. We always watched Perry when he would do the Kraft Television Specials, and we so admired his beautiful voice.

Well, that particular day, Mr. Altschuler was producing a session on a guy who was singing a song about a tangerine. I thought to myself, "That's strange, he's singing about a tangerine and we live in a house in the middle of an orchard in the Valley that has a few tangerine trees."

Mr. Altschuler left the control room and went into the recording studio and asked this artist if he would mind taking a short break and let the Nash Family make a demonstration tape.

We still had no clue what this all meant or who that guy playing the piano was. I had never even been inside a real, professional recording studio except that one in Corpus Christi where my dad had to swat my bottom to get me to sing.

It turns out the artist was so very nice and agreeable and got up from the piano. As we made our way in, we were introduced to him; his name was Dave Brubeck. I sincerely do wish I had known who he was at that time so I could have gotten his autograph. His song, "Take Five," is one of my all-time favorite jazz numbers now.

So, mom sat down at the piano and had her own mike, and Dave and I shared a mike. They were both made in Germany by a company named Telefunken. We noticed everything like that. We had never seen a strange name on a mike like that. We found out later that was one of the best brands of microphones in the world. We sang a few songs and ran straight through them, and afterwards we got back in the limo and headed back to NBC and then our hotel.

The rest of the trip was pretty much just singing at night in the ballroom for the little grandmas. When the convention ended, we climbed back into that new Edsel of Granny Ogden's and headed back to Texas. We arrived home, and Dave and I went back to school and couldn't quit thinking about New York and wondering when or if we would ever hear anything about our little demo tape we made at Columbia Records.

After a couple of months went by, we finally got a call from Gene Rayburn telling us that we were being sent contracts from Columbia Records to record for them. We were very excited and were waiting impatiently for the contracts to arrive. In those days, it was all snail mail, and we hurried to the mailbox every day.

Finally, the contracts arrived and I'm sure mom and dad tried their best to understand all the "legalese" embodied in their pages, but since we couldn't afford an attorney, it didn't matter anyway. We just signed them and sent them back to New York.

This was obviously a lot bigger deal than we had ever had before and a real shot at taking our music to the nation and the world.

The date was subsequently set for our recording session at Columbia Recording Studios in New York City, New York.

Once again, we were on a limited budget. There would later be an advance on royalties, but for the moment, we had to come up with the budget to get back to New York, and that meant three days of driving to get there, once again, and obviously three days back. It took a full six days of hard driving.

My folks started praying and thanking God for opening this big door for the Nash Trio to take our Gospel music to the world, and they were asking God to supply the means for us to get there. We had a preacher friend who was an evangelist named C.M. Ward. He had held revivals for dad several times and dad was telling him about our need. He said he had preached at the Rock Church, a famous church in Manhattan, and knew the pastor, Pastor Vick. He set it up for us to have a week-long revival at the Rock Church where an offering would be taken for us after each service, and in this way our need would be supplied. The church also had guest quarters where we could stay on the third floor of their building. What a blessing, thank you Jesus for providing the means through the offerings they would take at each service in New York.

Chapter Three

COLUMBIA RECORDS

ONCE AGAIN, WE SET OUT FOR New York. We were up at the crack of dawn to get in as much driving as possible in one day. We always started out our car trips by reciting the 23rd Psalm, the 91st Psalm and the 103rd Psalm. Then dad would pray. That's how we always did it; I have now resumed that practice with my own family when we get in the car to go anywhere.

The radio was the big deal when we traveled, and in certain areas where we could get no reception, momma would read true stories to us for miles and miles. We would listen to the Reverend J. Charles Jessup who broadcast from Ciudad Acuna, Coahuila, Mexico. That station had 100,000 watts of power and in the early evening and at night you could pick it up mostly anywhere across the U.S.A.

As we headed up the East Coast, we were all pumped about the recording session, and also that we were set to sing and stay at the Rock Church. I have such fond memories of that beautiful church and that wonderful Pastor Vick who treated us like royalty. When we arrived there at the church, they got us situated in the quarters they reserved for evangelists and missionaries, and it was very nice. Church services were held in the two-level auditorium and we sang on the second level and were able to look out over the crowd. Our living quarters were on the third floor. The next time I'm in New York City, I would really like to find this church again just for old time's sake. It's one of the things on my bucket list.

New Yorkers were known to be a bit more conservative in their church services, but these New Yorkers were a very lively and receptive congregation and seemed to really love our music and dad's preaching. They were quite more demonstrative and welcoming to our style of music.

As Monday morning rolled around and we headed over to Columbia Studios to record, once again, the question arose of us being in the union. We obviously were not union members, and Mr. Rayburn was very knowledgeable about these things since he himself had to be a member of AFTRA, American Federation of Television and Radio Artists, to be on NBC TV. He came to us and so graciously offered to be our manager and also offered to front the money to pay our initiation fee and applicable fees to join the union and thereby satisfy their requirements in order for us to record. We took him up on his offer (what else could we do?), and we became full-fledged members of AFTRA in New York City...the BIG TIME!!! We were now professional. I will always appreciate what this wonderful man did to help our family from Pharr who was just trying to work their way up the ladder to a better and richer life.

While we were in New York, we also needed to get an album cover photo of the three of us. We went to the Columbia Records Photo Studio and met Henry Parker. He was working out what kind of shots to get when he came up with the idea of white pullover shirts with ascots for Dave and me. Mom had a white blouse that went under her black dress, and the pictures came out great. Now we were ready to go to the studio and record. I don't even remember being nervous or at all concerned about the recordings. I had my mom and my big brother, and I depended on them a lot. It seems incredible, now that I've been recording all my life, that we could do that entire session in only one day, but that's what we did.

We cut 15 songs with a bass player and a rhythm guitar player. Those guys were great, and I'm so sorry I don't even recall their names. We did take a break in the middle of the session to have a hoagie sandwich. We had never heard of a hoagie at that time, but it was sure tasty. Mr. Taubman came by to check on us, and he could see that we had been working very hard and needed a bit of a break. So he sat down at the piano and proceeded to play a tune for us and intentionally missed the top note of the chorus and verse of that song and acted like it was right.

It is, obviously, one of those location jokes again--you would have to have been there. We just laughed and laughed. It was a very needed respite from the singing and playing.

He then invited us to come to his restaurant called The Penthouse, which overlooked Central Park. We didn't have the appropriate dress clothes most of his clientele usually wore to a fancy place like that, but he said not to worry about it. So we dressed in our album cover wardrobe, the pullover white shirts with ascots, which to us was quite smartly dressed. We didn't see

any chicken-fried steak on the menu, which was the greatest thing you could possibly order back home. It was only steaks and stuff with very large price tags. We could have eaten for a month on what that meal for the four of us cost. Mr. Taubman was so gracious to give us that wonderful meal and experience. He came over to our table and we had to

Nash Family Trio in NYC - 1957   ask him what he recommended for us to order since we saw those prices and they didn't have anything like Junction Café did in Pharr. He suggested the New

York strip, and that's what we ordered. That was the first time in our lives my brother and I even knew that there was any other kind of steak in existence. I remember Grandma Nash with her meat cleaver beating that old thin piece of meat we called steak. She would beat it and beat it until it surrendered, I guess, and that was how she tenderized the steak before it was dipped in batter and fried. Thank you, Mr. Taubman! He was so understanding of two boys from the country and our first time in the big city eating a big city meal.

The only time we got stuck during that first session in New York City was during one of the songs we'd sung forever and we had to do it 15 times before finally getting it right. It's called a studio block where you zone out for a minute and can't seem to get it together for a while even on material you've done over and over again.

The studio is a different "animal." You just have to take a break and relax, then go again and it will come to you. All the other songs were done in mostly one take which is just a phenomenon which I've never achieved again in my life.

As I think back about my mom and her piano playing, there she was playing that grand piano with two highly accomplished musicians from New York who were hired by Ernie Altschuler for our session. Columbia and Ernie only hired the best and greatest of musicians and my mom was actually the leader of that session and was in their league as a musician. In retrospect, I am so proud of my mother for having the self-discipline it took to achieve that level of musicianship. There she was, recording with the best in the world.

We finished the session and we were absolutely exhausted, physically and emotionally. I had never sung that much for that long at any given time and my voice was very tired. As I look back on it all, I recall that that is the last time I ever hit some of those notes I used to hit in my "little boy" voice without going into my falsetto. My voice began doing that age-old thing all boys' voices do. It never did dip down deep like Dave's voice, but it did start to change and my voice cracked on every third or fourth word. How frustrating!

Be that as it may, we finished our revival at the Rock Church that week and headed home. We owe that Church a lot, and it really helped make all that possible. They even invited us back a few months later because they really seemed to like us and my dad's preaching.

Our first album, "Lord Hear Us Sing," was so successful that Columbia immediately asked us for a second album. On our third trip to NYC that year, Mr. Taubman got us invited to sing on the courthouse steps of New York City, an outdoor event that he was helping put together. That was when we had the great honor and privilege of working with Cab Calloway, the famous Vaudeville performer and with Bobby Colt, a new, hot artist of the day. That album also got us invited to do several other shows across the country.

We were asked to be on the Eddy Arnold television show, which was filmed at NBC Studios in the Merchandise Mart Building in downtown Chicago. It was the replacement show for the Red Foley TV show, which went into summertime hiatus. We arrived there on a Tuesday and rehearsed every day, all day long until Friday when we came in later to do the actual taping. Then we had to wait around until the show went on the air in case there was any default on the part of the videotape. This videotape was the newest thing out on the market, and they didn't trust it totally yet, so in case the tape should break, we would have to sing live on the broadcast. This was pretty early on in the days of television. That Ampex Video machine was as big as a car. The show would emanate from Chicago to be broadcast nationwide. It aired in New York City at 6:00 am.

It was quite a great time for me to get to stand around just behind the cameras and watch Eddy Arnold work. He sang a brand new song that day called, "It's a Big Land." I never will forget how smoothly he would go down and hit the lower range notes in that song, and then come back up with that smooth crooning voice he had. I would get those goose bumps just hearing him sing. He was so very nice to us, a very genteel Southern gentleman. He had just been given a big award from RCA Records for many years of hits, and we stood around and talked and joked with him.

Nash Note 🎵

I was so young at the time that I didn't recall certain figures. My brother, Dave, was 4 years older than me though, and he reminded me that the day they presented our first album, the distributors ordered 13,000 copies, which was quite a lot for an initial order of a gospel album on an unknown family. He also reminded me that shortly after the release, we received a feature in Seventeen Magazine on the strength of our sales and the subsequent press push by Columbia.

This was also the first time I was introduced to riding a train into the city to go to rehearsal or work each morning. We still had not received a big royalty check yet from Columbia (it can take years sometimes), but this event produced another miracle in God's provision to make it possible to do this show. There was a Winter Texan from the Chicago suburbs who attended our church when she came to the Rio Grande Valley as the winter got too cold for her. She opened her home to us for the duration of our TV taping in Chicago. She lived just across the Illinois and Indiana line.

We hoped this opportunity to appear with Eddy Arnold on national television would help get us bookings that actually paid real money so we wouldn't always have to depend on being able to stay with friends or relatives or depend on booking a church where they took an offering. We were learning that, even though we were singing Gospel music and for all the right reasons due to our love for God and Jesus, there was still another aspect to this whole dynamic, and that was the business side of things that had to be fulfilled.

Unfortunately, neither mom nor dad had much of a business

background to help embolden them to ask for a fair amount of money or even to reach out to a booking agent who would know how to ask on our behalf. The other challenge we always faced was the fact that we lived in the southern-most tip of the United States just seven miles from the dividing line between the U.S. and Mexico.

It was 350 miles north to Houston, roughly 230 miles to San Antonio and 500 miles to Dallas. It was a tremendous disadvantage to live so far from all destinations that had cities and venues we should be cultivating to sing in. That's why so many music people gravitated towards Nashville. There's about an 800-mile radius with cities around Nashville you could book into where large amounts of people live, people that you need to reach with your music to make your trip financially viable and promote your group.

We've said many times that we should have moved to Nashville at that time. I have this vivid memory of Ben Speer, head of one of the most famous Gospel families of all time, who happened to be at the Ryman Auditorium the morning we were pulling out of Nashville to head back to Pharr. He saw our record album in the back window and he stopped and introduced himself.

He asked to see the album and as he looked at the cover and perused the credits on the back liner, he paused for a moment and said, "Why don't you guys stay over and come sing at our big concert tonight?"

We looked at dad and then back and forth at each other. Would we stay or not? We should have stayed, but hindsight is 20/20. Dad was so loyal to his congregation back home that his decision was to get on home to be back in time for Sunday services at Friendly Chapel.

There's no way to know the outcome of an invitation like that, but we have wished a thousand times that we would've stayed and sung. Only God knows the "what if" factor.

One of the other great things we did get to do on the strength of our first Columbia album was to perform on the Louisiana Hayride in Shreveport, LA. This was a live show that resembled the Grand Ole Opry in Nashville, and all the country stars performed on it. We received an invitation and set the date, but for some reason which I can't remember, the only way we could make the show on Saturday night in Shreveport and get back to Pharr for Sunday service was to fly. My mother had a great friend, Mrs. Stinnett, who owned the Stinnett Jewelry Store on Main Street there in Pharr. It just so happened that she had a friend who had a small private plane who offered to fly us there if we would pay for the gas.

That was really not within our budget, but Mrs. Stinnett said she had family in Shreveport and would be happy to fly with us and pay half of the gas for the plane. What a great gesture and what a great friend she was.

So the day came and we headed to the McAllen Airport and loaded up our stuff on that little plane and flew to Shreveport. I know this sounds crazy now to say that all I mostly knew about in those days were the rock 'n roll stars that I listened to on our rock station in McAllen, KRIO Radio.

So, when we got to the auditorium to do the Hayride, we met the other acts that were also going to be on the show. As I look back, I really can't believe that we were opening for two of the greatest legends of all time, Minnie Pearl and Roy Acuff, the father of Country Music. The other act was a disc jockey who was soon to become a star: Nat Stuckey was his name, and his first hit was, "Don't Give Me No Plastic Saddle."

As I type their names, it makes me want to stand up and hold my hand over my heart and give it a moment of silent prayer. I have wished a million times that I had known who they really were and gotten a whole roll of pictures taken with each of them. And were they nice? Oh my, yes, and a thousand times yes. Minnie's husband was a pilot and he flew her in their plane to all her performances. Mr. Acuff and his band traveled in two cars, both Chrysler Imperials. After we opened the show, we hung around backstage to watch and listen to the rest of the show.

When Mr. Acuff, obviously the headliner, started to close the show, he looked around and we heard him say, "Where is that Nash Family? I really like them."

We were stunned and we ran back out on stage. He said for us to sing with him on the closing number, a Gospel song written by A.P. Carter, head of the Carter Family. The song was, "Will The Circle Be Unbroken."

Mr. Acuff loved the family aspect of our group and the close harmony we had. After the show, he took Dave and me out back of the theater to show us his cars. He took such a liking to us; it was unbelievable.

He opened the back door to that 4-door, white Chrysler Imperial, and stuck his hand in to touch the white leather seat. He turned to us and said, "This leather is just so soft and it's so comfortable. I just ride here in the back and relax."

Dave and I are both big car nuts anyway and the Imperial was the very top of the line in the Chrysler lineup, so we could only imagine what it would be like to fly down the road in that Imperial like Roy Acuff. I can still picture that big bass fiddle on top of the lead car in that procession...a humorous and wonderful memory.

Meeting Roy and Minnie at such a young age is surely one of my greatest childhood memories.

We left the theatre that night and little did we know that Minnie Pearl and her husband were staying in the same hotel as we were. When we went down to breakfast the next morning, there they were in the restaurant, Minnie and her husband. They invited us to join them for breakfast and we got to visit with them. We talked mostly about their airplane and flying and stuff. Dave was and is still a big airplane nut.

The memory of that show and the Louisiana Hayride are big in my mind. About this same time, Bill Anderson, or Whisperin' Bill, as he's better known, came to Houston as the headliner for a Grand Ole Opry show starring him, Charlie Louvin, and The Nash Family Trio. We were the show opener for these two famous Country acts.

I was so paranoid in those days about my breath. I don't know why, but I was. I bought a package of Clorets, the breath chewing gum, and while we were waiting for the curtain to go up for us to open the show, I managed to get most of those little gum squares in my mouth just to be double-dog sure I had good breath, even though at the Houston coliseum the audience was never going to be that close to me on stage. Go figure.

As I was pacing around backstage, one of Bill Anderson's band members took a look at me and said, "Hey, your teeth are green, what's the matter?" I was so embarrassed, and I told him it was just Clorets, but I ran to the water fountain and rinsed my mouth. I was just 15 or so and still don't know what I was thinking; it may have had something to do with the nerve thing that can happen when you are on a big show like that.

The next thing that happened was that Dave showed up in gray Hush Puppy shoes to wear on stage. They had paint splotches on them and were just plain ugly. Mom and I severely chastised him. I don't know if he had another pair of shoes with him or not, but as I recall, he walked out on stage in those shoes. It didn't seem to matter to the audience, though.

We got a great reception from the crowd and did our part of the show and came off stage. We were met there by a guy from the coliseum merchandise sales team who historically went out in the crowd and sold albums for the acts performing on stage. He said it would be a 25/75% split, 25% for him and 75% for us. So we loaded him up and sent him out there with a whole arm-load of our albums. He was back in no time to grab more albums. He even came back one last time to get even more. He sold us out of albums and made us all a very nice bonus we didn't expect. We had just never had any experience like that, especially marketing albums one-on-one to that big of an audience.

The Second Columbia Album for the Nash Family Trio

After that, our producer, Ernie Altschuler, thought it best that we record our second album in Nashville instead of New York. He told us who our new producer would be, Mr. Don Law, producer of some of the biggest stars in Country Music, stars like Johnny Cash, Marty Robbins and many more. We then started working on songs for that album and started planning the trip.

In the meantime, Columbia decided to have us come in for what they called the Disc Jockey Convention in the month of October. This would have been in 1960 because the second album came out in 1961. I remember traveling from Pharr the first day up to Houston and staying the night with my mother's younger brother, Uncle David Johnson, and his wife, Aunt Helen. It took another couple of days to reach Nashville from there, but it sure was nice to break up such a long trip with a little rest at "Unkie", as Dave and I affectionately named our uncle, and Aunt Helen's. We finally did make it all the way to Music City, USA, Nashville, Tennessee.

CASH, CARTER, AND CARL

One good thing that came about at that time was that Columbia sent us a check for $1,250 in royalties from our first album, so that helped on expenses for the trip.

We stayed in the Noel Hotel, just a few blocks from the Andrew Jackson Hotel, which was the host hotel for the convention.

For three full days, shows were put on by all the major record companies to showcase their artists, the established ones as well as the new, up-coming ones, to the disc jockeys that were there from all over the nation. It was really quite a time with fans and disc jockeys from both coasts and everywhere in between.

The show we were on was done at the original home of the Grand Ole Opry, the Ryman Auditorium. It has quite a history and now we were going to be a part of the Grand Ole Opry "Columbia Records Parade of Stars" show for all the disc jockeys. Several things stand out in my memory: first of all, Jimmy Dean was there and he happened to have the hottest TV show at that time on national TV, so he really got the attention. I remember him at rehearsal taking an old-fashioned flash bulb from a Kodak Camera and inserting it into his nose and saying, "I have a code" (cold). We thought that was hilarious. He was never at a loss for something funny to do or say; he was a really friendly guy to all of us at rehearsal.

The next thing that was such an incredible honor was that the Jordanaires, Elvis's back-up group, were going to be our back-up group on the show. They filled in the background music where real strings and such might have been played if we had had an orchestra. We had the regular Grand Ole Opry band plus the Jordanaires. I wish I had a video of the Jordanaires and that great Opry band backing us up. It was a night to remember.

The last thing I recall about that show was that Johnny Cash and June Carter and family were the closing act. However, the opening act and emcee of the show was a Columbia Records star named Carl Smith. Columbia had released an album with 12 of its biggest stars including Carl Smith, the Chuck Wagon Gang, Johnny Cash, Marty Robbins, Lefty Frizzel, the Nash Family Trio and several others.

Bill & Clara Nash with Flatt & Sruggs

So that day at the show Carl was once again the emcee for all of us. The "kicker" to this last remembrance is that Carl Smith used to be married to June Carter who was now married to Johnny Cash. As it came time for Johnny to go on, Carl started his introduction and said a couple of things about Johnny and then ended it with a crazy remark about how he had been married to June first, and he knew her better than Johnny did. Well, you should have seen it all go down.

Johnny, who was standing in the wings beside June on one side, and me on the other, was waiting to go on and sing. When Carl made his little remark, I watched in shock as Johnny just took off running toward Carl at center stage.

Carl was standing on that famous middle part of the Grand Ole Opry stage that was later cut out and transplanted to the new Grand Ole Opry House adjacent to the Opryland Hotel. Carl had been keeping watch over his shoulder monitoring Johnny's reaction, and when Carl saw Johnny take off toward him, Carl took off running to the opposite side of the stage. These two men, great Country Music Stars that they were, reverted to boyhood, and played chase around and around that stage with us and the audience all looking on wondering what would be the outcome.

Well, Johnny never caught Carl and finally quit chasing him. He stopped, put on his guitar, and walked to center stage all out of breath. I don't remember him saying a word, he just started into his first song and was soon joined on stage by June Carter and the rest of the Carter Family.

I was standing right beside Don Law, our producer, and when Johnny hit his low note on the song "Were You There?," Don commented to everyone around us in an admiring voice, "He's hot today, he's hot." Man, what a show, what a time in a teenager's life to be around Country Music royalty like that and get to know some of those folks.

We ran into Johnny later at the Noel Hotel as he got off the elevator. He just simply smiled and said a friendly greeting, "Hi."

I got to work with him a couple of times later in life and he always was that same, genteel guy with that down to earth, humble spirit. That's one of the things that made him so great.

I also got to meet people like Jean Shepherd and Hawkshaw Hawkins. They were the hot couple in the news because of their tempestuous marriage and goings on. In fact, the day we met them at the Andrew Jackson, Hawkshaw had a Band-aid over his

Clara Nash with Marty Robbins

eye from where she had whacked him good for staying out too late or some kind of thing like that. We thought it was kind of funny, and it was all over the social, word-of-mouth news media of the day.

I remember waiting at the bottom of the staircase for Faron Young to appear. He had just had a huge hit on "Hello Walls," a song written by Willie Nelson. We knew him because we had opened the show for him when he came to Dallas to headline a show called "The Big D Jamboree." It was in the big coliseum there in downtown Dallas, and we were excited to be opening for him.

As Faron walked on into the hotel ballroom to get ready for the festivities, Doyle Wilburn of the Wilburn Brothers fame walked in. We had previously met him at our recording session earlier that week, and he came up and said hi. Our producer, Don Law, asked us who our publishing company was, and my mom told him we didn't have anyone to publish the original songs she had written for the new album. Doyle piped up and said, "Hey, I'll publish your songs." We had no idea about publishing and all that it entailed, the air royalties, the mechanicals, and so on. We just thought to ourselves, "What a great guy to go to all that trouble to publish mom's songs." Surefire Publishing Co., the Wilburn Brothers, were guys of great integrity and honesty. We admired Teddy and Doyle greatly.

Back at the Andrew Jackson, WSM-Radio was broadcasting live from the lobby, so Doyle Wilburn just went over to the disc jockey, Ralph Emery, who was on the air, and busted in on his show.

They all got a big laugh because they were all big buddies, and he got us involved and talked about the Nash Family Trio. He was a really great guy, and he and his brother, Teddy, were very popular in country music at that time. Loretta Lynn came in right after that with her husband who was dressed in coveralls like you would wear to milk the cows or work on the farm. Loretta had just  *David Nash with Loretta Lynn* had her first big hit, and guess what? Doyle Wilburn was the one that got her record deal for her.

Loretta was so down to earth, and we just loved meeting her, so humble and sweet. The story as told to us by Doyle was that he had had a meeting with Owen Bradley who was producing Brenda Lee and Patsy Cline, two of the biggest female stars on the planet, and Owen wanted one of the songs that Doyle & Teddy had the publishing rights to.

Doyle told Owen that he could record the song if he, Owen, would agree to produce Loretta. From what I remember, there was some back and forth for a bit and then the deal was made. That's kind of how Nashville ran for many years, there was a "good ol' boy" network of guys that had their fingers on the pulse of the business and they could make or break whoever they wanted.

The last great person we hung out with that day came in a little later, and it was Eddy Arnold. He was so glad to see us again, and we kibitzed with him for a while, and he told us another one of his famous jokes. We all laughed and, as he walked away, I asked my mom and Dave to explain the joke to me.

By the way, some of the players on our second recording session became big stars such as Floyd Cramer, who had a hit on a song called, "Last Date." He played piano on our session. And there was Grady Martin, the guitar player who played that great introduction to "El Paso" and all those great Spanish sounding "licks" on the Marty Robbins Gunfighter albums; he not only played guitar for us but did some over-dub work on our songs on the Hammond B-3 Organ.

We had the crème de la crème for that memorable session. I remember standing over to the side watching the guys work on the songs, and Don Law coming over to me. He asked if I would ever consider a solo recording career. I asked my mom about it and she said that was perfectly OK with her if that's what might happen. I'm sorry to say I didn't get that chance to work with Don. We just never did work it out for us to live in Nashville, and I was too young to move by myself. Other opportunities would later come my way, but for the time being, it was back to Pharr.

Chapter Four

Things Go Back To "Normal"

S WE HEADED BACK TO THE "end of the world," in Pharr, we left Nashville behind. Our recording contract was not renewed for a third year. We just never found that "right" manager who would help pick a booking agent, and would have coordinated our radio promo tour, etc., to keep our career going.

It doesn't just happen in show biz, it usually takes lots of P.R. and someone who has a vested interest in you and your career to make it a successful venture. We were so green and lived so far down in the Valley, and the small amount of money the Gospel promoters were willing to pay for a semi-known Gospel group was not enough; it hardly paid for our expenses to get back to Nashville or elsewhere to do a show with other artists.

The one other show we did do was with the Blackwood Brothers Quartet and The Statesmen Quartet. My Uncle Joe had a radio show in Corpus, and when these two famous Gospel Quartets came to Corpus, Uncle Joe helped to get us on that show. We had the honor of singing right after Uncle Joe and Aunt Ellen with their daughter, JoEllen, and her husband, Ernest Maxwell, in their ensemble.

I remember meeting James Blackwood, and him giving us a check for a whopping $100. We endorsed it and he in turn gave us cash that paid us for the show. If we had lived closer to Nashville, we could have worked every weekend for pretty small money just to get heard by the huge crowds those stars drew to concerts, but you have to be able to pay for gas and food and hotel and keep a good enough car to travel those thousands of miles it takes to build the fan base that buys your records and builds a rapport with you.

After not being renewed for a third year on Columbia, it was kind of a downer, but at least I was able to go back to school. Dave got an offer to be a disc jockey at a radio station in Raymondville, and then he got a different shift simultaneously at the country radio station in Edinburg, KURV Radio. He had two jobs now.

Momma just had a really hard time with it because her dreams of success and music-making on the "Big Stage" in life seemed to be at an end.

Soon after, my Uncle David in Houston offered to help us get bookings in Houston and surrounding areas.

We did this for a couple of years and even put out an album we recorded in Corpus with our cousin, JoEllen and her husband, Ernest, so that we could offer them for sale at our concerts and performances.

The Nash Family Trio Post-Columbia Records

We still got some gigs around the Valley as well, especially for the Winter Texans, and some radio and TV things, but nothing with the potential like Columbia Records gave us.

A little while later, my brother got drafted by Uncle Sam to fight in Vietnam, and that pretty much ended the Nash Family Trio's career.

Mom still was not ready to give up or quit; she just kept taking bookings even without Dave in the group, and she and I would travel to Houston about every weekend for a while to sing in another church.

That's the part I so admired about my mom, that even in the height of her "quiet desperation," she never gave up; she just wouldn't let that dream die. Eventually, it had to be vented in a new and different way.

For the moment though, I was at the end of my first real music career. Gospel singer Billy Nash would soon, of necessity, morph into Country singer Bill Nash. Before this happened, though, I remember going back to high school after having dropped out for a year to tour with the National Safety Circus (which never came to fruition) and then to promote our music at every radio station we saw along the highways and byways when we were on Columbia.

I can say honestly that I was truly glad to go back to being a full-time student because the "road" can get really lonely when you don't have any of your pals around to do things with. I really missed my friends, and was actually elated to return. The only challenging part was that my class had moved up a grade and I was now an underclassman to all my peers. They all seemed glad to have me back though. I worked so hard to excel and study and let my teachers know how much I appreciated them. I was almost back to being just a normal teenager.

I had so many great things happen for me at P.S.J.A. High School. I was honored to be asked to join Mr. Pollard's Concert Choir as a freshman, and he started teaching me things that I would later need for survival in my singing career like voice control, breathing from my diaphragm, and supporting that high note by tightening your buttocks.

Do not lean your head back and point your eyes toward the upper-most part of the ceiling; you will strain those vocal cords and ruin your voice due to stretching and straining to hit those high notes. Make the crown of your head point up at that ceiling with your chin a bit down so your neck is in straight alignment with your spine. Support that note with deep breathing and you will never be hoarse. I will never get through thanking Mr. Pollard. I just had a blast in concert choir.

Bill Nash Back In High School - 1963

My greatest honor was the year I made All State Choir, and I got to represent P.S.J.A. at the state level in Houston that following year. I had such a need to excel at everything I did, and as I look back on it now, it had a lot to do with my self-image. I had this tremendous need to prove to my teachers and classmates that I was part of them and wanted to be somebody in their eyes. I volunteered for everything, studied so hard to make it into the National Honor Society for 3 straight years, got to go to Boys State, an honor sponsored by the American Legion in Austin, Texas for a week the summer of my junior year, and sang for the sock hops, civic clubs and anything else I could get up to sing for.

This is at the time when we were still singing some on weekends in churches out of town, and it was kind of difficult to get enough sleep after driving all weekend to get to Houston, or wherever, and back. I tried my best to be nice to everybody, and it seems like that's all it took in those days to have everybody be nice to you also. It was a different day and time back then.

THE MELODY LOUNGE

After graduation, I contemplated what to do next with my life. My mom and I decided that I did need to go to college so I wouldn't be, as mom called it, "a singin' dummy." Now I had to start thinking about how to pay for college. My Aunt Audra owned the Melody Lounge in Pharr, which was more of a neighborhood "Cheers" type bar. It was brand new, with a neon sign out front you could see for miles with musical notes on the sign. She had just built it, and she called me and asked me to come out and sing one song, "He's Got The Whole World In His Hands." Naturally, my mom went with me to play piano. I was just a novice on the guitar since she was just now teaching me to play.

That "one song" turned into several songs, but the only songs I really knew how to sing were Gospel songs; I had never sung any other kind to an audience. It didn't seem to matter to the folks at the Melody Lounge, they seemed to like my singing and they accepted whatever I sang.

A real unique thing happened that first night. I found out about a great invention for aspiring artists. My Aunt Audra put an ice bucket up on the piano and made me a little sign that said "KITTY." As I sang, people would come up and put a dollar, $5, $10 in the kitty. There was a wealthy farmer who put a hundred dollar bill in one night and requested a song. This was a totally new experience for me, and it was exciting to think that I might be able to make some really great college money this way. We got invited back again the next night.

Aunt Audra made me a deal: she would pay me $20 and I would get the kitty as well. This was an answer to my prayer about how I could afford to go to the University of Houston. After a few more nights of this, it just got more and more exciting as more people found out that mom and I were singing and playing at the Melody Lounge. We even decided that we should learn some of the good old country songs as long as the words to the songs were all in good taste.

There were two waitresses in particular that were so tremendously helpful to me and I will never forget them. I don't think I knew their last names, but their first names were Jeannie and Jeannette. These two ladies took me under their wings and started teaching me country songs. They got me a blue, spiral notebook, and started writing the words down to some of the great old standard country songs like, "Your Cheatin' Heart," which is actually one of the greatest anti-cheating songs ever written. Then came "Hey Good Lookin'," "Jambalaya," and on and on.

As the crowd grew bigger and bigger each night, I would be asked for a song I didn't know, then I would write down the title and learn it. And as more and more folks liked the fact that I would take the time and trouble to learn their favorite song, more and more folks would come up and ask me for their song request. I would tell them to give me a couple of days and then come back and I would sing it.

This was really working. You must realize that in my hometown of Pharr, there was hardly anywhere to go to hear live music. The Melody Lounge was the perfect place to bring a date and listen to music, especially if the musician or singer dedicated it right to you.

As mom and I gathered a larger and larger following, it started to get harder to get a seat in this really nice, but semi-small place. They would be lined out the door and stuffed in the bar area as well. Our popularity had grown to the point that everyone in our small area of the world started to talk about it and it got back to some of the folks in dad's church. They got upset over the fact that their preacher's son and wife were singing and playing in a bar where people were drinking alcohol. They called dad in "on the carpet." Their verdict turned out to be an ultimatum: get your family out of that bar or you are fired.

'JUST A CLOSER WALK WITH THEE' — Billy Nash, accompanied by his mother, Clara, on the piano, sings a gospel song to an appreciative audience in a Pharr lounge. The appearance in the lounge of the young singer and his mother, members of the Nash Trio, which has recorded several religious albums, led to the release of Rev. L. L. Nash as pastor of the People's Chapel. (Monitor Photo)

Clara & Bill Nash at the Melody Lounge

My dad had always been one of the calmest people on the planet and I remember him reacting to this turn of events in the same manner as always. When, from time to time, he would come to hear mom and I play and sing, he would invariably be asked spiritual questions by some of the folks at the bar, and then would be asked to pray with them right there. These folks didn't think they were good enough to enter the doors of a church.

Dad let them know right off the bat that God loved them. That was his message always. However, now dad was facing a decision that concerned not only his livelihood, but his career as a minister of the Gospel. But he refused to forbid me from singing at the Melody Lounge and also refused to tell my mom she could no longer play piano for me.

So here we were; dad now had no church to pastor. Even when he did still have that pastorate, he was only paid $50 per week. He had to sell cars on the side to continue to make a living for us. So, for the next several weeks as mom and I sang every night, I would save my money for college and help my family with groceries and rent. I paid the rent on our house for several months while dad was trying to decide what to do. Most nights in my kitty I would make more in that one night than the church paid dad for a whole month.

To our surprise, some of the folks from the church came to dad and told him they would stay with him if he decided to start a new church. Well, this was very gratifying, and dad said yes. He then proceeded to explore the possibilities of renting a building where we could have church.

Wouldn't you know, there was just this type of place about a quarter of a mile from the Melody Lounge. We all found that interesting and, frankly, quite amusing. Dad's church was just down the road from the Melody Lounge. I would sing until after midnight at the Melody Lounge on Saturday and then be up early for church on Sunday morning to sing for church.

So then, the next thing that no one in a million years would have expected happened at the McAllen Monitor in McAllen, which was the newspaper that allowed all the churches to advertise their services and locations on Sunday for free.

Dad had always turned in his ad in person for his church, The Friendly Chapel, by the deadline each week. So, this week he went to the Monitor and turned in a new address for his up-coming Sunday service. The man that he dealt with there had become friends with dad and asked him why his church had a new location. Dad just told it like it had happened, that he had been asked to leave the church because of his wife and son singing at the Melody Lounge.

8   CHICAGO SUN-TIMES, Mon., May 17, 1965

GOSPEL SONGS PLUS BOOZE

Church Ousts Minister Whose Wife, Son Entertain At Tavern

PHARR, Tex. (UPI- — A church board told its preacher the doors were closed to him Sunday because his wife and son were mixing gospel songs with booze.

A spokesman for the People's Chapel (nondenominational) said the Rev. L. L. Nash had been fired because his 19-year-old son, Billy, and his wife were entertaining with gospel songs at a local tavern.

Mrs. Nash plays the piano and Billy sings. With another son, they made two gospel albums under the name "The Nash Trio."

The Rev. Mr. Nash stood behind his family. He said he went along to the pub as a "counselor."

You can save more sinners if you're where they are, the Rev. Mr. Nash reasons.

"I'm ready to offer help to anyone in the crowd that needs me," he said. "Many members of that church were

I still don't know exactly how to say what transpired next, but somehow this Monitor man wrote an article about dad's story and put it in the paper the following week. In those days, everyone read the paper on a daily basis and really got into the Sunday paper. There were two world-wide news services connected with the print media and one of them was the U.P.I., United Press International, and the other was the Associated Press, A.P.

Well, both entities picked up on the story and interviewed dad and then came out with the headline, "Pastor Ousted Due To His Son Singing in a Bar." I don't know why this caught everyone's attention, but it did. It even caught the attention of the NBC Television Network. They called one day and said they were sending a film crew down to cover our story. They set up a time and came to the Melody Lounge one evening and set up all their lights and turned the cameras on.

They also interviewed my parents about what had happened with the church. The place was packed and the crowd was so supportive of us. I sang several of our Gospel songs and they picked "Shall We Gather at the River" to use in their segment. NBC aired that piece on *The Today Show with Hugh Downes* and received lots of positive feedback from many of their viewers.

I still have the original NBC film, which can be viewed on

our website, www.bknash.com. How funny that this South Texas family was on NBC yet again! It probably wouldn't even get noticed in these days and times, but back then we were still in somewhat of a Victorian Age, and the three great sins were smoking, cussing and drinking. Anything to do with the church in association with any of these three things was quite sensational.

My whole family had been deeply affected and hurt by the rejection of our close friends in the church. Years later, when mom and dad would come out to hear me sing in some club where I was playing, my mom and I would always go on and on about those "d*** church people and hypocrites," as we called them, because of the bitterness we both still held in our hearts. Of course, she and I were both having a bit of "communion," or drinks, as we talked about those times. I was bitter for a long time.

CASTING A LIGHT

Bitterness is a heavy load to carry, and it only ends up hurting you much more than the initial blow you were dealt. I heard it said once that it's like drinking poison and waiting for the person who wronged you to die. It just keeps building and building inside of you if you don't release it. The Lord's Prayer plainly says, "Forgive our debts as we forgive our debtors." That's easier said than done, and it's a hard lesson to learn. I certainly wish I could have managed it at that time in my life, but it was so much easier to embrace the hurt. That bitter feeling stuck with me for more than 20 years. If I could go back and give myself any advice at that age, it would be to just let it go, and give it all to God. Sometimes, though, I guess we all just have to live through it and find our own way to do so, and thankfully, God is patient with us.

Chapter Five

College Bound Headed to H-Town

I KNEW I FINALLY HAD TO LEAVE the Valley in order to get to the rest of the world, and that journey had to begin with college.

My high school pal, Penn Gaines, had gone on to college ahead of me, and was now a junior at the University of Houston. I had quit one year during high school to travel and sing, and laid out one more year to decide what to do next. Penn urged me to enroll at U. of H., so I did. I bought a 1957 4-door Plymouth from dad's used car lot that I paid $350 for. Dad had rented a space to sell used cars and worked out the particulars with the bank. Mr. Cooper at Security State Bank in Pharr let me borrow the money and he set me up with easy payments of $35/month. I had so much anticipation, excitement, fear and trepidation, apprehension and so on and so forth, never having lived away from home, and I was a tightly wound ball of emotion. I hugged dad goodbye, and then mom cried as we hugged. Then I got in my gold and white Plymouth and drove down our street, Richmond Drive, and turned left onto the back highway. I took a right on South Cage Street and headed north. Tears welled all up in my eyes, and try as I might, I could not stop the flow of them as they went rolling down my cheeks all the way to Edinburg (7 miles) as I drove toward my new life.

There were approximately 19,000 students at U. of H. the year I enrolled in 1965. If there was any scholarship money or help from the government in those days, I was never told about it. However, Mrs. Ty Cobb, wife of our TV talk show friend in Weslaco, a wealthy socialite, offered me a scholarship, and in my literature from U. of H., it said tuition for in-state students was $50, so I told her it was $50. WRONG! No one had told me about the $900 per semester cost to live in the dorm, no one had said anything about the $350 cost for books which are provided by the state at the high school level, but not at college, and no one had mentioned the lab fees. I didn't find out about this additional information until I got to registration. None of my immediate family had ever graduated from college, so I didn't have a clue and didn't know to ask.

The little efficiency apartment I thought I was going to live in was not going to be possible now. I was depending on what I had saved up from the Melody Lounge to help me have a few months to find some kind of singing gig to support myself.

That plan became a thing of the past rather quickly as my money started to run out. I began contemplating what in the world I was going to do. I had to come up with a new plan. It never entered my mind to just quit and go home; momma always taught us to never give up.

Then I remembered a lady pastor that mom and I had sung for in Pasadena, a city that is adjoining to Houston, on one of our weekend trips to Houston. In talking with her and her husband about my plans to attend college, she told me that they had a spare bedroom and would love to have me stay with them if I should ever need a place to live.

Well, should I call them, or should I not? That was quite

a question for me at the time, trying to be Mr. Independent. However, when my rent came due for the next month in that little efficiency and I didn't have it, all I could do was become that humble guy who needed some help, swallow my pride, and break down and call this pastor and her husband.

So, I called Johnny and Mrs. Dr. Fanny Nevers in Pasadena and asked them if that bedroom was still open to me. I was so relieved when they said absolutely yes, and she was excited about the possibility of my singing in her church on Sundays as well.

It took me three more days of pondering until I finally called them back once more just to be sure. Dr. Fanny said, "I've had your bed turned down for three days now just waiting for you."

Wow! So, I drove on over there, and when she opened the door, she said, "Come on in and make yourself at home"; then she showed me to my room.

They had such a nice home, and the other great thing was that she opened the refrigerator and told me to eat anything and everything in there, and all I wanted of it. You know a young skinny guy like me at 20 years old was hungry all the time, and could never fill what my dad called, "a holler (hollow) leg."

You would have thought I was their only son, and that they were there just to make sure I had everything I needed to go to college. Thank God for Dr. Nevers and her husband, Johnny. I could never put into words what their love and generosity meant to me at that time in my life, and still means to me to this day.

That first week of registration at U. of H. was capped off by a Friday night talent show that was advertised via leaflets tacked up around the campus and in the buildings where we all registered, all 19,000 of us. I decided to sign up and sing at that show on that Friday night at the Cullen Auditorium. It was not a competition thing; it was just a chance for the new kids to ply their talents and meet one another. The auditorium was packed, and they had several other folks there singing and dancing and whatever. Then it was my turn. I was used to having mom beside me on the piano, but this night it was just me and my guitar that I had bought the previous summer; it cost me $188.50, and the store let me pay it out at $10/week, which I did.

I remember deciding to sing the old Hank Williams song,

"Long Gone Lonesome Blues." I am told that the first night Hank sang it on the Grand Ole Opry, he got six curtain calls and sang it all six times. So, there I was singing that same song Hank sang, and the same thing almost happened.

After the yodeling and less than great guitar playing (I'd only been playing for a few months with mom teaching me guitar chords), the audience erupted into loud and boisterous cheering and chanting--more, more, more--and they wouldn't stop.

The emcee called me back out and said to sing another song.

I don't remember what my encore song was, but it probably only had three chords with no minors — what a reception for my first week in Houston. The photographer for the Daily Cougar was there and took my picture and put it on the front page the next

Daily Cougar Article After Bill Nash's First Performance at U.H.

week. That was a real pump and an encouraging thing for me as a single artist, finally, on my own.

MY FRATERNITY DAYS

My High School friend, Penn Gaines, who urged me to apply to U. of H. also persuaded me to join his fraternity, Pi Kappa Alpha. I had no idea what that was all about; it seemed like it was going to be like one of those clubs I was a member of in high school like the Key Club, sponsored by the Kiwanis Clubs International. It turns out that the comparison was not even close.

The Pikes were known as the biggest beer drinking fraternity on campus and one of the biggest "hell raisers," as well. How was I to know that? I also didn't know about "dues" and the initiation fee. That took a chunk out of my meager earnings my first couple of years, and I sometimes needed to stretch my dues out, which they always let me do.

This is where I learned about "syrup and Wheaties." Oh my

goodness, the initiation into the fraternity!!! They got all of us potential pledges into the large garage adjacent to the frat house and we had to strip down to our undies and lay on the garage floor while they poured syrup all over our backsides and then box after box of Wheaties was applied to our cold and shivering bodies. Wouldn't you know this happened in wintertime, which made it an even rougher experience since we had no warm clothes on.

Then the command was given by our soon-to-be "brothers" to roll over and over each other, thereby driving those Wheaties into our backs. Oh man, we were howling and groaning until they finally let us quit all the nonsense. Then we ran around to the front of the frat house to turn the freezing cold water hose on to wash all that syrup and Wheaties off of us. We didn't even care that a Norther had blown in; we just wanted the stickiness to be gone.

How silly, actually, and you have to be as green as I was to put yourself through all that hazing. No one was ever hurt, though, and it really was all in fun, and our new "brothers" respected us highly for our grit that got us through it. I was later inducted as a full-fledged Pike. One of the advantages the Pikes gave me was that I now had a whole new social realm of folks, family, so to speak, that surrounded me here in my new life at college. Then they found out I was a singer. I played for the whole crew one day at the frat house at the behest of Penn Gaines, and the guys really liked my music. When we had the sororities come over, the guys would push me out front to sing and play for them. It got to be quite fun. Now all I needed was to find a paying job as a singer somewhere, somehow.

COLLEGE JOBS

My first job was at Pop's Poolside Motor Hotel Club on South Main Street in Houston. It was a roadside motel that had a small piano bar, and it was owned by a retired gentleman named Pop. I would drive all the way from Pasadena to South Main and play one night a week on Sundays for $10 per night. I only had to sing for four hours, but I got a 15-minute break every hour. One particular Sunday evening, the piano bar was full, and the folks were really into my songs. I explained that I was working my way through college and was also working on my music as a career choice. I had a great first set. Then when I took my break, they all disappeared. I remember thinking to myself, "What did I do wrong? Where did they go?" When my break was over, I went back up on the little stage and sat behind the piano on the bar stool and started to play and sing again. After a few more minutes went by, one of the couples that was there earlier came back and sat down and ordered another drink. I thought, "Wonder where they went?" I was so young and green. I just didn't understand. After another song or two, in came another couple and another until the bar was once again filled, not with new patrons, but with the same people that had been there earlier. Well, the next week as this sort of thing happened again and then the next week, I started to put two and two together. I can't remember how exactly I confirmed my suspicions, but I found out that they rented those rooms by the hour! They all seemed like such nice folks, and they also liked my singing. What can I say?

About this time, I had also found a second job at United Record Distributing Co. on St. Emanuel Street in downtown Houston. The recording artists of the day would come by to see Steve Poncio, the owner, and I got to meet B.J. Thomas who had come by after his first album, "I'm So Lonesome I Could Cry," went platinum. B.B. King also came by to shake everybody's hand. It was very exciting to meet people that were doing what I aspired to do.

United was the largest in the Southwest and Steve had some Nashville connections through Monument Records, the label Roy Orbison was on. Steve agreed to record me and try to get me signed at Monument, but in the meantime, he gave me a job as a stock boy to help me with college. He paid me $1.25/hour. I would go to my first class at 8 a.m. in the morning, then head downtown to St. Emanuel Street at noon and work until 5:30 p.m., and then drive to Baytown to sing at a Pizza Joint until midnight. I got this job through the help of Pam Phelps, a really cute gal who was a great piano player and whose family attended Dr. Nevers' Church, Pasadena Gospel Temple. She and I became a duo for that period of time, and she played piano and sang with me, as well. We split the $10/night and got to eat all the pizza we could hold.

I'm not sure how I ever found the time to study, but I somehow managed a 2.6 G.P.A. that first semester and was able to maintain it so I could stay in the fraternity. I only did one recording session with Steve Poncio at Gold Star Studios with a group called the Impellas. They played great, but nothing ever came of the session. It didn't help that I had rehearsed for far too long the day before and was rather hoarse. Note to self, don't over-sing the day before you record.

Another opportunity arose because I used to "sit in" with my friends, Don and Dixie, at a restaurant/bar where they were playing. Dixie was my first crush from Pharr, Texas when I was just a kid, and her mother, Lottie Eubank, was my mother's best friend.

Dixie would always have me come out to sit in and sing with her and Don, her husband/drummer extraordinaire, on a Saturday night when the club they were playing was packed. She was determined to help me get my start in Houston and she did just that. That particular night, a fellow in the crowd told me of a club in Pasadena that was looking for a new singer. He even set up an appointment for me to go and meet the owners of the Bawana Club, Paul and Betty Clack.

That was an interesting time for me because Paul and Betty really liked my singing, but they said I would need a band in order to play for dancing at their club. I had some friends I had played a couple of private parties with, and they became my first band. I was now playing with four other musicians and learning how to deal with being the bandleader.

Paul Clack was a very quiet and soft-spoken man, and he didn't like for the music to get too loud. The problem with that was that his definition of loud was just a bit above a whisper. He had the main amplifier to the mikes and speakers right under the register at the main bar where he sat. When he felt like I was singing too loud, he would just turn me down.

One night we had a potentially dangerous incident when Paul happened to be out of town on business. Betty, Paul's wife, had some customers who were causing trouble this particular Friday night. They had refused to pay their bill, and as they were leaving, they were spouting off some very loud and ugly words to her. She ran to the bar, which was way across the dance floor from where the band and I were playing, and got on the intercom and called for me to get back there to help her.

I hastily threw down my guitar and ran to the back of the room across the dance floor. When I arrived at the door, I looked around, and my whole band had come off the bandstand to back me up. When I arrived on the scene, there was a guy talking very loudly to Betty, and when he saw me, he pointed his finger right in my face and said, "I have a bullet for you, and for you, and you" as he said pointing to me, the band, and Betty.

Well, I really don't know exactly what I said, but I just kept my arms down to my side with my hands open. I told him we were not a threat to him and didn't want to fight or anything, and asked if I could help him somehow.

When he saw we weren't going to try to throw him out bodily, and he heard my "softer tone," he began to settle down a bit. He then told me how bad he thought the place was and went on and on about some other stupid stuff just trying to justify his threatening attitude.

I responded with my voice in a calm manner and in low tones that I was sorry he felt that way. I took my cue for this situation from a Proverb dad had taught me, "A soft answer turns away wrath."

After a couple of minutes, he actually calmed down, and as he surprisingly went ahead and paid his bill, he stuck his hand out to shake my hand and thanked me for being nice about it all.

I must admit I was a bit shocked at his turn-around behavior, but I sure was thankful that no one got hurt, especially me. I shook his hand and told him goodbye.

That experience was opposite of what I had ever encountered in the church world, but to me, it was just one of the ways that I knew God was still looking out for me. The Bawana Club held some other interesting nights for me.

During a break one night, a couple of guys approached me and asked me to sit and talk with them a minute. One of them was albino, and I recognized him due to the fact that I had been downtown to a nightclub where he and his brother, also albino, were playing in a band that was just tremendous.

This night, however, I had Johnny Winter and his friend, Mark James, sitting in front of me wanting to visit about a proposition they had for me. Mark did all the talking; Johnny was very quiet and soft-spoken when he did talk. Mark said they wanted to be my back-up band. They wanted me to be the lead singer, and they would be my band. They really "dug" my singing.

At that time, I had no idea what a great compliment that was just because of who these guys were; I was just glad they thought that much of me and my sound. I actually wanted to work with them because we were looking for a new band at the Bawana since the guys I started with were still in high school, and the late nights were not conducive to attending high school. I thanked these two guys for the compliment of "digging my pipes" (that's exactly how it was said that night), and I told them I would ask Paul what he thought about it. Paul barely let me get the question out of my mouth before he said a resounding "No." He just didn't understand Johnny's appearance, him being albino and all (how small-minded), and he was not in favor of them being in his club.

I was extremely disappointed because Johnny's looks didn't bother me at all. That's just how he was born and how he looked, and my goodness, how could you not appreciate his talent? I had heard him play with that other band and I remembered how great that band was; they were simply sensational and I mean it, SENSATIONAL! I really hated to tell Mark that Paul wasn't interested, but I let him know at the same time that I considered it quite a compliment that they actually wanted me to front their band.

I wonder if Paul would have said yes if he had known that just about four years later Johnny Winter would become this huge rock star on Columbia Records, my old label. Mark James would end up on Scepter records out of New York and would write several songs that would become big hits, especially one called "Suspicious Minds" made famous by Elvis Presley, and another he co-wrote with Wayne Carson that Elvis and Willie Nelson both recorded, "Always On My Mind."

Oh, well, that's another one of those things you put in that category entitled, "What if?" I wish I had been able to at least jam with those guys. I did get part of that wish fulfilled later when I finally got to work with Johnny's brother, Edgar Winter, within the next year or so.

There were obviously many more memorable things that happened at the Bawana Club, but this last one I want to share was by far the most exciting. Paul Clack had booked Conway Twitty to come and play a "one-nighter" with us (BTW, Conway's real name is Harold Jenkins). Conway had just made his transition from rock and roll to country music. His first song that I recall was called "Workin' Girl." He had his own plane, and they flew in the day of the show and set up. Conway stayed in his dressing room until show time while my band and I opened the show; we sang for about an hour. Then Conway made his way to the bandstand, stepped behind the mike, and without a word he started singing, and that packed place went wild. He never actually spoke a word to the crowd in those days. His bass player is the one who talked and introduced each song.

Conway invited me to sit and visit with him after the show. He was absolutely the nicest guy you would ever want to meet, so complimentary and kind to me, and I'm sure he remembered his early, start-up years as he noticed me picking up every bit of information and guidance from him that I could. Little did I know that, many years later, I would be the artist who represented him at the official opening of Trinity City in Nashville when TBN, Trinity Broadcasting Network, purchased Conway's property, Twitty City. TBN asked for someone who knew him or had opened for him to come as a rep from the music community to help unveil his bronze statue on that property. It is still there to this day, and so is Conway's mansion just like he left it. It is one of my fondest memories.

As I come to the close of my Bawana Club and Pasadena days, there are a couple of interesting things left: one is the fact that Paul Clack believed in me so much that he paid for me to make a record at Doyle Jones' recording studio on Blair Street.

The record never did anything, but the significance to me is that I got to meet two of the greatest guys named Mickey in music history. One of them was the great Mickey Gilley, who, at that time, was playing music at night at a club on Spencer Highway in Pasadena called the Nesadel. He was also an engineer by day at Jones Recording Studio. So, when I went there to record, he was the person they introduced me to. We really hit it off. After the recording session was over, he invited me to come out and sit in with him at the Nesadel, which I did several times. There, I met another one of Houston's greatest talents, Mr. Johnny Williams, who fronted the band for Mickey and played piano and saxophone. Mickey even came over to the Bawana Club to listen to me and my band one night and he was so complimentary and supportive. He sincerely encouraged me to continue to work toward my music career. Later when Mickey moved to his new nightclub, "Gilley's," I got to sing with his band on numerous occasions. We have remained friends to this day.

The second guy I met at Jones Studio was a singer/songwriter named Mickey Newbury. He came strolling through the studio between takes during my session, and he stopped me and said he really liked my singing. I thanked him and went on. After awhile I noticed he kept hanging around and listening. So, I went over to Gilley and asked him who that guy was. He said, well, he wrote a big hit for Engelbert Humperdinck called "Funny, Familiar, Forgotten Feelings" and he's also had several other big songs recorded. Kenny Rogers' first hit, "Just Dropped In" (To See What Condition My Condition Was In), was also one of his songs. After the session that day, Mickey Newbury asked me to come into his little office there at Jones Studio; he wanted to play me some of his songs. There was no furniture, so we had nothing to sit on, so we sat on the floor. As Mickey began to sing for me, song after song, all I could think was, "Wow! Who is this guy?" I'd never heard of him and yet he was obviously a very successful songwriter already and was from Houston. His voice was so beautiful and his guitar work was exquisite. I could have listened to him for hours, in fact, we were in his office for at least an hour that day.

As our friendship progressed over the next couple of weeks

and months, he offered to write and produce a recording session for me and take it to Nashville to see about getting me a record deal. I was really pumped about it, and so we set a session date. I was to record three songs that Mickey was going to write for me.

However, on the Saturday before the Monday recording session, I got a letter in the mail from Mercury Records in Nashville, Tennessee. It was from the legendary producer, Jerry Kennedy, offering me a recording contract. I then remembered back to the night at the Bawana Club when several country artists came in after they had finished opening a show for Marty Robbins in downtown Houston. That's the night I met Mercury recording artist, Dave Dudley, whose truck driving song, "I'll Take Anything Leavin' Town Today," had made him a star. His booking agent was with them, and after he heard me sing, he asked me for a tape to take back to Nashville to present to someone. I didn't realize that it was Jerry Kennedy at Mercury Records, Dave Dudley's producer, that he was talking about. Jerry heard my less than wonderful demo tape and sent me a recording contract. Well, now the dilemma: do I record with Mickey Newbury or do I accept this Mercury deal? All I knew to do was to call Mickey and just ask the question. He told me straight away, "You should take the Mercury deal." His whole plan was to get me a record deal, and there it was right in front of me. So we called off the Monday session, and I signed the Mercury contract and sent it back to Nashville.

Signing the Mercury contract was of course the right thing to do, but I still wish I could have worked with Mickey Newbury, as well. Looking back, I thought to myself, "Why couldn't I have still taken those 3 songs he wrote just for me and present them to Jerry Kennedy at least as possibilities to record?" I don't know why that thought didn't occur to me, especially since we were going to have to look for songs anyways, but it just didn't.

About that time, Paul Clack decided to go out of business and closed the Bawana Club. The way I found this out was when I went to work on that Monday night there were chains on the front doors, and the band and I couldn't get in. We were banging on the doors and hollering for someone to let us in and hopefully explain what was going on. Besides that, we all had our guitars and amps and all other kinds of equipment that belonged to us in there. Paul finally came to the door and let us in. He gave us the news that he was going out of business. What a bummer! There went my job and my livelihood. Now I needed to find another way to pay my bills and continue college while looking forward to a great new start with Mercury Records.

At the same time, my family had finally persuaded my dad to make the big move to Houston from the Valley and start a new life for him and my mother. Dad was able to make a down payment on a nice but small home in Channelview near where Uncle David and Aunt Helen Johnson pastored. They offered to help dad get started in something meaningful in the Houston area. They were so very gracious and a vital component in dad and mom's decision to finally relocate where dad could find a good job pastoring or something else meaningful.

There were so many different things going on in my life at that time. I got a new job downtown on Market Square at The Golden Fleece and started my first solo major recording career with Mercury Records. But at the same time, I had to maintain my 2.6 G.P.A. at U. of H. or they would send me to Vietnam. I had a IIS deferment from the draft board; that means as long as I stayed in college, I wouldn't have to go to Vietnam like my brother already had.

That war was really raging at that time and several of my friends had either been killed or incapacitated. We really grieved over those wonderful people; they are forever etched in my memory. Our banker, Mr. Cooper, and his wife, lost their youngest son, Ned, to that awful war. He was one very special individual who had such a magnetic personality, and I actually loved him as we all did at P.S.J.A. I first met him in the second grade at Carnahan School.

My own brother's copter blew its engine as he was co-pilot that day about a mile into enemy territory. With the engine blown, they came down by auto-rotation, but somehow plummeted from 50 feet up; Dave and the pilot barely escaped with their lives. They had to do some creative hiding for three days before they could be rescued. The crash had left Dave paralyzed from the waist down, and it also caused a compression fracture of his spine; he came home almost two inches shorter than when he left.

Thank God the feeling finally came back into his lower body, and he was able to walk again, but there's no way to overcome a compression fracture. Our country owes him and all the other vets that fought alongside him a great debt of gratitude.

Meanwhile, here at home, I started working a new job on Market Square at the Golden Fleece. A man by the name of Marshall Stewart owned the Fleece, and he had a partner named Herb Stelter whose wife, Liz, loved music, and she came to the club almost every weekend. There was a revival of that old downtown part of Houston at that time and many clubs sprang up of all different kinds in the mid to late 60's. The Golden Fleece had a Viking motif and was down two flights of stairs into a sub area of that building on Congress Avenue. Herb and Liz Stelter became my best friends and confidants in those days; they actually became like a second mom and dad to me.

My band at the Fleece was headed by none other than Johnny Winter's brother, Edgar Winter. I just have to stop right here and

tell you the Edgar Winter I knew was the most soft-spoken individual I have ever worked with. He barely talked above a whisper, but when he did, everybody got quiet and listened because he was a musical genius. He used to write my music charts for me for the three new

Bill Nash with Edgar Winter & Gene Kurtz

songs I learned each week. Edgar would take the three records I would choose into the dressing room and listen to each one individually just one time. He then would proceed to write the chord chart without even listening to the song a second time. Then he would bring the chart out, everyone would gather around Ed to make their own copy from Edgar's chart, and we would play the record one more time for the band to go over their chart. Then they'd rehearse with me singing the song.

When I sang, he would sing harmony with me on an old country song like "Fraulein" and then turn around and sing a loud rock and roll song with a singing voice from who knew where. He talked so softly and then could sing so loudly. He was, hands down, the greatest musician I have ever worked with in a club situation. He later became this huge rock star when Columbia Records signed him to their label where he produced and performed the "Frankenstein" album that is still a monster (pardon the pun) rock album, one of the biggest of all time. My bass player, Gene Kurtz, co-wrote with Roy Head Roy's million seller hit, "Treat Her Right" in 1965.

We had a lot of interesting people come through the Fleece in those days. It kind of became one of the hot spots in town. We had the folks packed in there every weekend and many times during the week, as well. One night as I finished my first set, I walked off the stage and somebody said they had someone they wanted to introduce me to. Lo and behold, there stood Willie Nelson with a drink in his hand wearing a suit and tie with his hair cut short like a doctor or lawyer would wear. I obviously knew of him and the hit songs he had written for everybody else, but he himself hadn't had the singing career he would later have and become even more famous for. He was complimentary, polite, and very soft spoken. He really liked our music. He had another famous songwriter, Hank Cochran, with him at the time, and Hank was there with Grand Ole Opry star, Jeannie Sealey. I shook their hands and welcomed them to our club. I then asked Jeannie if Hank had written her big hit record

Nash Note 🎵

Roy Head called me a little while back all excited and said, "Hey, they're using my song in the new Leonardo DiCaprio movie." Well, he was talking about *Once Upon A Time In Hollywood.* They licensed "Treat Her Right," and ended up starting the whole movie off with Roy's song. It's amazing to me after all these years how one song can change your life, and it can just keep going.

that was still hot about that time, "Don't Touch Me." She replied, "Hank writes all my songs." Not a bad deal to have a great songwriter in your corner.

Chapter Six

Mercury Records Nashville

THE BIG DAY CAME WHEN I was to fly to Nashville to record my first session with that famous producer, Jerry Kennedy. Jerry was producing Roger Miller, the Statler Brothers, and had just rejuvenated the career of Jerry Lee Lewis, taking him from rock and roll to country western. Nobody thought it could be done, but Kennedy did it. So things were rocking at Mercury Records, and I was assigned to one of their subsidiary labels called Smash/Mercury. I asked Jerry on the phone before I left Houston if I needed to find some songs I liked or if that was something he would do. He said not to worry, he was going to have some of those "big time" writers write some songs for me, and it would be great.

I flew up there and met with him on a Tuesday morning at 10 a.m. right there on Music Row on 16th Avenue South in Nashville.

At that time, Mercury's offices were right across the street from Columbia Records Studios, which had been built by Owen Bradley who produced Patsy Cline, Loretta Lynn, Brenda Lee and so many more.

As Kennedy sat down behind his desk and stuck his feet up

on one corner, I took my place in a chair in front of him. He didn't say much after we shook hands. He just proceeded to pick up the phone and dial a number. Someone answered and Jerry asked if he could speak to the janitor. There was a short pause and then someone came to the phone and I heard Kennedy say, "Bill's here and he wants to hear your song." I didn't know

Bill Nash Departing for Nashville - 1967

what to think. We hadn't even talked about someone bringing me a song, much less a janitor bringing me a song. What was all this about? In about 5 minutes, no exaggeration, Kennedy's secretary, Ellen Wood, announced the arrival of the janitor. He had a military type burr haircut, and came in carrying a black guitar and wearing a faded pair of black jeans, black t-shirt, and on his feet were Hush Puppy type shoes with a hole in the bottom of one of them (I noticed the hole when he crossed his legs while we talked).

Then the "janitor," as I knew him, started to strum down on his 6-string, and his opening lines were: "Don't look so sad, I know it's over, but life goes on, and this old world will keep on turning. Let's just be glad we had some time to spend together. There's no need to watch the bridges that we're burning."

Just about there I had goose bumps go up and down my spine. My thought was, "That sure is a great start line of a song. If the rest of it is just as good, it sounds like a big hit to me."

Then he got to the chorus: "Lay your head upon my pillow, Hold your warm and tender body close to mine. Hear the whisper of the raindrops, blowing soft against the window, and make believe you love me one more time, For The Good Times."

Oh my goodness, what lines and what a song. I had goose bumps on my goose bumps. I'd never heard anyone say/sing such positive lines to such a negative, heartbreak situation like the breakup of two people in love, and he did it in such a simple, succinct and poignant way, so down to earth. I don't even remember hearing the rest of the song. Those lines were so earthy, the melody so haunting, how could I not love it? When he finished singing, he looked at me, waiting for my response. It just came out of me as I blurted out, "I love it." Kennedy said, "It's a hit." The songwriter/janitor floated out of the office after I told him I wanted to record it. I asked Jerry what his name was again, and Jerry said, "Kris Kristofferson." Then he said right behind that, "He's going to be great one day."

What I didn't know until later was that Kris was a Rhodes Scholar and had also become a helicopter pilot after completing his Ranger training in the army. He sincerely was a genius who was only sweeping the floors at Columbia to be in closer proximity to the music business and have the chance to play his songs for artists and producers. Looks like his plan worked.

I invited Kris to the session the next day. He was truly excited, and he came to hear his first major label "cut" there at Columbia Studios. That day, I could see Kris through the large glass window that separated the studio from the control room. He was beaming. He was so excited, and so was I. I recall him celebrating with a few beers as he stood in the corner behind Jerry who was sitting at the control board. We cut four songs that day, and "For the Good Times" was clearly the one that stood out from the rest. Jerry said

Bill with Kris Kristofferson In Studio - 1967

he would send me the finished product when he got through with his guitar parts and the strings over-dub session.

I headed back to Houston on cloud nine, and waited to get a copy of my first single, "For The Good Times," in the mail.

Nowadays they can just mp3 it to you once it's done almost immediately. In those days it was snail mail, and we had no choice but to wait for it to come. One Saturday morning about 8 a.m., the doorbell rang at our little house in Channelview, and it was a package from Mercury Records in Nashville. I opened it as fast as I could, and it was what they called an acetate. An acetate was a vinyl product that they burned at the recording studio for you right from the master tape. I put it on the spindle of my record player and it started up. Mom was sitting near the stereo player and I got down on the floor right in front of the speakers. When it first started to play the sound was not a lot different than what I had heard on playback in the studio. Then, just before the chorus, there came the most incredible sound I had ever heard on any of my past recordings: the strings, made up of violins, cellos and violas came in. It was so beautiful!! The tears hit my eyes, and I

Bill Nash Receiving His First Copy of "For The Good Times"

sat there on the floor in the living room and just cried as I listened to the most glorious sounds I had ever been a part of on record. I looked over at mom, and she was crying too. We must have played that song over and over and over at least a "jillion" times; we just couldn't hear it enough. I will never forget that day as long as I live.

RELEASE AND PROMOTION

It was a unanimous decision at the label to go with "For the Good Times" as the "A" side, and the "B" side would be "We Had All the Good Things Going." Right out of the box, we got a pick to hit at Billboard Magazine, known as the Bible of the music industry.

The promotion man assigned to my record was a guy named

Rory Burke. He was a very likable guy with a very positive attitude, and he really believed in "For the Good Times." He immediately sent a telegram to all the radio stations saying, "It's a Smash." So the song was blessed by Billboard and went out to all the disc jockeys and radio stations. It started climbing the charts and, as it neared the 40s and high 30s, it started to pick up steam.

Then, from somewhere in left field, somehow, feedback to

First Mercury Promo Photo - 1967

Mercury from some of the Bible belt stations was negative. Their interpretation of Kris's line, "Hold your warm and tender body close to mine," seemed to offend some of them. You see, I don't recall any other song with a "body" line so descriptively put before Kris's song. That "body" line scared some of the disc jockeys off from playing it any further because of the feedback from some of their listening audience.

They kind of deemed it "that porno song." I couldn't believe it and nobody else at the label could believe it either.

My old pal, Bill Bailey, the voice of the Houston Livestock Show and Rodeo, started playing it immediately at his station, KIKK, and it made it to the top ten here in the Houston market. Well, we had very mixed reactions to the song all across the country, and Mercury became very hesitant to spend any more promotion money on this particular record. It seemed like we got off to such a great start, but getting that kind of feedback felt like a dream killer.

The next year, Mercury brought me to Nashville for the disc jockey convention. That's what they called it back then due to the fact that all the disc jockeys from all over the U.S. and Canada were invited. All the big country stars would come to town for that week, and each label would have a show featuring its artists. It reminded me of the Nash Family Trio days again. I sort of knew the drill. I would go to the suite in my hotel that Mercury rented for the week, which is what all the labels did, and I would make myself available for autographs and for meetings with the disc jockeys. Since I really was the newest Mercury artist, and hadn't had a hit yet, I was not that well-known nationally; but that's how you get well-known, by getting out there.

I was standing around the Mercury Records suite watching the ebb and flow of the disc jockeys coming and getting free drinks and roaming around to all the other label suites in the hotel picking up promotional items like pens, hats, and lots of junk, but fun stuff for memory's sake. It was the pre-designated time for Jerry Lee Lewis to show up and sign autographs.

As soon as he arrived, a whole crowd of people appeared. Jerry Lee also had his road crew park all five of his limousines out front of the hotel so he arrived

Nash Note ♫

Keep in mind during all this, I was still enrolled at UH. Looking back, I don't know how I managed to do it all, especially with the traveling back and forth, but I did. I was determined to be the first one in my family to graduate college, and still work on my career. This was the time when I learned how to "power nap" for 15 minutes at a time. That was a life-saving skill.

with all the pomp and ceremony someone of the British Royal Line would be expected to display. People were lined out the door of the suite to get Jerry Lee's autograph and picture.

So he's sitting there at a table signing everything they put in front of him, and meanwhile the juke box is playing records (they set up a Wurlitzer Juke Box filled with recordings by Mercury artists). It just so happened that lots of Roger Miller records had already been selected on the juke box. After about three Roger Miller songs in a row like, "Chug A Lug," "Dang Me," and "King of The Road," Jerry Lee stood up and said, "I like Roger Miller, but if they don't start playing some Jerry Lee Lewis on that juke box, I'm leaving." Whoa now, here came Jerry Lee's sister, Linda Gail, and his momma, rushing to the juke box, and rolling it away from the wall a bit to get to that eject button on the back of the machine.

They ejected the current one playing, then the next and one more until they got to, "What's Made Milwaukee Famous." When that started playing, Jerry Lee sat down and said, "Now that's more like it." It was just a hoot for me sitting on the sidelines observing this famous star and his family.

That evening at the Mercury Records Show, Jerry Lee and I were standing around backstage before his performance at the hotel ballroom where the disc jockeys had packed the room. He said to me as he showed me his ankle-high black leather boots, "I wear these pointed-toed boots so I can kick the 'blank' out of troublemakers in the clubs we play." I just chuckled, but he was serious.

Nov. 29, 1968

th Mendel Quidnunc

SMASH

and

LINDA GAIL LEWIS BILL NASH

NORRO WILSON

Welcome You to NASHVILLE and the CMA CONVENTION

The regard with which Smash records, a subsidiary of Mercury, holds Bill Nash was indicated by posters which the company used to welcome disc jockeys from through-out the nation to the recent Country Music Association convention in Nashville. Bill, star of the revue at the Golden Fleece, also recorded three more songs when he was in Nashville.

I will say this about the concert: you must remember that Jerry Kennedy had taken a chance on Jerry Lee when he signed him and had cut straight country songs instead of the old rock and roll he was famous for. No one realized that Jerry Lee still had at least a million fans out there waiting for him to do something else because he was back on top of the charts again, but this time with traditional type country songs.

However, at this particular show there were lots of die-hard country disc jockeys that resented the fact that Jerry Lee used to be rock and roll and was now transitioning to country; they viewed him as an opportunist who had turned to the Country side of music in order to save his career.

They didn't believe that he sincerely cared about Country music at all. So when he took the stage, some of these kinds of folks started to boo him. He made it through about the first verse of his first song, and when the booing didn't stop, he abruptly quit playing his piano right in the middle of the song. He stood up and kicked the piano bench backwards and hollered (that's country talk for "shouted") at the crowd, "If any of you 'blanking blankers' don't like my music then get the 'H' out." I was sitting in the audience by this time just to see the show, and I thought there was going to be a riot, sincerely. However, the malcontents just got up and exited the ballroom booing as they walked out.

After the air cleared a bit, I looked around to see that more than half the crowd had chosen to stay. He sat back down at his piano and proceeded with his concert, and after he was done, the crowd gave him a standing ovation.

The next night at the Coliseum in downtown Nashville, the big closing banquet was taking place. Jerry Kennedy and I were sitting with all the Mercury folks, the president, Charlie Fach, etc..., and we decided to go out to the lobby area to get drinks. That's where we ran into Roger Miller (Jerry Kennedy was the producer that made him a star). I had two glasses in my hand, and as Jerry introduced me to Roger, I said to him that I would shake his hand, but couldn't because I had two glasses in my hands at the moment. He replied right back to me so quickly, "Just pour your drink on me."

I didn't expect that at all, and I looked at Jerry, and we kind of laughed and walked on back into the auditorium. I asked Jerry if I really should have poured my drink on him and Jerry said, "He would've loved it." That tells you a bit about what a fun-loving guy Roger really was.

I met Dolly Parton that same night. I used to see her on the Porter Wagoner Show on TV, but when I saw her in person that night, I realized that the early television cameras really didn't do her justice. She was just such a beautiful woman!

I remember getting up my gumption as she and Porter were walking by our table. I stood up and stuck my hand out to her and said, "I think you are beautiful." It was one of those things a 23-year-old guy just can't help when he sees someone like her who is just naturally so pretty. She stopped in her tracks and shook my hand and said, "Why thank you, honey."

Meanwhile, Porter just looked over his shoulder and didn't say a word. He just kept walking. She looked at him like, "Hey, this guy really admires me and I'm going to stop for a second and speak to him." What a sweet individual and incredibly talented star she was back then, and still is now. Many years later, she actually became involved with a song I wrote, but I'll share more on that when we get there.

THIRD SESSION WITH MERCURY RECORDS

My second Mercury session came and went without much happening except that Kris came by and we hung out. He said he didn't have anything to submit for me to record yet. So I was scheduled for about six months later in 1968 for my third session.

I headed back to Nashville, and when I arrived at the production meeting at Jerry Kennedy's office to listen to new, original songs for my session, Kris came by to say hello again. My first question for him was, "Do you have another song for me to record?" In his vernacular he said, "I 'bout ruined your career with that first one." He was meaning, "For the Good Times," which hadn't hit for me or him, though a couple of years later Ray Price released it, and it became a huge hit (oddly enough, since my version was the only recording, Ray actually learned it from my record).

Kris and I laughed, and I said, "No man, I really dig your writing and I sincerely want to record something else by you." So he said these very words, "I have another song, but I have to get real drunk to finish it."

So, being the good preacher's kid that I was, I handed him three bucks for a 6-pack of beer, and as he started to walk out, Jerry and I reminded him that the session was set for 2:00 p.m. across the street at Columbia, and he needed to be back before then to have his song considered.

So from 10:00 a.m. that morning we kept looking at the clock and wondering if Kris would actually get back in time and would he even finish the song. It was about ten minutes until 2:00, and just as Jerry and I started to head for the door to walk over to Columbia, in walks Kris.

He said, "I got your song, Bill." We sat back down, and Kris sat across from me in a chair and Jerry sat back down behind his desk.

Kris proceeded to sing these words: "Take the ribbon from your hair, shake it loose and let it fall, lay it soft upon my skin, like the shadows on the wall. Come and lay down by my side, 'til the early mornin' light, all I'm takin' is your time, help me make it through the night."

I loved the verse right away, and then he sang the chorus to us, and Jerry slammed his fists down on his desk and declared, "It's a smash!" I concurred and told Kris I was going to record it.

He was in disbelief and a bit shocked at our instant acceptance of the song, but somehow Jerry and I both knew it was truly a great song. We cut it within a half hour of Kris's singing it to us, and Ellen Wood, Jerry's secretary, took the words down on paper as Kris repeated the words to her, and she typed it up for me to have at the session. Ellen kept a copy of the lyrics, and decades later, she told me how she had donated them to the Country Music Hall of Fame.

Jerry Kennedy, Bill Nash, Bob Beckham in Studio

Kris came across the street with us and played it for the studio band, and they picked it out, wrote the music charts, and I sang it.

Now that I've spent some years in Nashville writing and pitching songs to producers, I can only imagine what was going on in Kris's mind when his song was not only accepted but recorded within minutes of his having written it.

On a humorous note, I objected to singing a word in the line, "Let the devil take tomorrow." I told him, "My momma told me to never sing about the devil." His response was "you little self-righteous S.O.B. (more like "somebeach"), then just sing, 'Let whatever take tomorrow.'" So that's how I sang it.

At that same session, I also recorded, "She Even Woke Me Up To Say Goodbye." It had been written by my old friend, Mickey Newbury. A day before the session in Kennedy's office, the three of us, Mickey, Jerry and I, were standing around listening to the new cuts on Mickey's soon-to-be-released "Looks Like Rain" album. As we were listening and talking between songs, Mickey told Jerry to let me have first choice of anything on his new album for me to record on my up-coming session. That album is still one of the greatest Country albums ever created, and I'm so proud I was one of the first people to hear it that day.

I loved "She Even Woke Me Up To Say Goodbye", and so did Jerry, so we cut it the next day along with "Help Me Make It Through The Night." That really was an amazing session. Mickey was a wonderful friend who believed in me back in Houston, and here we were, both now recording artists on Mercury Records. Thank you, Mickey, rest in peace, I still love you, man.

And Kris, thanks again for the second song. Unfortunately, I

Kris & Bill on the Phil Everly Show - 1970

didn't get to stay with the label since shortly after returning home I got my draft notice in the mail from the Army. In fact, sadly to this day, I don't even have a copy of the session. My best guess is that the label just recorded over it, since those 24-track masters we recorded on were quite expensive.

What a shame, but sometimes, that's just the music business.

Subsequently, Jerry Lee Lewis recorded "She Even Woke Me Up To Say Goodbye", and it was a big hit for him. Sammi Smith later recorded, "Help Me Make It Through The Night," and had a million seller. A few years later in 1970, Phil Everly had Kris on his TV show in Los Angeles, and he brought me in to sing "For the Good Times" with Kris. Phil asked questions about the song, and Kris told the world our story. Thanks, Kris, for always remembering me as the first person to record one of your songs. What an honor.

Chapter Seven

Thanks Uncle Sam

THAT DRAFT NOTICE BROUGHT EVERYTHING TO a screeching halt as far as my career was concerned. Here I was, facing this letter from Uncle Sam that said, "Greetings." I was drafted into the Army and was given a time to show up. However, the draft board did say I could go ahead and finish the current semester at U. of H. My last semester in college would have to wait.

I said okay. What else could I say? The one place for some wiggle room was in the fact that I was allowed to join a military branch of my own choice if I did so before I was inducted into the Army.

It just so happened that my dad had become the chaplain of the Civitan Club in Channelview, and mom started playing piano for them for their meetings and gatherings. One of the guys they met there was Major Dave Halpen who was in the Air Force Reserves at Ellington Air Force Base here in Houston.

Upon talking with my folks at a meeting one day, he found out that I had been drafted, and he suggested that I apply for the Air Force Reserves, and he walked me through the whole procedure. I believe God gave me favor with him that day through my music that he liked so well.

So, at the end of my next-to-last semester at U. of H., I got on the bus in downtown Houston with several other recruits and we headed to Lackland Air Force Base in San Antonio, Texas for 5 weeks and 5 days of basic training.

I had butterflies in my stomach much like the ones I usually got when standing in the wings at a concert waiting to go on stage. I faced a lot of my fears for the first time. We had to run the obstacle course, which we were all very afraid of because they told us it was real machine gun fire over our heads, so keep your head down as you crawl under the barbed wire and through the mud. When I successfully finished the course, I was proud of myself and realized a lot of things by facing the challenges head on. At the end of basic training, I got on a bus and headed back to Houston where I would start my Ellington Field assignment as an Admin Specialist and spend the next 6 months on active duty.

I'd like to acknowledge that I was far more fortunate than most when it came to the Vietnam War. My brother came so close to death multiple times on the front lines, and many other friends and classmates never made it back. I was extremely thankful that I could fulfill my duty to my country at Ellington Field in those perilous times.

Another thing that greatly helped me was that I was the only guy in my whole outfit that could type. Very few guys took typing in school in those days, but it just so happened that I needed an elective my junior year of high school, and typing was offered as one of my choices. Since I really liked Mrs. Koch, the typing teacher, I decided to sign up for her class (I will always be grateful to her for teaching me to type). That's what got me an office job in the air-conditioned office at Ellington instead of out on the tarmac or in the hangars where our mission was to fix and refurbish the C-130s that were returning badly damaged from Vietnam. Of course, I'd get teased for having it so easy indoors, with everyone else out in the Texas heat, but somebody had to type up important documents for the officers, and I was literally the only one who could do it.

I made great friends of those "lifers," as we called the career military guys on base, and they actually became fans of my music. I would bring my guitar to the base and play music after work at the non-commissioned officers' club. It was another way for me to contribute that helped build morale for the crew and for the others stationed on base. Once my guitar player from the Golden Fleece, Randall Dollahon, joined the Reserves as well, he and I orchestrated several different music events together with our other music guys to play at the NCO Club for dances.

My "Top Kick" was Master Sergeant Jim Gifford, and he was a great friend and terrific example of excellence in top form in our U.S. military. He helped Randall and I get it all together for these functions, which actually did raise the morale of the guys stationed on base with us. They made good use of our music. Music would always continue to open doors for me in the most unexpected ways.

As I mentioned before, though, ultimately, that enlistment caused Mercury to drop me from the label. I don't blame them. It was a time when we were losing lots of men on the front lines in Vietnam and if you got drafted, there was a good chance you might not make it back.

Mercury couldn't be sure of my availability since I was subject to being called up and shipped off somewhere around the globe at any time. They felt like there definitely wouldn't be any opportunity at all for me to go out to the radio stations or promote my records anymore or be on the "watts line" at Mercury in Nashville to call the disc jockeys at the stations.

I was sad because my music dreams were now officially on hold. However, I will forever be grateful that I was able to do what was asked of me by my country, while staying Stateside, and once again, still getting to use my music to bring joy to those around me.

I was also very sad to be dropped from Mercury, because

I had really grown to admire and respect Jerry Kennedy, who took me under his wing and offered so much moral support. My memory of Jerry telling me in the studio, "Sing it ignorant," still stands out in my mind as a prolific piece of advice. I know what he meant; he meant to sing it honest like you would sing it, not like you think people would want to hear it. Sing it so your individuality will show up and people will know you for you. This is a pearl of wisdom I still try to pass down to other young singers I meet, because it was so helpful to me at that age.

LIFE AFTER MERCURY RECORDS

I wondered and asked God, what is next? I was serving my 6 months of full active duty, after which I would be required to serve one weekend a month, and I was so close to getting my degree at U. of H., but that was on hold. Basically, it felt like my whole life was on hold.

I was devastated about the end of my Mercury deal. I was despondent, depressed, and had no idea how to proceed with my career, which was my life. Then, one night at The Fleece, I was introduced to a wealthy businessman named Don Shepherd who had friends in Hollywood.

Don ended up introducing me to a guy named Nick Brainard who came in to Houston to hear me sing and consider being my manager. I signed a management deal with Nick and Don Shepherd as our backer. Nick took me to L.A. and introduced me to a famous disc jockey at KHJ Radio Station named Sam Riddle. That's how the wheels were set in motion. Nick and Sam and all the crew back home were aware that I was still in the military and had to be in Houston one weekend a month no matter what, but they were okay with that and I was glad.

The next step in Sam and Nick's plan was to find a record producer and make a production deal with him and get me placed on a record label. I remember going to Sunset Strip to Johnny Rivers' Publishing Co. and meeting a guy named Dallas Smith who headed up that company. Johnny had had the good fortune of finding a new young writer who would write huge hits for him even before he was 21 years old. His name was

Jimmy Webb, and he was the writer of Glen Campbell's biggest hits including "By the Time I Get To Phoenix," "Galveston," and "Wichita Lineman."

By this point now, I was through with my 6 months of service and was just serving one weekend a month, so three weeks out of the month I was free to fly back to L.A. and record and do television shows. Sam and Nick worked out a deal with Dallas Smith to produce four songs with me at the United Artists Studio there in L.A. He picked a Jimmy Webb song and three other songs. He set up the players and they were the best L.A. had to offer. Anybody who knows anything about music in the 70s will know who Artie Butler is. He was a short, rotund guy who had short, stubby fingers but with a reach and technique that rivaled Elton John. I also remember a famous female bass player named Carol Kay. She used to take the strings off of her bass guitar once a week and boil them. She actually became part of that famous crew of West Coast musicians deemed "The Wrecking Crew" of which Glen Campbell was a member. We also had a guy who used to play for Ricky Nelson on lead guitar; he was soon to play for Elvis when Elvis returned to the live concert stage. His name was James Burton. He was an amazing player, and a really nice guy.

With the tracks now recorded, it was time for me to turn in my best performance on the project. The pressure was immense as I think back on it. I had Nick Brainard over my shoulder, and he was not the most patient of guys, and all he had on his mind was partying and women. I was kind of a commodity to him to be bought and sold to the highest bidder. Sam Riddle, on the other hand, had more of a people approach with me, and we had a really good working relationship. Sam was already working on what TV appearances he could get for me to promote the record and was a great thinker; he knew what it took for an artist to "make it." It was also decided at that time by Sam and Nick that I should change my name to a more "pop" sounding name since I had already had a career at Mercury as a country artist. "Bill Nash" sounded too country to them, so they re-named me "Michael Brennan," pop artist.

Well, there's nothing wrong with the name, Michael Brennan.

It's a fine name, except for the fact that it wasn't mine. My dad was particularly upset for me not to be carrying the Nash name, at least in terms of my career. It became quite a hassle for me, too, especially when I tried to open a new bank account and couldn't prove I was Michael Brennan, mainly because I wasn't. I certainly wasn't legally going to change my name, but Sam and Nick felt strongly about it, so I let them use it as my "showbiz" name, or what is known as an "AKA" (also known as) at the union.

Dallas Smith set up the recording sessions for my vocal overdubs and we got to work. I recorded my voice on those four songs in a couple of days. Now Dallas Smith would mix the final session and make it ready to present it to all the record companies. With this last step complete, the next item on the agenda was to find a major record label that would sign me and release and promote the songs. Sam Riddle had many contacts in L.A. at all the labels because they were usually at his office at KHJ trying to get him to play their records. Sam got some appointments set up and we went to several, but it came down to two major labels.

Nash Note ♫

Somewhere in the midst of all this, after my full-time service at Ellington was completed, I went back and finished my final semester at UH. If you asked me to lay out the exact timeline, and how I managed my schedule to make it all happen, I'm not sure I could line it all out from memory. All I know is at long last I had my college degree, and I've always been very proud to have stuck with it and saw that through to completion.

One of the labels of interest was Capitol Records, and the other was Pierre Cosette Productions. At the time, Pierre Cosette was producing some of the grandest productions in Hollywood for award shows like the Grammys and Oscars. Even though they were not technically classified as a label, more a production company, they had a large presence in the music industry, and Pierre's senior record producer had great interest not only in our project, but in me as an artist. He told Sam and Nick that he would really like to work with me and develop me as an artist. He had Mr. Cosette's permission to offer us $15,000 for our four-song project and offered to produce me himself and help develop my career.

Bill Receiving His Diploma In The Mail - 1971

The other offer then came in from Capitol, and they offered $20,000 for the project. Sam and Nick chose Capitol, and I guess their decision was based on the money. I remember the day I went to that landmark tower in L.A. that we see in all the movies filmed there, the Capitol Records round building, and picked up a check for $20,000. When I arrived, I went to the floor where the lawyers all have offices, and there I met an attorney who had everything ready for me. I had to sign several pages of a contract, and then he very unceremoniously handed me the largest check I'd ever personally seen in my life. I sailed out of that place and back to Sam Riddle and Nick Brainard's office that they had newly rented, and we celebrated that signing and the check. Then we started making plans to promote me as an artist, which meant getting me to L.A. more permanently.

Chapter Eight

The Life and Death of Michael Brennan

W E WERE RUNNING ON MR. SHEPHERD'S backing, and Sam and Nick wanted me to live in the Hollywood Hills for the prestige of it all, so they rented me a beautiful home with a swimming pool just up the semi-private road from Phil Spector's house. Cary Grant and Eartha Kitt lived further on up the hill. Sam and Nick's idea was to keep me "under wraps" until the appropriate time to "unveil me" to the industry. So I moved in and there I sat, just waiting for "what's next?" Nick Brainard happened to have an extra car, a red Jaguar sports car, and he brought it out to L.A. for me to drive while I was there. I felt like one of the Beverly Hillbillies, my living out there in a home with a pool (a cement pond as Uncle Jed would say), driving an expensive sports car, and tooling around Hollywood. But I was so attached to my family and friends back home in Houston that I just felt lonesome all the time.

Capitol released my first record, and the song was called, "It's My First Day In The World Without Her." When the record came out, Billboard gave it a "Pick to hit." I wasn't sure anymore if that meant anything at all since I had "picks to hit" on every one of my previous record releases, including the Nash Family Trio albums.

Sam booked me on several TV shows like the *Steve Allen Show* where they asked me to be a co-host for a week after my first appearance on the show. I was so privileged to work with stars like Lucille Ball, who kissed me on my forehead after the taping and said she loved my voice. Then there was Buddy Ebsen (Uncle Jed) of the *Beverly Hillbillies'* fame, who asked me for some of my press kits so he could help promote me. There was Bob Crane of *Hogan's Heroes* who was kind of aloof, Rod Serling of *The Twilight Zone,* and then there was that world-famous comedian, Jerry Lewis. He was sitting next to me on the set as we all sat around the grand piano. Since I was co-host and announcer that day, they cued me to read my script with the name of our next guest. As I held the script up to read, Jerry took out his cigarette lighter, and proceeded to set it on fire. It started to burn from the bottom up, and I had to read faster and faster to get done before the whole thing was just ashes in my hand. The audience got a big laugh out of it all, and Steve Allen just chalked it up to something only a comedian like Jerry Lewis would do on live television and get away with it. Diana Dors was such a beautiful movie star we had on the show, and she was very memorable for a young guy like me who had seen her in the movies on the big screen. I remember her as someone who looked like Marilyn Monroe with her long blonde hair and compelling eyes. There were others that I can't quite recall, but working with all these show business legends really was a thrill.

Sam also got me booked on the *The Mama Cass Television Program* with Cass Elliot (of The Mamas and the Papas fame) at ABC TV Network. She was very jovial and said I had a "sexy smile" as she introduced me to her national TV audience. I was actually taken aback by that intro. Perhaps I didn't always have the best self-image, but I just didn't see myself in that way. I had to "lip-sync" the song I was to sing, and it felt weird to be mouthing the words, but that's how they started doing it to save money on a studio band. She was absolutely one of the sweetest and most down to earth, real people I had ever met. Besides all that, she said she really dug my singing. Sam also set up an appearance on a show in Philadelphia at WCAU TV, Channel 10. It was the *Betty Hughes Show*. Betty was the wife of then-governor of New Jersey, Richard Hughes. She really liked me and asked Sam if he would consider letting me co-host her show. Sam said yes, and I moved to Philly at the end of the record promo tour and lived there for a whole season. I worked with Jerry

SON OF A PREACHER MAN BY ANITY BRODY

The first time I saw the name Michael Brennan I immediately forgot it. I was skimming the weekly T V listings and noticed an ad for a T V special "Hand in Hand With Michael Brennan," Two weeks later I remembered the name and was talking with the star of the show.

Michael Brennan is a tall, lanky Texan, Pharr away from home. Pardon the pun (couldn't resist it) but home is in Pharr, Texas, a small town east of Laredo. Mike, a minister's son, has been singing since the age of three in his dad's churches. "They used to make me sing--they'd spank me!" No one has to force him to sing now--"That's my calling to be a singer." Mike can be heard singing daily on "The Betty Hughes Show on W C A U-T V and on Capitol records release "First Day In The World Without You." He has already had his own T V special, the afore mentioned "Hand in Hand With Michael Brennan." The show may be called a "generation gapper," if there is such a term, with appeal to both young and old. Mike's future plans include appearances on Merv Griffin's show and the "Jim Franklin Show" in New York and also a recording session to be produced by David Gates of "Bread."

Mike has been following his "calling" from Texas to L. A. and east to Philadelphia and New York. "It takes one big record or T V show and perserverance." The record is here and the name is Michael Brennan. Don't forget it! I won't.

MICHAEL BRENNAN
"They used to make me Sing"

Lewis once again and also "The Schnoz," world famous, Jimmy Durante, one of the last Vaudevillians from that era who came in to do the show. My mom had come to stay a few days with me, and I introduced her to my producer, Stewart Crowner. He quickly took a liking to mom and her piano playing, and she became a part of the warmup for the studio audience.

When Mr. Durante came in that morning, he didn't go directly to his dressing room because he was intrigued with mom and I and the music we were singing and playing for the studio audience; the music was from his era. Back then it was dubbed "Gay '90s Music" (as in the 1890s), but he had sung many of those songs himself. He applauded at the end of each song, and when it was time to "Stop the music" (Jimmy Durante fans will know what I just said), he wasn't quite ready for it to end and he asked for "just one more song." What a great and lovable guy. It was a very meaningful time in my life, and my mom and I absolutely loved Jimmy Durante (God rest his soul).

Everything came to a screeching halt when Capitol Records,

after only 6 months with the new president, decided to change course once again, fire the new guy, and get another new CEO. When they let the guy go who had been so high on me and my sound, they also cut all the acts that were signed under his

regime, including me. They offered to put out a second record, but they said it wouldn't matter since they had no plans to go forward with me, and they did not intend to promote it. It would only be to fulfill their contractual obligations.

I was back at square one. Don Shepherd had come into some money problems and was over-extended on some of his investments and was now

Bill on the Betty Hughes Show with Dionne Warwick

officially in a money crunch. Something had to be cut, and it was going to be me. However, one of the quick fixes that was proposed in order to salvage everything had to do with a product called bat guano.

Right here I just can't help but make an analogy between what bat guano is, and what my career seemed to be at the time. Bat guano was bat droppings that had built up in the numerous caves in Nevada, and these caves were just full of this stuff due to the large bat population. Don Shepherd and some associates were going to "mine" this stuff and sell it as fertilizer.

We flew to Las Vegas and met with a couple of guys from one of the big hotels that were approached with the deal, and they actually had the sheriff there, Sheriff Lamb. He sat in on the meetings. He was a really nice guy and I just sat there in my suit and tie in that Las Vegas casino and listened to the "plan" to help pull Shepherd out of his money crunch.

Here's how I was to fit in the picture: the hotel was going to sign me up to sing in their showroom and pay me $25,000 per week. However, I was only to receive $5,000 per week and the other $20,000 was to go to Shepherd as an investment for the hotel guys. They would then mine these bat droppings and market them and supposedly make lots of money because this stuff was being touted as extra special fertilizer, even richer than cow dung.

It never worked out, and I don't remember any more talk about it. The money had run out, and no amount of guano could save my deal.

Shepherd and Capitol Records were now history. I was still living in Philadelphia and doing the *Betty Hughes Show* at this time, so that's what I hung on to for the moment. My most challenging interview there was with Astrud Gilberto, the Brazilian artist who sang the hit, "The Girl From Ipanema." It was a good thing I had had some training at U. of H. School of Radio/TV on how to conduct an on-air, live interview. I didn't get a lot of advance time to talk with Astrud, but I had her biography. I asked her my first question, which was, "Isn't it great to have a big hit like "Girl From Ipanema?" She pondered the question a minute and then answered with that dreaded, one word response, "Yes." That was it, no excitement, no bubbly exuberance that usually comes along with that kind of question about an artist's success. Note to self, ask more open-ended questions to get a longer response. I asked a few more questions, but never got any more than a one-word answer. I pretty much had to ask and then embellish, having to imagine for myself what it must be like to be in her shoes. That was definitely the most difficult interview I have ever done, bar none. It taught me more about interviewing and drove it home to me about being prepared.

One of my other guests turned out to be Lucille Ball's daughter, Lucie Arnaz. After the show, I remember her coming to me and telling me "Your voice sounds like an instrument. I just love your singing." It's hard to forget those kinds of compliments that encourage you so much, and sometimes you have to live on them during the dry spells. Discouragement has been the death of many music/showbiz hopefuls. How great also to receive such wonderful, sincere compliments from both Lucille Ball and her daughter, Lucie.

I worked that season, January through May, and when the show went into hiatus for the summer, I took off to come back to Houston. I knew I would not be able to fly back and forth to fulfill my obligation to the Air Force without Mr. Shepherd buying my plane tickets each month. Mr. Shepherd was done, and with Nick not wanting to invest his own personal money at that particular time, I was once again asking myself the question "what's next?"

Sam Riddle continued to believe in me and be my friend, though. Years later, Sam took on a position as producer of the new talent showcase hosted by Ed McMahon there in Hollywood. It was called *Star Search*. Sam offered to let me be a contestant on the show, but he cautioned me that you could never tell who the judges were going to be. Since many of them were not even music people, there was always that chance that you could lose, and then the record companies would really look at you in a negative light. We decided that show was not a good fit for me at that juncture in my career.

While I was still living in Philly, though, Sam came up with the idea of me doing a music special. WCAU liked it, and it was scheduled.

We hired a great band with horns and all kinds of instruments. Sam found this "new" girl that was playing on Broadway with Danny Kaye in Mr. Kaye's new musical. Her name was Tricia O'Neil. Sam had no idea that I had met Tricia when she sang at a beauty contest at my school. It was wonderful to see her again, and I was thrilled to have her on the show.

The next act we signed for the show was the Supremes. Diana Ross had left them to pursue a solo career, and Jean Terrell stepped in and joined the group in her place. So I met with the new Supremes in New York to go over the show. We had the best time just hanging out and getting to know each other; they were just so much fun to be around. By the day of the taping of the special, we were all good friends, and it was a fun show. It was called *Hand In Hand with Michael Brennan*. It later aired on CBS

Bill with The Supremes - 1971

Television nationwide. What I learned from that experience is that a "one-shot deal does not a career make." Good experience, disappointing outcome.

Before moving back to Houston, I did get an invitation to appear on the *Mike Douglas Show* out of Philadelphia. The idea is that you keep stepping through each open door in the hopes that this next one will get you that big break that will launch a tremendous career for you. That was my dream. I was still pretty torn up inside after all that happened with Capitol because I really thought that was going to be my big break. But I somehow mustered up the courage to plod on through the negatives, and thank God I did. I realized it was something God had instilled in me through my mom, "NEVER QUIT."

The day of the *Mike Douglas Show* in Philadelphia, I arrived for the rehearsal and met the other folks on the show. I felt so privileged to have the honor of singing on the same show as the Sons of the Pioneers, Roy Rogers' famous back up group that were in the movies with him and on records. They sang their famous song, "Tumbling Tumble Weeds." Their harmony was so tight, so rich and beautiful, and I was mesmerized as I stood on the sidelines next to one of the TV cameras just watching and listening.

The other special guest was a movie star, Janet Leigh, and her teenage daughter, Jamie Lee Curtis. Janet Leigh was so very beautiful on the big screen, and even more beautiful in person; she was warm and friendly to me. I didn't get to talk much with that teenage daughter of hers, but she was very nice and kind of shy in her teenage sort of way when we were introduced.

With those last experiences, Michael Brennan was no more. What's next?

CASTING A LIGHT

Through all my time in L.A., I don't really remember ever asking myself, "Is this where God wants me to be?" I've never doubted that God called me to sing, but I was so consumed with being a star at the time (and for many years), and that was only multiplied by all the glitz and glamour of Hollywood. I had what most would consider some pretty great opportunities arise, but in the end, none of that was meant to continue. If it had all turned out how I wanted it, I would be in a completely different place now, and I would have missed out on my destiny. It reminds me of the Garth Brooks song that says, "Some of God's greatest gifts are unanswered prayers." If that title were not already written so well in song, it could have been a very appropriate alternate title for this book!

Chapter Nine

The '70s Houston Club Scene

NOW THAT I WAS BILL NASH again and moved back to Houston, I needed to get back around the club circuit and see where I could play. Buddy Williams was my brother-in-law at the time; he was married to my sister, Alice. He introduced me to the manager of the piano bar at the Kings Inn, Sharon, and she hired me. The Kings Inn was in the "NASA" area south of Houston. I hired a guitar player named David Koon. I then bought a new musical invention called a drum machine to augment our sound and keep a beat for whoever might dance. We gave our drum machine a name as if he were really our drummer; his name was "Arthur." I guess it was easier to call it Arthur as opposed to the "drum machine." I would always tell the audience to wait for the next song while I programmed Arthur. It was funny to us and our audience.

I remember one day in particular during that time when I received a call from Sam Riddle telling me that Steve Allen was going to re-run one of the shows I was on, so I tuned it in on TV that afternoon and watched as I co-hosted Lucille Ball and the rest of the guests that day.

As I got dressed to leave for the Kings Inn, I couldn't help but

BILL NASH

Bill Nash Promo Photo 1970

think of the past and my near-miss with Capitol and the life I had always dreamed of and how, instead, I was preparing to drive down to NASA to sing in a piano bar to folks who didn't even know me or my story. They just came in to have a good time, have a drink and forget the troubles of their day. I had to learn not to put my sorrows about my career on them; I just needed to do my best to lift their load and help them have a good time. As I did that more and more, it also helped to relieve me of the pain I felt in my heart and soul over such life-shattering reversals in Nashville and Hollywood and all the dreams that almost came true.

What was I to do now, for my career, or even my life in general? I felt so lost, depressed! I prayed in those days, but my lifestyle was not congruous with my prayers. It was kind of like I wanted God to give me everything I wanted and make me a big star, but I wasn't interested in living the lifestyle that Jesus had laid out for a person who called himself a Christian. I still held the bitterness of dad being booted out of the church. I couldn't seem to shake that bitterness. However, I still had a dream, and I had to come up with a new way to make it come true. I never quit believing in the gift of music and singing that God had given me, I just had to re-group and figure out my future plan. My mom's words kept ringing in my ears, "NEVER QUIT," she used to say.

Dad used to quote the Proverb from the Bible that says: "A

man with no dream will perish." I had a dream alright, and I can almost thank my lack of finances for getting me over the hump because I couldn't afford to just quit. What would I have done then? I just hated the thought of being anything other than the singer that God called me to be. Life just held no intrigue without the music, so I persevered.

The Kings Inn ended up holding a breakthrough night for me, though I had always been mostly a singer who stood behind the mike and sang. I was not blessed with any dancing ability like my long-time friend, Roy Head. I was just a "stiff white guy." One night, though, I was bored with the scene in this small bar at the Kings Inn, and it seemed like no one was paying attention to me as I was singing to them. David Koon urged me to climb up on top of the grand piano in the middle of my song and keep singing. I don't know what came over me, but I thought that was better than just sitting on that bar stool and trying to sing over the noise of the crowd. When I did, the crowd stopped all their talking and turned my way to see what I was up to.

Then they started listening and clapping, no longer ignoring me, but responding to my antics. It brought the house down, and I've never forgotten it. The whole attitude of the evening took on a big fun-type feeling.

That was the beginning of the end of me being inhibited in front of an audience. From then on, people would keep coming back just to see what I would do next and invariably would ask me to jump up on top of that piano one more time. I usually always complied. It broke the boredom of the night.

Eventually I organized a full band in the early 70s and worked the local club scene in Houston where I also recorded several albums on my own. My first club was located in the high-rise Holiday Inn Hotel Downtown Houston. They created a great looking nightclub with the Indianapolis Speedway motif. With the permission of A. J. Foyt, a Houstonian who happened to be one of the world's most famous racecar drivers, they filled the walls with all kinds of pictures of A.J. They named the club "The Checkered Flag Lounge." They also installed a red, plastic racetrack that circled the entire room. That's when I first met A.J. He came out a couple of times, and even brought his family once. That's how I met his little girl, Terry. In later years, she became a great friend and even wrote a couple of songs with us. She's still a great friend of ours to this day.

This is also where I met my first wife, Gwen. I know it sounds like a Country song. I can hear it now: "I met my wife down at the Checkered Flag Club." Well, I did. I was working 6 nights a week, and she'd come into the club, and we ended up dating. After 6 months or so, we got married way too soon. Neither one of us was ready, but unfortunately, that didn't stop us from rushing in. All my friends were getting married, and I always wanted to start a family and have kids, so I tried to help God's plan along before it was time (because that worked so well for Abraham and Sarah in the Bible). I'll tell more about that as we go.

Aside from that, the night that sticks out the most is when Kris Kristofferson and his then wife, Rita Coolidge, came to my show. By this time, Kris finally had huge hits on both "For The Good Times" and "Help Me Make It Through The Night," among others, and his singing career had also taken off. He was one of the co-stars at a music concert downtown at the old coliseum.

My pal, Doc Fields, had met Kris when he accompanied me to Nashville and was present at the session where we cut "Help Me Make It Through the Night." Since he knew Kris, he went to the concert and got backstage. He told Kris that I was playing just up the road. Doc invited Kris to come by after he finished his show at the coliseum.

Well, Kris did even better than come by; he announced to the whole crowd that he was heading to my show at the Checkered Flag Lounge right after he was done with his show. What a night that turned out to be with limousines and Cadillacs circling the hotel and people all jammed up in the lobby trying to get into the show.

They seated Kris and Rita right on the front row to my right along with their promotion man from Kris's record label. I remember coming out on stage when I was introduced wearing this yellow, polyester pant and vest outfit custom made by Duke's Tailors on Market Square. My shirt had that real high collar, and I'm sure it was of some kind of matching color (who knows).

I wore my patent leather blue, short-topped boots that

zipped up the side. I had three pairs of them, one black, one blue and one white. I was set for any outfit I might wear. I thought I was "hot" (oh my goodness). I took the microphone off the stand on the stage, and as they played my opening song, I started to walk toward the audience. As I did, my mike cable got under my foot somehow and I stepped down on it and, when I raised it up to my mouth, it pulled the mike right out of my hand.

Bill, Kris, & Rita Coolidge - 1972

As I looked down in disbelief at having done such a dumb thing, then hearing that awful, loud "THUD" as it hit the floor, I know my face had to have turned several shades of red because I was so embarrassed. I couldn't believe my old friend, who used to pitch me songs, had caused me to be so nervous...lol. I had to pick up my mike and laugh it off, along with Kris and Rita, and continue singing where I left off.

Rita Coolidge got up and sang with me; we sang "Amazing Grace" a capella, no band. She was a preacher's kid, as well, and she knew we would both know that song. Kris turned me down when I asked him to sing. He said he didn't like to sing in front of me (go figure). It was a great night, and I've always been grateful to Doc Fields for getting Kris and Rita to my show.

CASTING A LIGHT

Looking back in broad strokes at my life, it seems that God has always had a purpose for me in Houston. I've lived in the Rio Grande Valley, I've lived in Nashville, Los Angeles, Philadelphia, and New Orleans, all for a time and a for a season, but I keep coming back to Houston.

Every time life has hit me hard, Houston has been the place I needed to recuperate and regroup. The people, my friends, my fans, my family, they have always been here for me, and God always blesses me here.

I think in all our lives, God has specific places we need to be, specific places where He intends for us to be blessed and be a blessing to others. The more I read in the Bible, the more I see this. I don't know what it is about Houston, but I know it's always the place where God shows me my next step.

Chapter Ten

GRC Records 1974 & 1975

WHEN I WAS PLAYING AT THE Checkered Flag, a guy by the name of Sam Camarata came to hear me sing. He was managing several other artists that he had done well with, and I, naturally, was looking for representation like that. After we met a couple of times, I signed up with him. He had record label connections as well as Las Vegas hotel connections. The first thing he stirred up for me was a gig in Las Vegas at the Hacienda Hotel where I opened the show for Jim Backus, better known as Mr. Magoo in cartoons, and as Mr. Howell from the *Gilligan's Island* TV show.

Sam got me signed up with GRC Records out of Atlanta owned by a Mr. Michael Thevis. I recorded for them in 1974 and 1975. I had three releases. The first one did okay, but the second one brought me some great notoriety due to the fact that Al De Lory produced it for me in L.A.

Bill in Las Vegas - 1973

I remember GRC flying me to L.A. to meet with Al. He was quite indescribable, the music man of the hour at that time, having produced all of Glen Campbell's biggest hits. The song he produced for me was called "Mississippi Song," and it was written by Jim Weatherly, who also wrote, "Midnight Train to Georgia" for Gladys Knight and the Pips. The first time I heard the finished track, I was on stun. It was unbelievably great sounding with all those L.A. strings and horns.

GRC released it and put a bit of a push on it. They set it up for me to fly down to Jackson, Mississippi to get my picture with Governor William Waller and to present him with his copy of the record. Governor Waller then made me an honorary Colonel in the Mississippi Militia.

That's when an incredibly impactful, life shattering incident occurred in my life and career.

The producer GRC then put me with was a great guy named Jeff Lee. Jeff had been one of Joe South's producers. Joe was a great writer and had some big hits on Capitol Records like "Games People Play" and "Walk A Mile in My Shoes." Jeff and I hit it off really great, and I even stayed at his house when I went to record in Atlanta for GRC.

I played him a song I had written with Mr. Bill (William) Francey, an older gentleman who was my first songwriting partner and had worked at the Coca Cola bottling plant in McAllen, Texas with my brother. Jeff loved a song we had written called, "Honky Tonk Bar Room Blues." We cut the track in Atlanta at the GRC studios on Peach Tree Street with Shane Keister and the band that recorded for the group, Lobo.

After the GRC Studios session in Atlanta, Jeff hopped a plane to L.A. and overdubbed background voices (he called them "chicks") and a Dixie Land band horn section. The gals did yeehaws and so on while the horns played the solo in the middle of the song. This is long before Garth Brooks did "Friends in Low Places" with a similar type of vocal backgrounds. Jeff was very innovative.

So while I was headed back to Houston to close out a weekend, Jeff finished up the L.A. session and headed back to Atlanta. Then the band and I hit the road for Albuquerque, New Mexico to perform at the Four Seasons Hotel for a two-week stint.

When I arrived, I got a phone call from Sam Camarata with the most terrible news. I will never forget that moment. He said, verbatim, "Jeff is dead." I said, "What?" He repeated it, and then I sat there on stun with the phone in my hand. I got this big lump in my throat, and tears began to roll down my cheeks. My next question as I was trying to clear my throat and keep my composure was, "How could this be? What happened?"

Camarata told me that Jeff had been shot in his home in his own bed, and there were no signs of forced entry. What is puzzling about that is that Jeff had this large German Shepherd guard dog that I had had to make friends with when I stayed at Jeff's house. Someone would definitely have had to get past his very large dog.

Just weeks before when I stayed with Jeff, he let me have his room with the waterbed, and he slept in his guest room. I had just been in that very bed; it could have been me they killed. To this day, no one has ever been arrested or charged with his murder.

I learned later that Camarata knew that Mr. Thevis, the owner of GRC, was considered the porno king of America (dubbed by Reader's Digest as the "Sultan of Smut"), but failed to inform me of that tidbit of information. I thought of all those people in Pharr who were upset just by me playing in a bar. Imagine if they knew I was now recording for the porno king. Their heads just might explode. I knew nothing about it though.

I was so naive! I can't believe it! I hadn't once seriously questioned Sam about this guy. Mr. Thevis had flown down to hear me play at Hilton Head Island and get acquainted with me. He was a really bright guy and very engaging. He had to walk with a cane due to a motorcycle accident he had had a few years earlier. He carried huge wads of cash in his pockets and handed out $100 bills like they were Monopoly money. He was a huge tipper. I just thought this wealthy guy really liked my singing and wanted to make us both a lot of money by making me a star.

I never did find out any more about Jeff but it seemed he had accrued a lot of inside knowledge about all of whatever had gone on in Mr. Thevis's business and personal ventures. I was not privy to any of it, and Jeff never told me anything more than that he was helping Mr. Thevis put together his case for a lawsuit with the Feds. Now Jeff was gone; the one man at the time who really believed in me and my songwriting. I was absolutely stunned and devastated! And there I was in Albuquerque. I can't describe the pain in my heart and my mind about the whole situation. Jeff Lee: he was a really big loss on so many levels.

Since I hadn't put my final vocal on "Honky Tonk Bar Room Blues," GRC flew me back to Atlanta to do just that. This time I stayed at the home of Mr. & Mrs. Thevis. Mrs. Thevis was so warm and friendly, and she made me feel at home.

Their mansion was located outside Atlanta somewhere about 30 minutes from the office and studio. It looked like a huge hotel with a guesthouse off to the side that had to be at least 10,000 square feet itself; the mansion dwarfed the guesthouse. The mansion sat on a large acreage, and was connected by paved trails for Thevis's golf cart to travel on around his entire property. The grounds were kept in a manicured condition by the full-time gardener. I just recently found out this mansion later became home to Whitney Houston and Bobby Brown in the 90s.

The first night I was there, they all went to bed and left me downstairs playing pool on this incredibly beautiful custom pool table. I was used to being up most of the night since I was on my nightclub hours, but they all weren't. Somehow, they didn't realize that I had stayed downstairs, so when I was ready to retire, I hit the winding staircase to climb to the second floor and all hell broke loose. The alarm went off, and the huge lights came on, and the next thing I knew, the groundskeeper had a shotgun aimed over the railing of the stairs right at me. Oh *****! Now what do I do?

Mike came hobbling on his cane as fast as he could out of his bedroom, and when he looked over the railing and saw me at the bottom of the stairs, he was relieved that I wasn't an intruder. The phone was already ringing, and it was the Atlanta Police Dept. Thevis answered and said, "false alarm" and gave the password.

That's one of the times I wondered who this guy really was. Before this incident, I really had no idea. He had such a nice and beautiful family. What does he really do? Sam Camarata would say, "Oh, he's in lots of different ventures," and leave it at that. I was young and wanted to be a star, so I didn't ask too many questions. Plus, there was no Google back then to look him up.

So I overdubbed my voice on the tracks that Jeff Lee had created (an emotional endeavor with him gone). Afterwards, I headed back to Houston to await the release of the next record. GRC picked "Honky Tonk Bar Room Blues." When they released it, they got an immediate response. Billboard Magazine gave my song a "Pick to Hit." This time I was more positive about the outcome than on my other "Picks to Hit."

The first week it came out, lots of stations added it to their play list, and the same thing happened the second week, as well. It started climbing up the charts really fast. The disc jockey

BILL NASH

Promo Photo - 1975

convention was coming up in Nashville, and a lady named Anne White was the promo person for GRC in those days. She had it all set up for me to fly in and do some things to promote the new record.

I remember the excitement in packing and thinking that this was finally going to be my time. I reflected on the night before when Moe Bandy had come to Houston to see me at the club I was playing, the Houstonaire, and he sat in with my band. Moe already had some hits, and he I were both on GRC, and that's why he came by. Moe was doing what I had always wanted to do. He was a great guy and a really good country singer. I got all packed that night after my show and was up early to get to the airport and head to Nashville.

I had started having stomach problems as I was getting dressed to go, and I barely made it to the airport and then onto the plane. I didn't know what I was going to do. I only knew one thing; I was going to make it to Nashville and promote my new record, and by all indications it was going to be my big hit.

My old friends at KIKK, Bill Bailey and Joe Ladd, encouraged me and were playing the song heavily on the radio, and it was selling big. We knew how fast it was going because Don's Record Shop in Bellaire kept us up to date. He couldn't keep them in stock. I was determined not to let a little 24-hour bug stop me from making it to the big time.

The plane lands, and as I rush to the rest room in the airport, I hear my name on the public address system. It said to please pick up a courtesy phone. I gutted up and trotted over to the phone, and when I said hello, the voice on the other end, Anne White, started apologizing saying, "I tried to catch you before you left Houston. GRC has closed its doors. Mr. Thevis declared bankruptcy for GRC this morning. I am so sorry."

Her words immediately sent me into shock. How many more times, how many more labels, how many more chances was I going to get? When will this ever end? I couldn't even think straight. I took a cab to the Hilton downtown, made it to my room, ripped off my jeans and shirt and shoes, and crawled under the covers with the air turned up high. I must admit that I cried like a big old baby. I was truly heartbroken once again. How much can a guy take? All that work, all that writing, all that recording, all that effort, all the pain over Jeff's death, how much more can I take?

I never left my room. After a nap, I called the airline, re-booked my ticket home, and the next morning I flew back to Houston. I don't think I spoke to anyone nor did I smile at all (which is not at all like me). I just couldn't lift my head. I made it home and laid back down just to rest and tried my best to think, but I couldn't. I just laid there until it was time to go to work that night. I called my sub and told him I was back and wouldn't need him.

I got to work barely in time to walk up behind the bandstand to let the guys know I was there and to call me up. They did: Ladies and Gentlemen, here he is directly back from Nashville, Tennessee, Mr. Bill Nash (applause, applause).

The intro to the first song started playing, and I walked out into the spotlight and took the mike off the stand, and when it was time for me to sing, I couldn't. I tried, but I couldn't make a sound come out. I was doing good to breathe.

Nobody besides another artist could know what that moment was like for me. They say in show biz, "The show must go on." But that night, the show did not go on. I just stood there, and in a minute the tears started rolling down my cheeks. I held on to the mike like you grasp at the side of a swimming pool when you feel like you have to hold on for dear life to keep from drowning. It seemed like an eternity, on and on, standing, swallowing, looking down at the floor of the stage, wiping the snot from my nose (not a classy thing to say, but it's the God-awful truth).

I really don't know how long I stood there and, frankly, can't remember what I finally did to get through that ordeal. Eventually, I just turned it over to my band and went to the bar and started drinking. I thought Jack Daniels was my best friend that night until a couple of hours later when he deserted me and nausea took over. I paid a huge price for drinking that much that night. I never did drugs because I saw the devastation it caused some of my frat brothers at U of H. Marijuana was the big thing at that time, but I never smoked anything because I was worried it would spoil my voice.

When it was reported to the music world that GRC had closed its doors, every radio station pulled my record with the exception of Joe Ladd at KIKK and the sister station in New York. It was ultimately over, though. In times like that, you just have to learn to plod on. I was mostly a zombie on stun for a week or two, and then somehow I made it back to the land of the living. What's next?

CASTING A LIGHT

At the time, I couldn't imagine anything positive coming

from GRC closing. Now, though, while doing some research for this book, I've realized just how fortunate I was to get out with my life.

As it turns out, not only was Mr. Thevis one of the largest pornographers in the country, he was also involved with the Gambino crime family, was arrested for conspiracy to commit arson, then broke out of prison, was put on the FBI's most wanted list, and committed double homicide before finally being apprehended and put away for good.

I'm sure that the answer to the mystery surrounding Jeff's death is wrapped up somewhere in all of Mr. Thevis' criminal dealings, and only God could have protected me through that whole situation. So many number of things could have happened to me in the midst of all that. To escape with only a bruised career, I now count a blessing.

Chapter Eleven

Life Has To Go On

THE BAND AND I KEPT PLAYING our dates and traveling. We played the beautiful high-rise Marriott in New Orleans. It had a club at the top of the Hotel called the River Queen Lounge. They liked us so well they booked us for the whole winter season in 1974. I had a suite on the 7th floor, and on one side was the den area that overlooked the Mississippi River, and the other side of the suite was the bed and closet.

I started writing more to try to get some of the feelings out of me and onto paper. I got everything I wanted off the menu for free as per my contract, so I would order coffee and food and sit and eat and write and watch TV. Through the large glass windows in my suite that overlooked the Mississippi river, I watched the ships as they came in and out of New Orleans. It was totally therapeutic and healing for me.

Camarata had previously introduced to me a very successful songwriter from L.A. Let's just call him D.J. He flew into Houston to meet me. He wanted to talk about writing and producing records on me. We hit it off well, and he said he really liked my singing. I ended up flying out to L.A. to spend a few days with him working on material and getting to know him better. He lived in a large penthouse apartment that was very beautiful and very well appointed, and we drank a lot of Blue Nun

Bill Nash At Live Performance

Wine. He had written hits for the Partridge Family and for some other great names, and he had connections that would help take me directly back into Capitol Records.

I came back home to continue playing six nights a week in various clubs in Houston, and he flew in again to see me. We had a party for him at Camarata's house on the golf course, and as Camarata and I and the other guests were visiting in the house, I could see this guy (D.J.) sitting outside in the porch swing with my then-wife, Gwen. As I touched on before, she and I had embarked on this thing called "marriage," under the wrong premise to begin with. Before we even got married we had said, "If it doesn't work out, we'll just get a divorce." It was destined to fail from the start. So, she and D.J. sat out there for the longest time, and it just looked like they were visiting and having casual conversation.

You can probably see where this is heading, but there was more to it than that.

All my life I had put the music first. I lived, ate, slept and breathed music and the dream of becoming a star. I paid more attention to music than I did my ex, and I was a terrible husband. I hate to admit that about myself, but in those days, it was just music and party time. I had no concept of a healthy marriage. I stayed out late and drank too much and didn't pay her the proper attention a wife deserves. That can get old really fast, and I am still ashamed to this day about it all.

A few days later, after the party, the band and I left to go play our gig at the South Park Inn in Lubbock, Texas. It was a long drive and, when we arrived, we had to hurry and get set up ready to play. It was a couple of days before I called home. Keep in mind that there weren't any cell phones in those days. When I did try to call home, there was no answer, and in those days we didn't have answering machines. I didn't think much of it at first, but then I tried again and again. Then I started to get worried, so I called my ex's mom. She said she didn't know where she was. That's when my brother called me and asked me what my white Cougar was doing at the Houston Airport. I told him he must have made a mistake. He insisted, he was sure it was my car.

He said, "It has the radiator hoses hanging down underneath the radiator. It's your car." I was at a total loss. I called her mom again and asked her to tell my ex to please call me. I didn't know what to make of it all.

Later, between shows, I got a call, and finally it was her. She said she'd just been busy and on and on, but wanted to sit down and talk about everything when I returned home; it was kind of left like we were going to try to work things out.

I talked again with my brother, Dave, and he knew I was upset about it all and was having trouble focusing on anything. So when the gig ended two weeks later, he flew to Lubbock and helped me pack to come home. I had clothes strewn all over that hotel room of mine when I left to perform my last show on that Saturday night.

Dave told me not to worry about it. He would have me all packed and ready to take off for home right after the show. As soon as the show was over, I went back to my room to change out of my stage clothes into my jeans.

Sure enough, everything was packed and had been moved out of the room. Dave said that we were ready to go. I asked him how he did it so quickly and he told me, "I got some big trash bags from the kitchen at the hotel, and put all your clothes and toilet articles and everything in them, and threw them in the car. Let's go!"

My show clothes and everything I owned were just dumped into those big old bags. That's just my big brother's way; get it done. But no matter, we were headed home.

After driving all night, we pulled into my parents' driveway in Spring, and I went inside and collapsed in dad's big recliner, and after a few minutes I called my wife's mom again. She said she still didn't know of my ex's whereabouts. I know now that she knew all along where her daughter was, but she couldn't violate that loyalty to her. I called my ex's best friend, Debbie, and she said she didn't know anything either.

A couple of days later, I called Debbie once again, but this time her husband, Allen, answered the phone. He and I were good friends, and I told him about my dilemma, and he said,

"Don't you know where she is?"

I said I had no idea.

He said, "She's in L.A. with your songwriter friend."

The guy who portrayed himself as my new best friend, and was supposedly going to get behind my career and help me become a star, the one who had me fly to L.A. and stay in his home with him? I can't tell you how long I stayed on stun. There went my marriage and my new career opportunity all in one fell swoop.

I know I was not the greatest husband, but I would have really appreciated an honest and open request for a divorce instead of having it all come down like this. Unbeknownst to me, Camarata had foreknowledge of the situation and did not tell me anything either. I now had to once again pick up the pieces of my life and my career and see if I could make any sense of it, another restart. What's next?

A DIFFERENT KIND OF "HIT"

A few weeks later, I was in my hotel suite at the Marriott in New Orleans when the phone rang. Now here comes a "you can't make this stuff up" story! My soon-to-be ex was on the other end of the line. Her voice was subdued but urgent.

She asked me, "Did you put a hit out on D.J."?

I replied emphatically, "No, I don't even know anyone that would kill someone for money."

I heard her say to D.J., "I told you so, Bill wouldn't do a thing like that, and he's saying absolutely that he didn't!"

She still knew my heart, and that that was not how I did things. She then shared with me the fact that D.J. was going to call his "connections" in New Orleans and have me disappear. Probably dumped in the Mississippi never to be heard from again. I wondered then who in the world could have even told him that I was out to get him. How preposterous!

However, what I didn't know was that Sam Camarata had a little something inadvertently to do with this. When my ex came back to Houston to get all her stuff and move to L.A., Camarata told D.J. that he was holding her hostage, and would not allow her to return to L.A. unless D.J. sent him $10,000. Camarata had actually extorted $10,000 out of D.J.

That played its own part in D.J. believing that I might have been part of that as well. I learned about this later when Camarata and I had lunch one day. He laughed and thought it was too funny that D.J. believed him and sent the money.

It kind of confirmed my suspicions about Camarata's ties to the underworld. It's one of the reasons I asked to buy my contract back from him, and suggested we part ways.

The end for Camarata came when he went to prison for some drug related trafficking charges, if my information is correct. However, he did have one last stand; while in the airport in Memphis, he became involved in a shoot-out right there in the middle of the airport. I thank God that I was not with him. A few months earlier there would have been a high probability that I would have been traveling with him.

Sam survived that incident, but still ended up in prison where he passed away. I knew all this because I was told by my good friend, Lee Ofman, who was the attorney for Camarata's wife, Mary. Lee had also been one of Camarata's clients in his showbiz days, and he knew the family before becoming an attorney. Mary knew he would be honest with her and help her out. BTW, Lee Ofman is also the one who wrote and sang the Houston Oilers' fight song, "Houston Oilers."

SONGWRITING SUCCESS & A NEW PRODUCER 1975-1980

My next recordings were picked up by A.V. Mittlestedt at Sound Masters Studios in Houston. A.V. was a very successful independent producer that had a national hit with Randy Cornor, a great friend of mine. Randy's song, "Sometimes I Talk In My Sleep," was quite successful.

Another great artist from Houston A.V. produced was Kenny Dale. He had a song called, "Bluest Heartache of the Year," which A.V. produced, and it got Kenny signed to Capitol Records.

With that kind of track record, I sought A.V. out and asked if he would be interested in working with me, and he said yes. My brother Dave got involved and invested in what we call the white album project because of the white, John Travolta type suit I wore for the album cover picture.

I wrote a song in New Orleans right after my divorce was final called, "I Can't Help It If You're Always On My Mind" (this is before Willie Nelson's "Always On My Mind" had come out) that received some radio play. During this time, I met a publicity agent/ publisher named Gabe Tucker, and he became my publisher. He worked for Eddy Arnold as his P.R. man and did that for many years.

Bill In His "Travolta" Suit

Gabe took my song and played it for Eddy, who loved it, and cut it on his newest album for RCA Records. He did a very nice version of it and turned my ballad into a mid-tempo song. It was a great honor to have Eddy Arnold cut a song I had written.

On one of Gabe Tucker's trips to Nashville for Eddy, he dropped one of my albums off to Dave Burgess who was the administrator for Hank Williams, Jr.'s publishing company.

We ended up making a deal with Dave to produce some recordings on me and to shop my stuff to the major record labels to try to come up with another record deal. In the meantime, I

had been working on an album project with my good friend, Tony Puccio, here in Houston. We had cut several things already and we finished it off with my most recent song, "Hold Me 'Til the Last Waltz Is Over."

Tony had just released my version to the Houston stations, and KIKK radio picked up on it immediately, and Billboard Magazine gave me another

Bill with Eddy Arnold

pick to hit, (just like every single I ever put out). I would always get a pick to hit from Billboard...interesting!

LIBERTY RECORDS

"Hold Me" was now moving up the charts nationally when Dave Burgess called and told me he'd gotten me a deal on Liberty Records. Liberty is a subsidiary of Capitol Records. The kicker was that they demanded that we pull "Hold Me" off the market so as not to interfere with their new publicity campaign with all the radio stations on a national basis.

Tony P. suggested they just take "Hold Me" over so as not to stop the momentum of what looked like it could finally be my

big hit. I told Dave that Tony was wide open to any kind of an arrangement with Liberty.

I still don't understand why that couldn't be done. I never did get a clear answer as to why we couldn't make that deal. It was either pull my existing record or Liberty was not going to go forward. I had to choose.

Bill with Producer, Dave Burgess - 1978

Dave was adamant about the power of a major label with their big budgets and promotion team, and he said a local recording wasn't going to make me a star or any money compared to what a national hit with a large company would make me.

So Tony pulled "Hold Me" off the national table at my request. However, my version still went top 5 at KIKK and number 1 at several other smaller stations around the South Texas region. I owe a big thank you to my good buddy, Joe Ladd, for playing my music which had its part to play in the smaller stations picking up on it. Gabe ended up pitching "Hold Me" to Eddy Arnold, and again, Eddy loved one more of my songs and cut it on his very last album for RCA. It was an honor both times to have Eddy cut one of my songs, and I will be forever grateful to him for that.

I was getting another shot at a big record label with Liberty Records. Dave Burgess set up the session in Nashville, and I went in as I had done several times before and prepared for a new session and a new chance at being a star.

Liberty was my fifth major record label, and I thought maybe the saying should go, "fifth time's the charm." The session went great, we were all pumped, and the record was released.

Liberty only had two artists on its roster, Kenny Rogers and me. I even wondered if there might be a possibility of my opening for Kenny.

Then there came this big announcement in the music industry trade magazines, "Kenny Rogers leaves Liberty Records and signs with RCA Records for over 20 million dollars."

That was wonderful for Kenny, and I can't blame him for taking the deal (I sure would have), but what about me? The announcement that followed read: "Capitol Records is shutting down its subsidiary label, Liberty Records."

It was happening all over again. They had advance knowledge that Kenny was in negotiations with RCA, and they knew if he jumped off the label that they were going to shut it down.

I was just at the wrong place at the wrong time.

What's next...again?

Chapter Twelve

A Brand New Life

I N 1979, MY MOM AND DAD had gotten into the Amway business, and had been talking to me about it for over a year. My Uncle David, my mom's youngest brother who had signed them up, kept telling me about it too.

He came to my house and showed me the Amway Plan. I really didn't get it at first, and I only took the meeting because Unkie, as I have always called him affectionately, was so special to me, having lived with us when I was a baby and in my growing up years. He had been the one who taught me to play baseball and football, and took lots of time with my brother and me. I didn't get into Amway then, and waited another few months until my mom invited me to a family get-together for us to talk more about Amway (just what I wanted to do on my night off). By this time, I had met a new gal that I thought I was going to settle down with and marry and live life happily ever after. That night at my uncle's house, I signed my future wife and myself up in Amway. We attended a few meetings, and I signed some great friends up in the business with me, and we were rocking along.

I met her at the first annual Tim Hearn Memorial Softball game that I put together with Dave Ward (my good friend and Houston TV anchor). Tim was her husband. He was a police officer who was killed in the street late one night as he and his partner were making an arrest of a drug dealer. It was an awful tragedy. She was so gracious at the tournament, and I presented her with a check in Memorial Park for $13,000 that me and my great/crazy showbiz buds had raised. A few weeks later, we started dating, and a couple months after that we got engaged.

Bill & Gary Smith at the Tim Hearn Memorial Softball Game - 1979

As the day of my second wedding approached, I started to get very jittery about it all. I couldn't help but remember my past failure at marriage, and how the showbiz life is just not conducive to marriage for the most part.

Bill at Bat - 1979

One night, as I was having dinner with her, I found myself struggling to look up at her at the dinner table. She asked me if everything was okay, and I nodded my head yes, but it wasn't really. I seemed to visualize mentally a large hand in a black glove pushing my head down into my plate, and each time I tried to raise my head to look at her, it just kept pushing me down. I should have told her right then how I was feeling.

Instead, I left to go sing at the club. But that hand would not leave me alone. I tried to get drunk at the club and couldn't.

This was on a Friday night. and by 2:00 a.m. that next morning, as I was driving to my home in the Heights, I just started to be overwhelmed with emotion, doubts and fears, and tears started to roll down my cheeks. When the dawn broke, I found myself still awake, walking up and down the sidewalk in front of my house, and for the first time in a long time, I was praying.

I recalled the first marriage ceremony as my ex walked toward me. I heard a voice in my ear that I hadn't heard before. It said, "Have you prayed about this?" I was stunned by the question, and then I realized I hadn't even thought of praying. I went through with it because it seemed like it was way too late to back out. Now, at least, I still had an option. The actual truth was that I was afraid that I would now ruin someone else's life. She had a 3-year-old son that I had become very close to (we'd watch cartoons together). This made it all extremely difficult and heartbreaking. I called my brother, and he came up to get me, and I met with this wonderful gal, and faced her with my dilemma. In retrospect, she handled it very well.

The next step was to cancel all the plans and then try to move on. She did not care much about the Amway business I had started to build, so we made a friendly business settlement, and I continued on in that business alone. I had already been booked to sing at the next convention for the "Champions" Amway organization the very next week in New Orleans on the 4th of July weekend in 1980. Champions was started by Keith and Jimmie Lee Belknap, who were very successful in Amway.

I decided to go on alone to New Orleans the following week, and I went a day early to spend some time with my old pal, Elario Lozano, who was the star singer and guitarist at the Royal Sonesta Hotel. I was feeling really bad about myself and incredibly guilty that I had caused someone else any pain that she certainly did not deserve or need in her life. With that mind-set, I couldn't wait to get back to my old stompin' grounds, New Orleans, and try to party away my depression and self-degradation.

Elario and I went out on the Wednesday night before I had to be at the Hyatt for the rehearsal the next morning at 8:00 a.m. We stayed out all night after his last show and went to Fat City and had drinks and saw a show, then headed back to Bourbon

Street to some all-night eatery that had fabulous food. Frankie Ford was playing there; he was a 50s star who had had a big hit, "Sea Cruise." Needless to say, that's not really the thing to do on the night before an early morning rehearsal.

On almost no sleep, I went downstairs that next morning to sign into the convention when I glanced across the lobby just in time to see the elevator doors open and Kim Belknap walk out.

Kim was Keith & Jimmie Lee's 19-year-old daughter. I had seen her picture on one of her family's music albums that my Aunt Helen and Uncle David had given me. I had always thought she was pretty. When I listened to the album, I thought to myself, "That girl can really sing." I truly liked her style and the sound of her voice. So when I saw her on this Thursday morning walking through the lobby, I couldn't take my blood-shot eyes off of her, and I probably shouldn't tell on myself, but I will anyway. I thought to myself, "She sure does have pretty legs."

What I didn't know until she told me later was that she kept playing the 8-track tape I had given her dad when he had come to Houston for some Amway meetings. She played it over and over, and that was part of the reason I was booked to sing at the convention.

I still felt really bad about my recent breakup and even felt a bit guilty that I would even be attracted to someone this soon after such an emotional breakup. It all felt very strange and bewildering, but I said to myself, "She's too young for me, and I'm crazy for thinking she would ever go for someone my age." I was 35 and she was just 19, after all.

I was then informed that the rehearsal had been postponed for another couple of hours. I had stayed out drinking most of the night, and now I had a huge hangover and was chagrined that I had gotten up after only a couple hours of sleep to make sure I was at that rehearsal on time. Finally, about 11:00 a.m., the rehearsal got started.

Kim was there and her older brother, Keith, Jr., was leading the rehearsal. Keith and Kim had been singing together since they were little kids along with their mom and dad. They had a gospel family group and had traveled all over the country for years.

Keith and Kim could sing beautifully and had that sibling harmony blend that I just loved. It reminded me of the Nash Family Trio.

However, there were four other singers who were not professional singers in the mix. They had been invited to sing along on a couple of songs due to the level they had reached in the Amway business, which resulted in one of the worst rehearsals I have ever had to endure.

Keith & Kim Belknap Promo Photos - 1980

We got stuck on the first song, and it took a lifetime just to get through it, or at least that's what it felt like at the time with my hangover and all. The only saving grace for me was that Kim was sitting just a short distance from me.

The rehearsal finally ended, and the next thing on the agenda was an afternoon river boat excursion on the Mississippi River planned for all the direct distributors and above. I was by myself so I asked my friends, Dr. Ken Tyer and his wife, Debra, if I could join them for the river boat trip, and they said yes.

Ken and Deb and I decided we would rather go down in

Keith & Kim Performing in Montreal - 1980

the bottom of the boat, get a pitcher of beer, and hang out there. I was sitting there with them drinking my troubles away, when I looked up and saw Kim coming down the steps. She took a seat at a table on the other side of the boat and was looking out the window at the shore as the riverboat slowly paddled down the river.

I looked at Ken and Debra and said, "Do you think I should go over and ask her to join us?" They agreed I should, so I walked over to where Kim was sitting. She looked up at me as I came over and smiled and agreed to join us.

I don't remember the conversation at all. I have, over the

years, accused her of looking all over that river boat for me, and when I was not up top she came downstairs to find me. She always denies it, but whether or not she did or didn't, we did end up together at that table.

After the boat finally came back into the dock and it was time to depart, we started off the boat. Suddenly I realized that I had all that beer in me and had to make a pit stop rather badly. I said to Kim as I headed into the men's room, "Wait here." The whole time I was in there I kept wondering whether she would really wait for me or not, plus, I didn't even say please (how rude). To my surprise, she did wait, and when I opened the restroom door, I saw her smiling face. She had waited. She had really waited. Then the thought came to me that maybe she did like me a little bit. This girl made me feel like I had never felt before in my entire life.

The convention rolled on through the weekend, and I sang with all the others on stage. I was very proud that Kim's mom loved how I sang "Everything Is Beautiful." In fact, she loved it so much that she asked me to sing it again.

Then came Saturday night, the final night, and we were all dressed in formal attire. I was sitting at the band table, which is usually placed a bit out of the way, and this time it was kind of behind the stage and to the side. All of the other singers were active "pins" in the Amway business and were all out schmoozing with their downline. That's why I was alone at this band table for ten when, to my surprise, I looked up and saw Kim walking up to my table. She sat down in the chair next to me. Was she really leaving her parents who were sitting at the head table and coming to sit with me?

She sat there by me for a few minutes, and I don't even think we said anything to each other. All I know is that in a minute or two we were holding hands. My heart was pounding out of my chest. Dinner was done, though, and the next thing that was to transpire was the baked Alaska. I had never seen baked Alaska presented to a convention before, but all of a sudden, the lights in this large ballroom slowly dimmed, and a long line of waiters came in through the large double doors with lighted candles that were burning brightly, stuck in the center of each portion of baked Alaska.

I turned toward Kim, and she turned toward me, and the next thing I knew we were kissing right there at the table during the baked Alaska presentation. Nobody was watching us, and we didn't give a hoot about the dessert. We sat a little closer as we held hands until the lights came back up and it was time for both of us to get back up on stage for the finale. She invited me to come up to her parents' suite where the other young people and single Amway distributors were going to have a bit of a celebration after the function to talk over all the proceedings of the weekend and have some fun getting to know each other better.

I got to the suite, and when I walked into the adjoining room there were lots of young, single people hanging out and having something to drink and visiting. Kim and a couple of other gals were sitting on the bed leaning up against the wall, and Kim motioned for me to come sit by her on the other side of the bed.

As we sat there, she reached for my hand and there we were, holding hands in front of all those people, including Kim's brother, Keith Jr., who would later become one of my best

Keith, Kim, & Bill - 1980

friends. I could feel all the eyes in the room staring, but Kim is one of those bold kinds of people who is not afraid to let her feelings show and not shy about it.

I could almost hear the thoughts of all those folks, "Isn't he much older than her?" They would stare and then look away as I looked their way, but I didn't care if she didn't. It started getting late, and it was time for the party to break up in anticipation of the morning good-bye service at 10:00 a.m.

I walked Kim to her door in her parents' suite, and we stepped just inside her room and just a bit behind the door, although the door stayed open, and I boldly took her in my arms this time and kissed her again. I floated out of that room and down the elevator to my room and tried to sleep to no avail.

The next morning, we all gathered in the ballroom once again for the last farewell and a Gospel song or two with a word of encouragement from Keith Sr. and Jimmie Lee. As I was observing everything that was going on, I was surprised by Jimmie Lee. She came out on stage and played some of the old Gospel hymns of the Church that I had been raised on. It touched me deep in my heart and made me know that this is the kind of atmosphere I wanted to live in from then on. I fought back the tears and the memories of my parents who had pastored so many churches and had sung those old, familiar songs. I simply loved it from the core of my being.

After the service which marked the end of the convention, someone came up to say goodbye, and with all the hustle and bustle going on, Kim and I got separated, so I didn't get to say a final goodbye.

However, I knew from the scheduling from Keith and Jimmie Lee's office in Tulsa that Keith Jr. and Kim were already scheduled to be in Houston the next week to do the weekly meeting at the Hyatt Regency Downtown. So I just decided to wait and see what would happen.

The next Monday night, they flew in and, to my surprise, they showed up at my hotel. I remember Kim opening that big heavy door to the club room and she rushed up to me and said, "Hi, baby." That girl had truly stolen my heart, and now there she was, right in front of me again.

I had two shows to do that night and I asked them to come up and sing a song or two with me and the band. In conversation with Keith, Jr. and Kim, I found out they knew lots of material since they themselves were a great duo. They sang with their beautiful harmony that night just like they had in New Orleans.

After my second show and a quick change back into my street clothes, we went to one of my favorite late-night restaurants to get something to eat, but there was no chance for me to be alone with Kim that night.

The next morning, I called the Hyatt and asked for their room and got Kim on the phone, and I asked her to dinner before the meeting. We went to a restaurant called the Mason Jar for our first official date by ourselves where we got to visit and just have a great time being together alone. She was kind of quiet and reserved, but that night we talked about everything, mostly having to do with music.

She knew all about rehearsals, traveling, setting up and tearing down, and performing in all kinds of circumstances. We talked about her experiences in showbiz from the age of 8 years old when she and her family opened for Gary Morris ("Wind Beneath My Wings") in Denver at an up-scale supper club. Her family did three shows a night, six nights a week. She told me about her special number, "These Boots Are Made For Walkin'." She wore her little white knee-high boots (a la Nancy Sinatra) and cute custom-made costume and "brought the house down."

She also talked about all the years they traveled across the country in their bus that would always break down somewhere like Arizona when it was 110 degrees outside.

The Belknap Family Touring In Their Greyhound Bus - 1968

I absolutely had fallen in love with this girl, and I barely even knew her. She was just so beautiful and talked so insightfully about the music business and recording and everything else we were both so familiar with. We really hit it off. We drove back to the Hyatt to attend the weekly Amway meeting, and I stayed at the meeting as long as I could before rushing out at the last minute to get to my club and walk on stage.

Later that night, my Uncle David and Aunt Helen brought Kim to where I was playing, and we got to have an after-the-show date as well. I just wanted to spend all the time I possibly could with her before she and her brother went back to Tulsa.

Two days later, after they left Houston, I called the Champions' office and her mom, Jimmie Lee, gave me the number where Kim was helping her dad pack up their belongings. The family was moving into their new 12,000 square ft. home in Tulsa, and

Kim and her dad were at the old place packing up some last-minute stuff.

When I called, her dad answered in his very business-like voice. He said, "Hullo" in his deep and sort of irritated voice like when someone disturbs you when you are trying to get stuff done and don't care to talk. I asked if I could speak to Kim. He said, "Who is this?" I told him. What I didn't know until much later was that Kim's brother, Keith, Jr., had gone and told her dad about how he had seen us holding hands in New Orleans, so Kim's dad had asked her if she liked me. She was kind of non-committal back to him, and then he said to her, "Do you know how old he is?" She answered, "No, do you?" Well, he didn't know either, so he just replied, "No, but he's got to be pretty old!"

So, after a few moments of her dad putting me on hold, she came on the phone and I heard her beautiful, hushed "Hello." She had such a pleasant-sounding voice, and when I heard it again, my heart leaped up into my throat. I wanted *Keith, Jr., Bill, & Kim - 1980* to ask her about my coming to Tulsa to see her and take her to dinner on a second date. If she said yes, I'd fly in, book a hotel room, rent a car, and ask her how to get to her house. What if she said no? What if she actually had a boyfriend she was dating in Tulsa and just hadn't told me. I had so many "what if's." So here's how I finally decided to pose the question to her. I said, "If I fly into Tulsa, would you pick me up?" She didn't hesitate a second. She said, "Yes." I was elated and overcome with excitement.

I booked myself on the earliest Sunday morning flight out of Houston to Tulsa. Saturday came, and I packed for the flight to Tulsa, and then it took several years for the next few hours to transpire, but I finally did my last show at midnight and headed home about 1:30 a.m. to get a couple hours of sleep.

My alarm went off at 5:00 a.m. and I was up and dressed and out the door for the 40-minute drive to Hobby airport. As I waited to board, it seemed like that old connecting flight would never arrive. I tried to catch a few winks, but I was too excited to sleep there in the airport. Finally, the plane to Tulsa made it in from Pittsburgh, and we boarded and took off (I made sure I was the first in line at the Southwest boarding gate).

We finally landed in Tulsa, and I was the first one off the plane. I walked out into that waiting area and looked around and no Kim. Maybe she overslept. Maybe she forgot? Was I just an old fool? You know what they say, "No fool like an old fool." All those thoughts were racing through my head. I jumped to the worst conclusions and felt humiliated. I decided to just head straight for the ticket counter to change my ticket and go right back home. My reaction was probably a result of my fragile self-image after one divorce and calling off another marriage, as well as me just being a bit jaded after everything life had thrown at me. My hopes were so high, and they immediately fell through the floor when I didn't see her.

I walked as fast as I could toward the ticket counter to change my ticket and figure it all out later. Then I heard this voice behind me calling my name, "Bill, Bill!!" As I looked over my shoulder, I saw this beautiful blonde running after me trying to catch up to me. It was her.

She was there. Where had she been? She said, "I had to use the ladies' room, and your plane arrived early and landed in the meantime, so I missed you back there." I went from despair to ecstasy in a split second. She gave me a hug. I was really there, and she was really with me, and we were on our own for more than just a couple of hours; we finally had a day and a half before I had to return home.

Our time together seemed so short since I had to return to Houston the very next evening to appear on stage. However, we made the best of the time we had and found out so much about each other as we talked and talked.

That next day, Monday evening at the airport, we waited for my plane to Houston. We sat in the bar area and I had a drink. I guess it gave me some courage to boldly proclaim to her, "I'm going to marry you." She didn't say anything, she just looked down at the floor and all around and then she said, "Where is your plane?"

Before I got on the plane to leave, I asked her if she would marry me. She responded, "I'm not prepared to answer that question at this time." I didn't hesitate. I said, "I'm going to marry you." She just smiled and gave me a kiss goodbye.

Now I think of Jim Carrey in *Dumb and Dumber* when the love interest he so desperately wanted said he had only a one in a million chance that she would ever be with him. He answered, "So you're saying there's a chance?" That's how I took her response.

After a couple of days back home (didn't want to seem too anxious or pushy), I picked up the phone and hoped beyond hope she didn't already have plans for the weekend. I wanted to return to her again and just be with her as much as I could. I did return for several weeks in a row; same drill each week as the first time. I would do my last show at midnight, head home and get a shower to get all that smoke from the club off of me and catch a few winks before heading to Hobby Airport.

It wasn't long before I was finally invited to stay at her parents' home. After a few visits, they figured out I wasn't going away so they might as well have us close by to "keep an eye on us" in their 12,000 sq. ft. mansion of a home.

There was a downstairs room where Keith had a custom made $10,000 pool table. He would sometimes keep me down there playing pool with him and Keith, Jr., until almost midnight. He knew I only came in to be with Kim, so I knew he was just being a bit ornery. I don't think he really wanted to play that many games of pool with me.

We still took our leave of the house to go out to eat and catch a movie and drive around. One of my most vivid memories from that time was the Sunday lunch her mom used to make. She would have a huge roast with all the trimmings and cherry pie with ice cream; she knew it was my favorite.

Her mom was insightful, and Kim talked to her about me and told her how it was almost impossible for me to eat when I was back in Houston, when I wasn't with Kim. I just missed her so much when we weren't together, so when the weekend came, and I was finally back in Tulsa for that incredible noon meal, I would eat and stuff myself. I only weighed about 148-150 pounds in those days and just didn't eat much at all when I was back home in Houston.

In those single days, it was like the Kristofferson song when he sings, "...and the beer I had for breakfast wasn't bad, so I had one more for dessert." I had always heard that you would know "the one" the moment you met her, and since I had already reached 35 years of age, and had not been lucky in love, I just hated hearing that old saying. My mother would say, "Every crooked pot has a lid." Those sayings would frustrate me most of all. "Can you just forget it," I would think. "It" ain't gonna happen for me. I truly had given up on finding someone and having a family.

I remember one night lying in my bed after my divorce just wanting the misery and heartache and ego to shut up and let me die. Now I never even came close to doing anything more than wishing I could die because as I contemplated getting out of this life and my circumstances, somewhere in the depths of my psyche, my sense of humor kicked in, and I started to laugh at myself for even thinking such a silly thing as willing myself mystically out of this life.

As I look back now, I know it was more of a spiritual thing, but at that time in my life I was not thinking very spiritually. I did pray each night before I would go to bed as I was highly intoxicated and would ask God to forgive me, knowing that I was going to do the same thing the next night.

When I found Kim, though, and started making those trips to see her, I just wanted to stay in Tulsa and be with her and her family all the time. I hated getting back on that plane headed for Houston, back to my next week of music and shows six nights a week. All of a sudden, I didn't need to get drunk every night because I had found a real reason to live and someone who I wanted to live life with.

Kim made all the difference in my attitude about everything in my life. My mom even loved Kim, and she had never approved of any love interest of mine.

Over the next several months, months in which I spent a fortune on airline tickets and phone bills for our long-distance relationship to continue, Kim and I got closer and closer. This is before the days of unlimited calls on a cellular phone plan. It was land lines all the way, and I paid by the minute (and every minute was worth whatever the cost). One day, after my asking her

several times to marry me, she finally said yes. She had told me she just needed time, but I thought that maybe she just wasn't serious about marriage. She was actually just trying to figure out if this was it, if I was really the real lifetime partner and if I truly was "the one." After all, she was only 20 years old by this time. She is a very deep person and thinks things all the way to the ground. Even at 20 years old, she was more grown up than I was

Kim Posing For A "Can-Can" Themed Photo in Vail, CO - 1980   mentally.

I was so used to entertaining and traveling, and at that time, drinking the night away with not much of a thought for tomorrow. I just wanted to have hit records and be a big star and have a party every place I played with my band. Now, it was all different. I had fallen in love for real, but I kept asking myself why she had to be only 20, and why did she have to live so far from me? I guess no one really knows those answers.

They say love is where you find it, and wherever that is, it is worth the price you have to pay to get it. I was willing to sell all that I had, spend all that I made, and do whatever it took to win this beautiful young girl's heart. As I look back on it all now, I see God's plan in our lives and the fact that He put us together.

Even though we had a 16-year age difference, we still "got" each other. We were raised the same way with a Pentecostal background of the Assembly of God Church and dads that were or had been ministers or pastors. Kim's grandfather, Reverend James C. Dodd, built one of the largest Assembly of God churches in the state of Oklahoma just outside of Tulsa in Broken Arrow. He was one of the first, if not "the first," to build an Assembly of God school and gymnasium alongside the church for the young people to gather and play and study and worship God.

We were both preachers' kids, and one Sunday at her home,

she started playing some old hymns of the church on her mom's piano, and we started singing some of them together. When we got around to that old Gospel song, "Power In The Blood," we both sang the same 'lick' or 'curly cue' at the very same spot the way we had both heard it sung as children a thousand times at church. We looked at each other and just laughed. I loved those Sundays.

Even though we were truly in love, it was very difficult for her to finally come to terms with the fact that marriage meant that she would have to leave Tulsa and her family and come to Houston to live and start a new life so we could get on with our future together.

The one thing that really was a strong common denominator was the fact that I had continued to build my Amway business in Houston, mainly because I wanted the favor of her family, especially her dad. Kim and I both felt that we should continue to build our own Amway business together and use those funds to build our music career together.

Our wedding was set for September 24, 1981, the day before my birthday and the weekend of one of our biggest functions, Free Enterprise Day. This was scheduled that way so her parents could invite their entire Champions Amway "family" to the wedding, since they would all be in town already for the convention. Kim and I would then sing at that function and help with the family duties, and then we could take off on our honeymoon.

We did have a huge wedding for which Kim's folks rented one of the big, old churches in Tulsa. Keith Sr. went out and ordered a stretch Lincoln limousine for us to ride in from the church to the Williams Plaza Hotel

Bill & Kim Nash Just Married

ballroom where the reception was to take place. That ballroom was huge, and the place was packed with around 1,500 people. Kim's grandfather, James C. Dodd, and my dad officiated at the ceremony together at the church.

We got so many beautiful gifts from so many wonderful friends, but the best wedding present of all was the honeymoon in Hawaii given to us by Kim's parents. The flight over in first class was just spectacular. Hawaii is truly one of God's most amazing places in

His creation. From the open-air terminal at the airport to all the incredible flowers and foliage all over that island of Oahu, it was just magnificently beautiful. All that was great, but the greatest thing of all was that I finally had my Kimmie girl all to myself for the rest of our lives.

Bill & Kim with Wedding Party and Leslie Nash & Rev. James C. Dodd Officiating

DON'T WAKE ME UP IF I'M JUST DREAMING

I was living a dream. I had found my soul mate, the love of

my life, my best friend, my partner, my wife with me all the time now. There's something about real love, no matter how syrupy it may sound to those who haven't experienced it. It is just an unbelievable feeling no words can explain. You never get

Bill & Kim On Honeymoon - Hawaii 1981   tired

of your mate, and you want to be together all the time. At least that's the way it was for us back then and still is even now; after so many years, nothing's changed. God knew what He wanted me to do in this life, and He knew who the perfect match for me would be. And did I mention talent? Kim turned out to be the

Bill & Kim On Honeymoon - Hawaii 1981

greatest songwriting partner a person could have and the greatest female singer of all time in my book. What did I ever do to deserve her? I surely don't know, but I am so very thankful to God that she's loved me enough to go through this life with me bravely hanging on through some of the most unimaginable twists and turns. She (and of course, God Himself) has been the key to any success we have had.

BACK HOME AND FULL SPEED AHEAD

Kim and I flew back from Hawaii to our home in Houston and started our new lives together as husband and wife. We bought a four-bedroom home with a swimming pool in west Houston and continued to work on our Amway business while I was playing the clubs. We were packed on Fridays and Saturdays and did really good on weekdays, too. However, I was bent on

building the Amway business. I originally had gotten in to gain not only my freedom from a full-time, six night a week gig in the clubs, but to have the money to promote my music recording career. I had seen other examples of people actually doing this in Amway and touring in their big tour buses and singing to large

Bill & Kim and the Belknap Family - 1981

audiences nationwide. That's what I wanted to do. Kim usually went to the club with me every night, and we picked up a few songs for her to sing with me and the band. However, our main focus was the Amway business. Reaching higher levels brought about many perks like the prop-jet aircraft Kim's dad had that gave another level of freedom I had never experienced before.

One of my best memories of Tulsa was sitting around Kim's family's indoor pool. We were all talking about Las Vegas. After a few minutes, Kim's dad said, "Let's go to Vegas." We all kind of looked at each other and said, "Really?" He said yes, so he called his pilot and told him to meet us at the airport in an hour. We all scuffled to pack and throw on some clothes. Within an hour and a half, we were in the air, and a couple of hours later we landed in Vegas and checked in to Caesar's Palace. We also went on a cruise with a lot of the Belknap Amway down-line. We had the whole boat to ourselves! It really was a very large organization.

That was the kind of lifestyle I wanted, and that's what I was working so hard for. This took all the energy I could muster on

a daily basis, but I so believed in it that I drove myself as hard as I could toward that goal. Kim and I would head out early each evening to attend a meeting almost every night, except Sunday, and then rush to one of the clubs I played to do my two shows. I was sometimes quite a few minutes late, but thankfully I had great fans who would wait for me, so the management really didn't say much about it, nor did they ever fire me for being late.

Bill & Kim Skiing after
Champions Event - 1984

Everything felt so fast paced because we were on a fast track and busy all the time. I was bound and determined to have a meeting with someone, anyone, as often as I could to present the Amway plan and ask them to join us in this endeavor; they called this "Dr. Pepper" since the goal was to schedule a meeting every day at 10, 2 and 4 (based on the old DP slogan).

Kim and I were working on all this together, and I'd never really had a partner like her before. Then Kim told me the great news after about fourteen months into our marriage that we were going to have a baby. What an incredible thing! Life just couldn't have been any better. I felt like I was on top of the world.

Bill & Kim On One of Many Cruises

When she was around six months into her pregnancy, we were honored to be invited to the White House along with Kim's parents and other leaders in Amway to meet with President Reagan. However, as the President entered the room, Kim began to feel like she was going to faint (very understandable at this stage of pregnancy). I quickly got the attention of a Marine who was on duty standing nearby, and asked for his assistance in finding Kim a place to sit down. He had to go over and talk to his superior to get that permission, but he finally did after a few minutes; it seemed like forever. He escorted her into a nearby room filled with plates and found a chair for her. This room was called the "China Room" where all the china from past presidencies was displayed. During the remainder of President Reagan's speech, this marine stayed right by Kim's side, never moving a muscle, standing so staunchly, we can only presume, to keep an eye on her and to make sure she didn't take any of those plates. He was totally devoted, which we actually appreciated.

Bill & Kim "expecting" Billy, Jr. on a Trip to Hawaii - 1982

A few weeks later, I retired from that six night a week show business grind in the clubs to go full time in Amway. About that time, we also reached that coveted level of Diamond (almost a million dollars in business volume in 1982), and there was a great celebration put on by our down-line. What great times!

Bill - First Time Holding Billy, Jr.

On November 30, 1982, Billy Jr. was born! He was the brightest spot (just under Jesus and right next to Kim) ever in my life! He was my first child, and I was an older dad, being 38 years old when he was born. He was the epitome of all I had ever dreamed of but had given up on finding when my life seemed to be such a failure before I met Kim. His birth was a joyous occasion to say the least; it meant more to me than any success I had ever had in anything else beforehand. I finally was a daddy!!! We were a family!!! Kim's parents and my parents, along with my little niece, Robin Christina, were standing right outside the door and got to hear his first very loud cry.

That December, Keith and Jimmie loved showing their first grandson off at the Champions Event called "Dream Night." Billy was a sharp dressed baby in his new tuxedo with tails as his grandparents introduced him to that large crowd.

These were the days when I bought myself a new Porsche

and bought Kim a new Mercedes. We were working the business and enjoying the rewards of the success thereof and living it up with our new baby boy.

We went to Hawaii at least three times in 1983 with him, and even turned down a trip on the Amway yacht to Peter Island we had earned for going Diamond. They wouldn't let us bring our baby along, so we declined. We were new parents, and we just

Bill & Kim with Billy, Jr. at "Dream Night"

couldn't leave our little Billy boy. We both had traveled so much in our lives that the allure of packing and going to some island in the Caribbean and hanging out for a few days with some strangers didn't even approach the joy we

Bill on his new Porsche with Billy, Jr.

felt having our new little baby son with us and playing with him every moment he was awake.

We were certainly flying high, doing what we wanted to do. I wasn't depending on just my music for a living anymore after countless years of traveling and booking and performing anywhere and everywhere, and that felt great. I could have more control over my own destiny.

CASTING A LIGHT

We made a lot of money very quickly and spent it very quickly also. It seems like human nature to come to a point in life where you feel like the good times will never end. Looking back now, we should have planned more for the future. It may seem like a negative mindset if you're thinking about things possibly going wrong one day, but it's not that we should expect bad times, it's that we just need to be prepared for life when it's unpredictable and be responsible with the gifts God has given us. The Bible has quite a few passages about being good "stewards" of God's money, because it all belongs to Him. Well, I can't say I was a great steward during that time, but I sure was great at spending it all. If I had known what lay ahead, I would have saved more, but unfortunately, life doesn't usually give you a warning when it's about to change.

Chapter Thirteen

Heartbreaking Times

I N THE MIDST OF ALL THOSE great days, and right before Billy was born, Kim's dad really started battling that awful and dreaded disease, Parkinson's. He was a very proud man who had built himself up from absolutely nothing and had only an 8th grade education. But he was the most gifted speaker I've ever heard in my life, and he influenced me greatly just as he inspired thousands of others. He could hold a crowd in the palm of his hand when he spoke like nobody I'd ever seen. Now at 45 years old, he was diagnosed with a debilitating disease. That was already very young to be diagnosed; plus, he had been dealing with symptoms that began a couple years earlier.

Our major challenge as a family now became Parkinson's disease. Since it was our leader, Keith Sr., who was in trouble, it affected all of us as a family, but just as importantly it affected our Amway family also. Parkinson's made it very difficult for Keith Sr. to get up in front of an audience and speak because it adversely affected his voice, and the tremors were increasingly difficult to keep medically in check. The timing on his prescription medication was paramount. It was the difference between controlled and uncontrolled shaking of his body.

It embarrassed him to think he couldn't beat this challenge. He was trying to deal with his good days and bad days, and the bad days were starting to win out over the good ones. Jimmie Lee, her parents, Kim and I, and Keith Jr. did all we could do to encourage him and help in every way as best we could. However, the situation continued to escalate. It was when he finally decided to become his own doctor and refused to follow doctor's orders or prescribed protocol that things got too far out of hand.

Suffice it to say, he didn't handle this health challenge well, but I never judged him since I had never been in any kind of similar situation. The disease took him in such a different direction in his thinking, and that tore up the whole family. Our leader, so strong and invincible, was now unable to cope or continue; his deep depression took him to an extremely dark place. When Billy, Jr. came in the room, he would come out of the depression for a little bit, but soon that was not enough (and he adored Billy from the day he was born).

The hardest thing for Kim was when her daddy no longer would let her or any of us into his life. He totally withdrew into his own world without us, and it took its toll on everyone and everything, including our combined Amway businesses.

Over time, we were forced to learn to face life and the future without him. This fact

Bill, Kim, & Billy, Jr. with Keith, Sr. 2 Years Into His Battle with Parkinson's - 1984

was made doubly clear after so many months when people started dropping out of the business left and right due to his unpredictable behavior. His success was what we pointed to and lifted up in our presentation of the Amway plan and the promise of a better life, free from having a boss or a company dictate what your future would be.

There came a life-altering decision for Kim and me to make. Do we try to keep building our distributorship? Could we really overcome this? The answer we eventually came to was "no." It just didn't feel right anymore. We could no longer point to that coveted life of freedom and happiness when the guy we were exemplifying was in such a downward spiral; there was no way to explain it all to the folks, especially the new prospects.

It made me physically ill for several days just trying to grasp this new set of circumstances that would dictate another dead end and life change, only now I had a wife and baby to consider in figuring out the future. Everything was in flux, and we were just looking for a solid footing.

CASTING A LIGHT

I didn't know it yet, but this was the start of my coming back to God. All I can say is people rarely come to God when everything is going their way. They already feel like life is good, and what more do they need? I had experienced highs like I never felt before and didn't think it could get any better. If we had continued on that same upward trajectory, well, who knows where we'd be, but I probably would still not be living for God. It's those difficult times when you start looking for a meaning to everything, and you just need some help to get through the next day. I was looking everywhere for help, but I should have been looking up. Once again, thankfully, God is patient. With me, He had to be.

BACK TO THE CLUBS AGAIN

What's next? Fortunately, the one thing that I knew that I knew how to do was sing. I had a wife and a son, so we had to go on! Even in the Amway business, our music had been a big part of our presentations at conventions and guest speaking engagements.

It was my solace, and I felt empowered when I was up singing in front of the folks. It had always felt like that was my ultimate dream. Kim and I made the decision to move back to Houston to our biggest fan base where I had the most confidence in once again earning a good living through our music. Houston, there it was again, always my saving grace; the one place I could return to and get back on my feet.

It took its toll on my pride to do so, but at least this time I was not alone. I not only had Kim, but her brother, Keith, Jr., who became a part of the group we put together that I would book into the clubs in Houston.

It was so gratifying when I returned to the nightclub scene in Houston and was still be able

Keith, Bill, and Kim Promo Photo

to draw capacity crowds on Fridays and Saturdays. I was so glad to be singing and performing for all the folks again. What mixed emotions rushed over me the first time I had to walk back out on stage. These incredibly wonderful Houston fans God had given me didn't treat me any way but great when they saw me.

Although I could no longer just hang out and fly here and there and take cruises and trips to Hawaii anymore, and even though I knew I would miss it, there still was that satisfaction of singing in front of a crowd and winning them over.

It took a while to acclimate myself to the six nights a week grind once again, but I did it. The 80s had brought a dip in the oil business, which affected Houston incredibly negatively, including the nightclub scene. We had to negotiate in a different way now, so cover charge was introduced in order to bolster up the budgets of the hotel showrooms we were playing.

We got the "door" as they call it, and the club got the bar revenue. We never knew from week to week what our income would be. If it had not been for our loyal Houston fans coming back out to see us, I don't really know what we would have done. We were starting all over again.

ONE HARD BLOW AFTER ANOTHER

One night, my mom and dad came to the club where we were playing and told us some hard-to-take news: my dad had been diagnosed with prostate cancer. I couldn't believe it: first Kim's dad with Parkinson's, and now my dad with cancer. He was my rock; the guy I knew I could count on to encourage me and help me however he was able. I don't think he ever told me no one time whenever I needed something.

What a year this was turning out to be. Cancer? My dad? What? I just couldn't wrap my head around it, couldn't grasp it at all. It just couldn't be! He had always been so healthy. But he faced the cancer with a positive attitude, which made it easier for me to take.

One morning a few weeks later, my beautiful bride announced to me that she was sure she was once again pregnant. In the midst of all this tragedy and other business challenges, we were going to have another baby!

We were all still struggling with the health issues of Kim's dad and my dad, but there was an undeniable, insuppressible joy that came with the news of having a new baby on the way.

However, during Kim's first few months of pregnancy, out of the blue, our son, Billy, started getting sick very frequently, and we'd get the pink "bubble gum" medicine from the doctor. But then a couple of weeks later, he'd come down with another infection of sorts that would send us back to the doctor who would prescribe more bubble gum medicine.

This lasted way too long, and we called his doctor at the time who assured us that this was nothing to be concerned about; nevertheless, we were still very concerned. Eventually, after a couple of months of him being sick off and on with no explanation, we went to a specialist we were referred to whose office was in Houston in the hospital district. We made the appointment. We had to find out what was really going on.

I remember that at that particular time I had been asked to be part of a benefit for the "Bubble Boy" (as the press deemed him due to the fact that his immune system was so fragile that he had to live in a "bubble"), on the evening prior to our doctor's appointment. The event was for the purpose of raising money for his medical expenses. Little did I know the scenario that would play out the very next day.

As Kim and I had always done after doctor visits, we would call our good friend, Dr. Ken Tyer, to get his take on the results of the tests and the doctor's analysis. So, on a Monday morning, February 18, 1985, a date that will live in infamy (to borrow a phrase) in my mind, we showed up at 10:00 a.m. at the specialist's office. As we topped the stairs and entered his office, we saw Dr. Ken Tyer and his wife, Debra. We asked them what they were doing there. Kenneth pretended that it was no big thing, but he and Debra just wanted to come down and meet us there. We found it highly suspect that Dr. Ken could take off on a Monday due to his large dental practice, but since the doctor was ready to see Billy now, we didn't stop to think more about it. We took Billy on in. The doctor had us there for a couple of hours and ran test after test, and finally came back to where we were waiting in his outer office and he said, "My suspicion is that it's Leukemia. I see some "suspicious cells."" At that moment, everything went black.

The doctor sent us straight to Texas Children's Hospital. I asked directions, and he told me, but I was in such a dark place by this time and couldn't put my thoughts together enough to think about how to drive there. Dr. Tyer just said, "Follow me." As we walked out of that office, I noticed that the entry nurse and the receptionist both had their heads down and would not look up at us. I didn't blame them; what could you say to a couple that was pregnant, and had a two-year old that had just gotten that kind of diagnosis? Just as I approached my car door, Ken stopped me and said, "Bill, you can't fall apart." He was right, and somehow with him telling me that, it helped me hold it together just enough to make it through the day and be strong for my family.

Billy, Jr. 2 Months Before Diagnosis - December 1984

We followed Dr. Tyer and Deb to the emergency entrance

at Texas Children's Hospital, and they stayed right there with us. When we finally got Billy all checked in and into his room, I decided to call my brother since I felt like I could talk to him, and he could better relay the message to my parents and sisters about Billy. So Deb and I found a pay phone down the hall, and I dialed my brother's number. When he answered, I couldn't speak. I swallowed hard and did my best, but couldn't get any words to come out. I just handed the phone to Deb, and she told my brother, Dave, the news.

Kim's mom had accompanied us to the doctor's office as well, thank God, and started calling everyone on her side of the family for prayer. You know what I remember right here? Deb and I went back to where Kim and Dr. Tyer were, in Billy's room, and we just sat there looking at each other for a few minutes.

Uncle Ken, as we affectionately called him, was able to talk calmly and help us through those next few moments. We didn't want to cry in front of Billy, and he kept asking me in his baby talk, "Daddy, when we donna doe home?" He didn't like being poked on and stuck with needles, having his blood pressure taken, and a cold stethoscope pressed against his little chest. He didn't know why his daddy and mommy couldn't just take him home.

We tried to be strong in front of him, and we made up some lame excuses for why we couldn't leave. I would disappear out into the hall and cry for a while, and then return to the room as composed as possible.

I don't know how many hours passed, but Dr. Ken and Deb soon had to go home themselves. He had canceled all his patients for that Monday just to be by our side when we got the news he suspected we would get. God surely sent him and Deb to us on that day. I don't know how I would have even found that huge hospital they call Texas Children's had they not shown up. We stayed there in that room with our baby boy that night--no way to sleep anyway.

The next day the specialist that had sent us to the hospital came by to see how things were going. He had come with a helium-filled balloon for Billy, and when he tried to hand it to Billy who was in bed under the covers, Billy looked away from him toward the window and immediately said, "Talk to B's daddy." He used to call himself "B," and at two years old he was smart enough to know that this doctor was the one who had sent him to the hospital, and he wasn't going to have anything to do with him. We took the balloon and tied it up at the foot of the bed, but Billy never would play with it. It reminded him of who had put him in this predicament. He was a sharp little cookie.

After extensive testing over a three-day period, a group of doctors and nurses called Kim and me into a little conference room. Dr. Starling started off the talk, and he had Billy's test results laid out on the table in front of him. He actually had tears in his eyes. He was such a kind doctor, and it hurt his feelings to have to give us this bad news. He said that Billy definitely had Acute Lymphoblastic Leukemia (A.L.L.), and that he had a 50/50 chance to live.

"Oh God, help me. Oh Jesus, please don't leave me!" was my inward cry. Sometimes when you get such awful news such as this, it's just impossible to even know how you are going to react. I was all dammed up inside. I had cried repeatedly over the previous three days as we were in the hospital awaiting test results, but now I just sat there on stun, still feeling and re-living the trauma I experienced from the meeting on Monday at the specialist's office. I have never been hit that hard by anything and I just didn't know what to do or say or how to react. I was more worried about my pregnant wife and how she would be able to stand this news, and then I worried about how it would affect our baby that was on the way due to her stress level being so high.

Dr. Starling then took us through the scenario and protocol of the up-coming events for the next three years. He said they would start with one shot of chemo and send us home. We would then return in ten days to start the chemo protocol. After this unforgettable meeting, we did our best to gather our senses about us and head back to our hospital room to be with our little Billy Boy. I just kept hugging him and caressing his little back and holding him and trying not to cry. Kim was so quiet and introspective, and I could see her heart was breaking, and at the same time she was thinking about that new little baby inside her.

For some reason that we don't understand to this day, the next thing we remember is that a grief counselor came to our room to talk with us in order to, as she couched it, "prepare us for death." Prepare us for what? We had only just gotten the doctor's report, and they were already anticipating the worst-case scenario? She handed us a book entitled, "If Death Must Come." Kim and I stood silent, in total shock when she did this in such a matter-of-fact way. We told her it wasn't a good time, so she left, and as she walked out the door, Kim simply tossed that book into the trash bin. After waiting so long for a child, after loving him with all of my being and every emotion I was capable of, was I now supposed to handle giving him up to Leukemia? The name of Jesus kept coming to me, and I was now starting to use it over and over again under my breath. It seemed to comfort me every time I said His name, Jesus, Jesus. Please help me. I need you so much. Please help Kim. Please help the baby in her tummy. Please help us all. It was my spiritual training that I received as a child that was resurfacing, coming back to help me in my greatest time of grief.

After a while we sort of gathered our wits about us as best we could, and we found a moment we were alone with Billy in that hospital room. I stood up and said to Kim, "Let's pray." We held hands right there at the foot of Billy's bed in that hospital room and I prayed, "Jesus, if you'll heal my son, I'll tell it everywhere I sing the rest of my life." Now I know and I knew then that you can't make deals with God. I just didn't know what else to do. I didn't know how else to pray. I just did the best I could. We said that simple prayer, uttering those simple words. The next day they gave Billy one shot of chemo in his little leg and then released us to go home to return in ten days to start the total protocol for Leukemia. Just before we left Texas Children's, there was a tap on our door. It was the Bubble Boy's mom and her friend I had seen a few nights before at the benefit we did for her son. He was in the same hospital, and there was his mom again dropping by to encourage us and thank me again for singing. You just never know how things are going to transpire. We really appreciated her thoughtfulness in the midst of her own personal grief and anxiety.

And so, we waited in anxious anticipation for the time to come for us to return to Texas Children's. Those next ten days became a time of deep reflection. By this time, every one of our friends and family knew about Billy and had started to pray for him. Kim's mom, who had been with us the day we got the news, moved down from Tulsa to stay with us, thank God, and to be there for Billy. I don't know what we would have done without her. I did my best to stay busy and talk positive, even though down inside I knew that Kim and I were facing the greatest battle we had ever faced at any time in both our lives. I fought off the made-up scenarios of "what if" because they all kept ending so negatively and gave me horrible feelings of grief. I learned that those scenarios can take a heavy toll on you.

THE MIRACLE

Finally, after what seemed like an eternity, it was Monday. Ten days had elapsed, and we headed back to Texas Children's Hospital to start the protocol. We checked in with the front desk nurse in that little brown building out on that parking lot, which is no longer there since all the new additions to TCH. We had to go through the procedure of getting the "finger stick" for some blood work. Since this was our first day of protocol, they proceeded to do the spinal tap and the bone marrow testing as well. I had to be on hand to hold my precious son's little body as still as possible as they inserted that huge needle into his spine. I petitioned the nurses for something to help alleviate the pain, but they said they didn't have anything they could give him. It's all changed nowadays. Today, they sedate kids who have to have these traumatic procedures. But in 1985, it didn't work that way yet.

I can't help but share the sheer agony I felt as I held him on that bed. It's hard enough for a two-year old to lie still at all, and now he was being told not to move or it would be worse, and the needle could injure him. Once again, my thoughts turned to God, Jesus, the only One who could help me now. I was doing my best to keep my composure and be Billy's dad, but it took everything I had and more not to scream and run out of that place with my kid. I just kept my head down not looking at anyone but Billy and fighting off the tears and feelings of anguish. We finally got done with all their procedures, and we went back out to the waiting room to await the results.

We kept waiting and waiting. It seemed like another eternity before Dr. Starling and his staff asked us to come back to the conference room. Oh no, what now? Is it worse now than they had told us before? My mind started to race with worst-case scenarios. I was so scared, but I tried to put forth a strong appearance for Kim. She was doing the same for me. We hardly talked on our way back to this conference room. As we sat down and faced Dr. Starling, we were wringing our hands and expecting the worst as the good doctor opened his mouth to speak. He held up a paper with test results, once again with tears in his eyes, but this time, with a smile on his face, and he said, "We don't know what has happened, but all of Billy's test results have come back normal." Normal? What? What was he saying? Could this be true? Could this be possible? Billy had only had one shot of chemo in his leg. Now Dr. Starling was telling us in an unusually emotional way that his blood had gone "normal." Every test came back normal! After regaining our composure and looking at each other in disbelief, we both exclaimed, in tears, "Normal? Is this a miracle?" Dr. Starling said he couldn't call it that; he couched it as "immediate remission." I didn't care what they called it as long as it meant that my son's life was no longer in jeopardy.

It took a few minutes for this information to sink in. We just sat there on stun not able to process the news completely. However, Dr. Starling told us that we needed to stay in the three-year program even though Billy's tests did come back normal. He said that the Leukemia cells have a tendency to hide in the base of the spinal column and then reappear at a later time, only the second time it would be with a vengeance. They couldn't, in all good conscience, let us just go home as if nothing had happened. They were very firm about this decision, and we got the drift that it was more than just a personal pleading on the part of the doctors; that it was, rather, mandatory protocol to make sure our child's life really was not going to be in danger, at least for the next three years.

Three years. That's how long this was going to take before they could pronounce him cured. They laid out a plan for six weeks, then every other day for another six weeks, then twice a week and so on until it got all the way down to once every 8 weeks, which they referred to as "maintenance." It seemed like a lifetime of dwelling on negative circumstances to us, but we didn't want any reports to Children's Protective Services due to lack of compliance to doctor's orders since it was a life-threatening disease. So even though it was with mixed emotions that we agreed to comply, the bottom line was that Billy was going to live and not die. We had received our miracle.

We knew that our own plans for the future in the music business were going to have to be put on hold due to the schedule of the TCH check-ups that were a must. Before Billy's diagnosis, our new life's goal was to write songs and pursue our writing careers in Nashville where I still had some friends from the past. For now, the new plan was to continue to work the Houston scene in night clubs and showrooms and save our money until it was time to move to Nashville, but not until we had passed the three-year mark for Billy with perfect check-ups and no relapse.

The first several months were the worst. As Billy went through treatment, he had to endure many side effects. The first was the expected loss of his beautiful blond hair. I recall Kim following behind him picking up locks of his hair as it fell on the floor with tears rolling down her face. At this time, she was about five months along with our second child, and due to the stress of everything, she was losing, not gaining weight. I felt so sorry for her, yet there was nothing I could do.

Kim with Billy, Jr. First Month of Treatment - 1985

Another disturbing side effect Billy had was mouth sores so severe that there would be blood all over his pillow every morning. Because of the mouth sores, it became impossible for him to brush his teeth. Many months later, we took him to the dentist and his mouth was full of cavities, just about every tooth. Fortunately, this only affected his baby teeth.

One night he had such a high fever due to the chemo that we had to hold him down in a tub of ice in spite of his screams from the discomfort. At two years of age, we could not explain to him why we had to do this, but we had no other choice.

Kim's mom had moved in with us right after Billy's diagnosis, and subsequently Kim's grandparents, James & Francine Dodd,

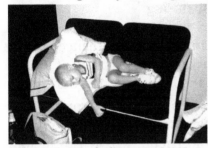

came and stayed with us for a whole month shortly before Kim was to give birth. She was finally able to get healthy. Somehow when her grandparents moved in and started cooking all the foods she loved as a child, she was able to eat everything they made, and started to gain weight.

Billy, Jr.'s First Month of Treatment - 1985

We got our second ray of sunshine when our son, Jimmy, was born on June 15th, 1985. Although the baby was healthy (and nearly 10 lbs!), Kim had a medical emergency at Jimmy's birth.

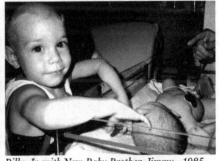

As I was standing by the hospital bed holding Kim's hand, I heard her doctor say in a panicky voice, "I don't know where all this blood is coming from!" She had a great doctor, though, and he found the source and was able to stem the bleeding, thus saving her *Billy, Jr. with New Baby Brother, Jimmy - 1985* life that day. I'll forever be grateful to Dr. Leroy Leeds.

Despite the negative side effects Billy had to endure, over and over again, all the tests continued to confirm the miracle we knew we had received. During the three years of our time at Texas Children's Hospital, Billy never had so much as even a cold; another miracle, considering that he was on chemo, which greatly decreases your ability to fight off infections and knocks down your immune system. That was an extra peace of mind that God gave us through that trying time.

Our little Jimmy really helped Billy through the remainder of his treatment. He had a very profound calming effect on him. One thing Billy did to alleviate stress after hospital visits was to play the drums, not just play, but beat on them very loudly. He would bang on those things for hours dressed only in his underwear and tennis shoes. Clothing irritated his baby skin too much during treatment. It was amazing how Jimmy

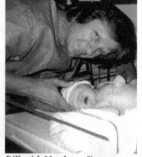
Bill with Newborn Jimmy

could sleep right through those amazing performances in his

Kim's Grandparents, Rev. James C. & Francine Dodd Holding Jimmy

Moses basket right in front of Billy's drums in the living room of our home.

When Jimmy was around five months old, a friend called and told me that my old friend, Kris Kristofferson, was going to be playing in Houston at Rockefeller's downtown. I was excited about the possibility of seeing Kris again, and thanks to Kim's mom watching the boys, we were able to have a night out. This was Kim's first time out of the house, basically, not only since the birth of Jimmy, but almost back to when Billy was diagnosed. I knew she needed to get out even if it was for just a little while. The load had been tremendous on her at such a young age, not only to be a new mom, but to have her dad's health on her mind, her

Billy, Jr. Enjoying Sharing His New Brother, Jimmy's "Moses" Basket

two-and-a-half-year old's TCH experience going on, and the dissolution of our Amway business still fresh on our minds.

So, we were going to have this big night out and showed up at Rockefeller's to see Kris's show; however, the lady at the ticket window said they were sold out! I told the lady in the ticket booth my story about me and Kris, and what Kim and I had just come through, and she was very compassionate. She drew closer to the other side of her window so she could talk softly, and she said that Kris usually takes a break between shows, and goes out back in the alley to get some fresh air. She suggested that I go back there and wait.

So Kim and I trudged around to the back of the theater and stood close to the back door in the alley where there was a 60 watt light bulb hanging on a wire above the door. We stood there and waited, and pretty soon the door opened, and Kris walked out with his very large bodyguard.

I just stood there looking, and he looked at me. He squinted his eyes and held his hand up to cover his forehead to help see through the light, and he said, "Bill, is that you?" I said yes and moved forward to hug him.

Then I introduced him to Kim, and I told him that the second show was sold out and we couldn't get in, so we would go on home. He stopped me from leaving and turned to the bodyguard and said, "Put that couch from the green room up on stage for Bill and Kim to sit on." What? We were going to sit right on the edge of the stage? Unbelievable! Kim and I were elated, and after we visited a few more minutes, we went on in and sat down on that red couch. I remember it as being a red leather love seat. We took our seats, and soon the show started.

Billy Swan was traveling with Kris and heading up the band, so they started the show off with his hit, "I Can Help." They did one or two more songs, and then Kris came on. He sang a couple of his hits, and then he started into the first line of "For The Good Times." Then he stopped the music in the middle of the song and held his hand up for the guys to quit playing. He said to the crowd, "The guy who did the first and best version of this song is sitting right here to my left. Bill Nash, let's get him up here to sing it again."

I was stunned and excited to have him ask me up to sing with him. I just couldn't believe it. So I did sing it and added a few flares that I wish I had done on the original recording in the 60s, and the people loved it.

Many of them knew me and were so excited to see me on

stage with Kris. He sang a harmony part with me on the chorus, and it brought the house down. They stood and clapped and clapped, and it seemed like they would never quit. Finally, it died down, and I took my place back on the love seat beside Kim.

So exciting after all the "junk" we had had to survive and the close to death issues with our baby, Billy, and so on. That night was so memorable and uplifting and encouraging.

We caught Kris a few years later in Nashville and told him

Bill with Kris Kristofferson at Rockefeller's - 1985 how much that night meant to us at that unusually emotional time in our lives. Actually, that time in Nashville, he was recording with the Highwaymen at Emerald Studios, and he stopped recording for a bit to come out and say hi to Kim and me. He's always remembered me, not only as a friend, but as a real fan of his writing from the start. What a night and what a great respite from what all we had recently been through. Thanks Kris!

MAMA'S PRAYERS

We hadn't called on or counted on God in a long time, but we both felt in our hearts that Jesus Christ had healed our son, and it was time for us to start going to church somewhere to get closer to God. We tried a different church every Sunday to find a fit for us. We weren't picky about what religious name they called it as long as it was based on Jesus Christ. We went Sunday after Sunday, but only in the evening since I didn't get through with my last show until around 1:00 or 1:30 a.m. on Saturday nights and didn't get to bed until 4:00 or 5:00 a.m.

After several weeks of churchgoing to no avail, we decided to check out what might be on television on a Sunday morning and at least watch that. The next Sunday morning came, and we flipped channels until we found a church service going on.

There was this preacher named John Osteen preaching from

Lakewood Church. He was so dynamic and said such uplifting things, things that we needed to hear. He only preached for about 25 minutes at the most, but he said more in those 25 minutes than some preachers do who go on for an hour or more. He was so down to earth, and it seemed like he really cared about the people. He was so passionate, and he preached the "love" of Jesus Christ and even got tears in his eyes when he talked about the Lord.

Later that Sunday evening, we decided to get dressed and head to Lakewood Church. We sat as close to the back as we could for two reasons: the first reason was that Billy was on chemo regularly, and that depresses your immune system, so we didn't want to sit any closer to other people than we had to for fear of Billy catching anything. The second reason was that I didn't want to be recognized by someone who might have come to hear me sing in the clubs in the past. Kim and I just wanted to be incognito and observe.

Be that as it may, someone still sent a note up to John and his wife, Dodie, and the note apparently just said that Bill Nash was there. It didn't surprise me that out of that large crowd someone was there who knew me from the nightclubs, but I didn't know how open Lakewood was to people in all walks and stages of life. The next thing I knew my name is being read from the note that was sent up to the platform and Brother John (as they affectionately called him) was asking me to stand and be recognized. I reluctantly stood up, a bit embarrassed due to the fact that I hadn't been to church in such a long time, and he told the crowd to give me a hand and they did. Then he asked me to stay around after church and come and talk with him. We really didn't know what to think since we didn't know the Osteens, but we were curious enough to find out what he wanted to talk with us about.

When service was over, we were escorted to his office where John and Dodie asked us all about ourselves. I introduced myself and Kim, and our two sons. Unbeknownst to me, my Aunt Ethel Johnson had asked Dodie, who we now lovingly call Mama Dodie, to pray for her nephew, Bill Nash, for God to get him back on track with Jesus and come back to church.

Dodie had been praying for me for several years. She would see my name on the marquee where I was playing around town, and she said she always called my name in prayer, and asked God to bring me back into "the fold." We shared with them the story of Billy's healing and how we had been searching for a home church.

We hadn't been talking long when Brother John abruptly stopped the conversation and asked if we would do a concert at Lakewood. I hadn't sung the old hymns of the church in such a long time, and the only songs our band knew were the two or three we had started singing in the night clubs that had some spiritual overtones.

It felt unbelievable, but I agreed, not knowing how it would all turn out since I hadn't sung in church in forever. However, we set up a time for the Lakewood concert and started trying to pull out some appropriate songs for a Gospel concert. The two songs I specifically remember us doing were, "I Believe," which I had heard Tom Jones's version of, and "You'll Never Walk Alone" which was the theme song for Jerry Lewis to sing at the end of his Labor Day Telethon. That's the only reason I knew those two songs. We leaned on a couple of old hymns, too. "Amazing Grace" is always appropriate.

John Osteen with Billy, Jr. 1992

The concert turned out to be an unbelievable night. I felt so accepted by that most incredible bunch of great people Lakewood had (and still has by the way), and a lot of our friends came out just to see what I was doing singing in a church.

Lakewood truly was an oasis in the desert for us, an oasis of love, and we started going to Lakewood even though it was located way across town from us on the east side of Houston. I started getting all the little booklets from the Lakewood bookstore that John Osteen had written and started studying in earnest. We were so excited to be on a great spiritual path. Lakewood became our church, and we were back to serve the

Lord as we played out our nightclub contracts in anticipation of moving to Nashville.

Brother John told me once never to come to church without bringing one of our music tracks with us to sing. He also told us to always come sit in the pastor's section right behind him and Dodie. That meant the world to us and we did that for many years. Their son, Joel, even called me one day (around 1988) and asked Kim and I to write a song for John's 50th Anniversary in the ministry. We were honored to do so, and wrote "It's Only The Beginning." Getting to surprise brother John and sing his life story in the form of a song as he watched, is one of my most beautiful memories at Lakewood.

One other blessing that came from Mama Dodie's prayers bringing me back to the church actually became a great blessing for Lakewood too.

One day, a few years after we had started going to Lakewood regularly, my cousin, Dowen Johnson, called me and posed an interesting question. He told me how he and his father, my Uncle Charles, had the last FCC license for a full-power TV station in the Houston market, but it was going to expire soon if they didn't get a station up and running, which would require a great deal of resources. So he asked, "Do you think Lakewood or anyone else you know would be interested in partnering with us?"

Well, I knew that John Osteen and Lakewood already had a far-reaching television ministry that went around the world, but

Years Later in 2010 - Jimmy, Kim, Dodie, and Bill

had no idea if they'd be interested or not in this proposal. I told my cousin, though, I certainly could ask and try to set up a meeting between them. The funny thing is that I knew many people who actually were in the field of television or entertainment or were successful entrepreneurs who would see the value of this FCC license, but I never even considered taking this deal to them. In my spirit, I just knew I was supposed to bring it to Lakewood and the Osteens.

So I went to Lakewood for Sunday service, and as it would

happen often, Pastor John would call me back to his office to talk before service. Joel happened to be the one that came to get me from the sanctuary that day, and on the way back to the office, I just asked him, "How would you like to have your own TV station?"

Joel was not only interested, but in a few short months, my uncle and my cousin completed a deal with Lakewood to launch Channel 55, "The Tube."

As any of you that live in Houston may know, that channel became very successful. Eventually, Lakewood made arrangements with my Uncle Charles and Cousin Dowen to buy out their share of the station entirely. My uncle and Dowen then used those proceeds to create a foundation called Shepherds for the Savior to benefit several ministries. This entity has made donations in excess of $100K to our Champions Kids Camp (which you'll read more about later) over the last nineteen years.

Bill with Joel in 2017

My cousin, Becky Johnson Thompson, still sits on the board there, and Tracey Magee is Foundation Director. They have been a real blessing and we sincerely appreciate their heart for children who have survived trauma. Love and blessings to Shepherds, Becky and Tracey.

Here's the really special (and amazing) part to me. A few years after Lakewood had bought the station outright, they ended up selling it for a sizable profit. I didn't know it until years later, but I heard Joel preach in a sermon how it would have been nearly impossible for Lakewood to have bought and renovated the Compaq Center if not for the proceeds from the sale of Channel 55.

Now, every time I go to Lakewood at the former Compaq Center and step into that beautiful sanctuary, I can't help but be a little proud that God saw fit to use me to make that simple connection that had such far-reaching implications. In a word, it makes me feel fulfilled. After all those years I didn't live for God, but He didn't hold it against me, it just built me up so much to think that I was still important to God and that He had used me for His grand plans. It reminds me that we're all just one small piece of a much bigger puzzle, and only God knows how it's all gonna fit together. Who else but God could have seen just how powerful a mama's prayers can be? Thank you, Mama Dodie, for praying me back into the fold.

Chapter Fourteen

Working For The Dream

AS TIME PROGRESSED AND WE FELT more and more assured that Billy was doing well (about a year and a half into treatment), we decided to sell our home in Houston and live in the hotels where we performed as part of our contract negotiation in order to save money for the next couple of years for our move to Music City, Nashville, Tennessee. We gave up the house with the pool that we had had so much fun in and were now living in two interconnecting rooms at the hotels.

We got ourselves a hotplate to cook small meals on and a little refrigerator to put in our hotel room, but still had to eat out a lot (we loved Luby's and Whataburger). It was kind of interesting how our little boys took to their surroundings.

The hotels always had a beautiful yard for us to get out into and run and play, and there was always a swimming pool. We really couldn't book out of town due to Billy's schedule at TCH, so we worked the hotels/clubs in the Houston area. We usually changed hotels on a monthly basis, so we would close on a Saturday (technically Sunday morning at 1:45 a.m. when the band shut down) and open on the following Monday at a different location. It was just our way of life.

At times those two rooms would feel like the walls were closing in on us. However, that was a small price to pay. We were set on pursuing the bigger dream of going to Nashville and having hit records either performed by us or by some major artist. The long-range money in the music is the writing and publishing side

Billy, Jr. & Jimmy Enjoying Hotel Life - 1986

anyway; they call it the rocking chair money.

Songs never die, and they have the potential to earn great amounts of money. We knew that some folks thought we were crazy, but it was our dream, and we were determined to follow it. BTW, we did pray about that decision this time and felt peace about it. John Osteen's instructions to us were that we "follow peace." It's been one of the best single pieces of advice I have ever received from anyone.

During this time, Judy Bunch, a friend I hadn't seen in many years, appeared out of the blue when she saw that I was back in the clubs. She had been a consistent fan, often bringing her clients to hear me sing.

After this reconnection, Judy started once again coming out on a regular basis with her work force, her entourage, and her friends. Her group took over our Thursday nights. Judy and Kim hit it off famously. Judy found out what we were doing about our future and our plans to move to Nashville and choosing to live in two hotel rooms with two babies to save our money. I think she respected that. She herself is a big dreamer and not afraid to take on the world. She far excelled the average guy in an executive position and found herself at the top of the heap due to her intelligence and hard work. That's what we knew about her.

One Thursday night at the club, she invited us to come to her house the following Sunday. She always had her close circle of friends over to eat her gourmet cooking (and unbelievable baking) and relax by her pool on Sunday afternoons.

Those Sundays at Judy's were like a great spell-off to the little two-hotel-room living arrangement and the hot plate or fast-food fare; it was a time to completely relax and a change of scenery from living in the hotel with two rambunctious boys. We ate until we couldn't and enjoyed visiting with all the other folks while the boys took over Judy's beautiful backyard. Sundays at Judy's was the greatest afternoon on the planet.

On one of those Sunday afternoons, Judy introduced me to a guy who worked at Channel 13 in Houston named Frank Elfland. He had bought a guitar and was learning to play it and write songs. We became very good friends with him, and our relationship grew.

Then on January 28th, 1986, the space shuttle Challenger exploded shortly after launch. We were all in shock and mourned, as the whole world did, for the seven crewmembers. When the Challenger blew up, Frank called and suggested we write a song to memorialize the crew of the Challenger. We got together and wrote a tribute, which we subsequently recorded and played for the powers that be at Channel 13. They loved it and decided to do a video to go along with the song. Once they had the music video done, they submitted it to the ABC Network for Ted Koppel's upcoming national news show that was featuring the whole story of the crew, the shuttle, and NASA.

We were so honored when we got word that they were going to use our song to commemorate these astronauts and the teacher who lost their lives. That song was called, "Seven New Stars."

Judy also introduced us to an organization she had worked with for years, The Exchange Clubs of America. These wonderful people are on the front lines of child abuse prevention. Their ESCAPE center in downtown Houston has gone a long way to help stop the cycle of child abuse. ESCAPE is an acronym for:

Exchange Supported Child Abuse Prevention Effort. Judy B (as we affectionately call her) then asked us if we could help put together a fundraiser for it called "The Great Escape." We said yes, and I started putting together a roster of friends that I thought might be available for a show.

We ended up on the parking lot of a bank in Northwest Houston on flatbed trucks with all kinds of things going on to raise money for the ESCAPE Center. It all kicked off on a Saturday morning, and I remember asking Pastor John and Dodie Osteen if they would consider coming out and starting the whole thing off with a prayer. Somewhat to my surprise, they said yes. They came that day and shook hands with everyone and talked and walked around to look at all the "stuff" available for auction.

Bill with Judy Bunch at The Great Escape

When it was time, Brother John just climbed those steps up to the top of that flatbed and said a great prayer to bless the proceedings and the Exchange Club's efforts to help so many children and their families. It was absolutely great. They spread the love of Jesus Christ that day. We noticed how the people were drawn to the Osteens, and some even asked questions about God and Jesus. They patiently answered their questions in an attitude of love and caring.

People know when someone is sincere about their beliefs, and this day that was evident to all who were there.

We wrote a memorable song for the occasion called, "The Tiny Seed." I invited all my music pals to come to A.V. Mittlestedt's studio, Sound Masters, to record it.

One of the stars that day happened to be Roy Head ("Treat Her Right"- 1965). He asked me if it would be okay if he brought his little boy along with him. I told him yes, and as it turns out, Roy's little boy, Sundance Head, has turned out to be the most famous of us all after winning *The Voice* on NBC in 2016, and we are so proud that his first recording session was with all the music family of Houston of that day and time at A.V.'s studio. We are all so very proud of you, Sundance.

So as our co-headliner with Roy, I called on an old friend of mine who I had helped out a few years earlier named R.C. Bannon. I asked him if he would come from Nashville to headline our show and he said yes. He happened to be married to Louise Mandrell at the time, and had been writing for The Barbara Mandrell Show on NBC TV. He offered to bring some of the wardrobe that Barbara and Louise had worn on TV so we could auction them off at the show. He did that, and they brought a lot of money.

We had some other great stars that came out in support that night: Warren Moon, quarterback of the Houston Oilers, local news celebrity Don Nelson, and Marvin Zindler. Marvin was not only a Houston news icon, but a famous movie was based upon his crusade to close the Chicken Ranch in La Grange, Texas, otherwise known as "The Best Little (you-know-what) House in Texas."

The event was a huge success! After the night was over, I was able to play some of the songs Kim and I had just written for R.C., and he was so impressed that he said we needed to get to Nashville as soon as possible and that he would be willing to help us in our endeavors. We were really pumped and encouraged to reach our goal of moving to Music City.

Judy also happened to be friends with one of the greatest songwriters of all time who lived in Nashville. I'm talking about Jerry Foster (of Foster and Rice). He flew into Houston to talk business with Judy, and guess where she brought him? I'm sure you know--she brought him to where we were singing. She later flew us to Nashville to meet with him before we moved there. We became friends, and we promised to meet up with him when we moved to Nashville.

We were finally preparing for our move to Nashville, which was about a month away, when we took Billy to his last check-up at TCH, something that seemed like an eternity away several years before. There is no way to describe our elation after his final perfect examination was completed! Thank you Jesus!!!

We'd made it to the end of his three-year protocol with no

relapses. That day we headed for the recording studio where my friend and former producer, A.V. Mittlestedt, was waiting for us

to record a Christmas album. When we stuck Billy up in front of a mike and turned on the track to "Jingle Bells," he sang along with Kim and me and did this cute little giggle as A.V. turned on the tape. We kept the giggle in the mix. We still have that album, "Christmas In Texas." We cherish that little voice at the beginning of that tape, and always thank God every day for Billy's miraculous healing.

When Billy turned five a few weeks later, we were singing at the

"Christmas In Texas" Album Cover

hotel we were playing at the time, and many friends came out to celebrate with us, not only his birthday, but his last perfect check-up at TCH.

Our drummer, George Weimmer, would always let Billy get up on stage to play his very expensive set of drums (something most drummers wouldn't think of) whenever we would take a break from doing a set. George, or Georgie as Kim called him, knew how much playing the drums had helped Billy through some really tough times at TCH. It was therapy for him.

So, on that special night of celebration, George surprised Billy with a brand-new full set of children's drums! A whole new beautiful set unlike the little set he had at home that he had taken all his emotions out on after his trips to TCH. He had worn that set completely out! George did a very special thing for Billy that night and for us. Billy couldn't wipe the smile off his face, which

George Weimmer with Billy, Jr. and His New Drum Set - 1987

made us so very happy! What a close friend and brother in music George has been to us. God bless you always, Georgie.

FINALLY, NASHVILLE!

Our New Year's Eve gig at the Sheraton Town and Country Hotel was our last night in Houston before heading to Nashville on January 1, 1988. I remember having packed that 26-foot U-haul truck I would drive and our custom trailer that Kim would pull behind our Suburban. We were packed so tight that I couldn't get the back doors of the trailer to close when we were trying to pull out of the Sheraton. There was our basketball in the way, and I tried everything humanly possible to get that ball on board, but it was a no-go. Goodbye basketball!

We had saved a whole $10,000 to start our new life in Nashville. We rented a house with a big yard for the boys for $675 a month, but had no idea how we were going to make a living after the $10,000 ran out. But we were so excited for whatever future plans God had for us. It's called faith! In the music business, you need a lot of it!

On the road to Nashville, I was driving the big U-Haul rented truck with most of our earthly goods in the back. Kim was following me in our Suburban, with all our sound system and instruments in our trailer. Little Jimmy, along with Kim's close friend from Sweden, Marina (who used to be our Au Pair for Billy in the Amway days, and Billy named her MeMe), were riding with Kim. Marina's boyfriend, Joachim (pronounced You-Uh-Keem), was in the U-haul truck with Billy and me. Those two had been helping us with the boys for that last year as we were playing in the clubs. Joachim would help sell our albums at night after each show (all the girls loved his accent), and Marina would take care of the boys. They came to Houston to visit for a couple of weeks and ended up staying indefinitely!

The Nashes with "MeMe" & Joachim

That was great for us, and now they were going to help us move and stay on awhile in Nashville. We were moving along, traveling toward our long-awaited destination until we got to Little Rock, Arkansas. It was a below freezing day on the roads, and there was ice everywhere. As we came around a slight curve in the road, and only coasting due to heavy traffic, I just tapped the brakes of that big ol' truck to slow me down even further just in case I needed to avoid hitting the car in front of me.

Well, no one told me about black ice.

However, that's what I hit. You couldn't tell it was there because it was transparent, and the asphalt just looked normal. So when I lightly tapped on my brakes, the truck started sliding and slid out of control to the left, and we started down the embankment of the highway into the large grassy area. There I was heading slowly downhill, so I tried to turn the wheel to the right to stay up as close to the shoulder as possible, but when I did that the truck started to "tump" over. I quickly straightened my wheel back out, and we slowly slid to a halt down in the ravine.

When Kim saw me do what I did, she also stepped on her brakes, and did the same thing as me. We both ended up in the ravine! I could hear all her dishes and the china she had gotten as wedding presents shattering as they fell all around in the back of that truck. I just knew there had to be a lot of "breakage." I just hated to open the doors to see what the inside of the truck looked like, so I didn't until we got to Nashville.

It cost us a bunch of money out of our stash we had saved for the move to get us out of that mess. We hated that part since we didn't know how long it would be until we found work again. However, the good news was that no one was hurt. A couple of wreckers pulled us out and we then proceeded to stop at the first motel we saw on the highway to crash (no pun intended) for a few hours and thank God for his protection. Only God could have protected us from rolling that truck and totaling the car and losing everything we owned.

The next day we finally made it to Nashville, Tennessee! Kim and I had both been in and out of Nashville many times in our younger days to record, and had always loved it, but to finally live there was a whole different experience.

After we got everything out of the U-haul and the trailer unloaded, Billy looked up at me as he rode by on his little bike and asked, "How many days are we gonna stay here Daddy?"

He was used to us moving every few weeks from hotel to hotel, wherever we were playing next. He just thought that was normal.

Once we moved into our house and got settled in, we proceeded to call our contacts and friends to see what we could make happen. We called Dave and Dion Burgess, friends from my Liberty Records days, and we met with them at their office. Dave was still administering the publishing of Hank Williams and Hank Williams, Jr. He told us about another old friend, Tom Grant, who had started a new

Jimmy & Billy, Jr. At Their New Home In Nashville - 1988

group called "Trinity Lane." They were having a showcase to present their new project that had been picked up by Warner Brothers Records.

My old friend, Norro Wilson, was producing them, and was going to be there with his co-producer, Jim Malloy. I called Tom, and he immediately invited us to come to the showcase as his guest and said he would introduce us to Jim Malloy. Norro was what the music industry calls a song plugger at that time. He had a great personality and winning ways, so it was easy to see why he had a job like that.

We met lots of industry folks there and Tom and his group, "Trinity Lane," were fabulous. After the show, we visited with Norro, who was really glad to see me again, and then with Jim Malloy. Jim's claims to fame were countless in the music world. He was Elvis's engineer, he produced Ann-Margret in the studio, he engineered the Pink Panther soundtracks, and he and his son, David Malloy, partnered in one of the most successful independent publishing companies there in town, Debdave Music (named after Jim's son and daughter).

After talking awhile that night to Jim and Norro, out of the blue, they asked us if I would be up for trying a thing with our old friend, Gary Smith, who had moved to town the year before we did and had worked with Malloy on an album project in the past.

We were up for anything and everything at that point, so Kim and I wrote a song with Gary and went into the studio with Jim and Norro co-producing. They wanted to try a version of the Righteous Brothers, only Country. We didn't score with that endeavor, but it was at least worth a shot with two incredibly successful music men who had hit it big several times before. We would meet up with Jim again a few months down the road, and Norro would later become Kenny Chesney's co-producer, hitting it "HUGE" that time around. In the meantime, we needed to make some money somewhere. We knew the money we had saved would only last four or five months with cars, rent, utilities, and babies to feed. We would have to do whatever it took to continue following this dream in order to stay in Nashville.

THE "SHOW PALACE" IN BRANSON

About that time, in the spring of 1988, we got an interesting invitation. Judy Bunch's songwriter friend, Jerry Foster, decided to try his hand at owning a theater in Branson, Missouri, and he wanted us to come to Branson and perform there as part of his variety show. We were approaching the summer season, and things usually slow down in Nashville in the summertime when all the big acts are touring and out on the road. We decided to take the deal and head to Branson; besides, we needed the money! We locked up the house and loaded up the car and took off for Branson.

Since Marina and Joachim had had to finally go back to Sweden, we knew we would need help with the boys when we had rehearsals and performances, so I called my parents in Spring, Texas, and

The Nash Family In Branson (Jimmy, Kim, Leslie, Clara, Bill & Billy, Jr.) - 1988

asked them if they would consider coming to Branson to live with us so we could make this happen.

They were excited to spend quality time with their grandbabies and also see the shows in Branson. We proceeded to rent a small, two-bedroom apartment and got set up. We were back to singing six nights a week and matinees on the weekends, but this time we had a whole cast and crew and great band. What a fun experience to be the duet segment of a big production.

We had a comedian, a Gospel quartet and a featured female vocalist. Jimmy was only three years old, and he especially liked the female vocalist, Chris Gentile. I remember Jimmy telling Chris one night after the show (he said it in his baby talk), "I Chris Gentile boyfriend," and then he blushed real big. He then told her, "I can dweth (dress) mythelf (myself). His first crush. I guess he thought that would impress her. We thought it was so very cute, and so did Chris.

We stayed through that summer, and then we felt it was time to come back to Nashville. We had added a few bucks to our savings, but we knew we had to get back to Nashville if we were ever going to attain the dreams of writing and possibly recording for a label again.

So, closing night came, and my folks wanted to go to one last show in Branson across town from us, so we took the boys to closing night at the theater.

Chris Gentile would help look after the kids in the wings

Kim, Jimmy, Bill, and Billy, Jr. at the Show Palace Backstage - 1988

of the theater while Kim and I sang. However, for the closing song when the entire cast was on stage, we had to take the kids out there on stage with us.

The big closing song for the show was "God Bless The USA." That night the lead singer and emcee of the show started the verse, and when we all joined in on the chorus, Billy, who I was holding in one arm (Jimmy in the other), reached out and took my microphone, and started singing into it in the loudest voice you ever heard.

Billy had heard me sing that song in our shows in Houston on many occasions, and he knew it as well as I did. Well, the crowd started running down all the aisles to take pictures. Flashes were going off all over the place, and the lead singer's chest swelled all up, and he started parading around the stage so proudly thinking they were taking pictures of him.

But those Branson audiences just eat up kid acts, and that's what they thought Billy was singing such a great, patriotic song. Then the lead singer turned around, took a double-take and started to laugh. He then knew what all the ruckus was about. It was a special moment, and the crowd just cheered and cheered as the curtain went down. What a finish to our stint in Branson. It was a memorable time in our lives and our career that we will never forget. What's next?

Nash Note ♫

One thing that still makes us laugh from our time in Branson is the "MeeMow at the Show Palace." This comes from us having our nightly prayers with our boys, and we'd tell them how they should pray for all their family and friends and others they care about. Well Jimmy really loved cats, and there was this one cat that always hung out around the Show Palace. He was only three, so instead of just calling it a cat, he called it a "MeeMow", which we took to be some derivation of "meow." Even after we left Branson, Jimmy kept the "MeeMow at the Show Palace" in his prayers for many years. We still laugh about the possibility that this cat might still be alive after 30 years, just because of all the prayers.

Chapter Fifteen

Winning And Losing In Nashville

A S WE WERE DRIVING BACK TO Nashville, Kim and I started to talk about what we should do to pay the bills until some music door might open for us. Then I remembered an old fan and friend of mine from Houston, Mr. Dave Rosenburg, an ex-football player who was now an Encyclopedia Representative. He used to come out to hear me sing before I met Kim and tell me he wanted me to get in the book business with him. He said to just give him a call if I were ever interested. He liked my people skills and thought I could really do well.

So, one day I called up Big Dave. He was so glad to hear from me, and he thought it would be ideal for me to get involved while I was in Nashville since I could write songs in the daytime and sell encyclopedias in the evening.

It was quite interesting how Big Dave sold books. First of all, I had to go to the courthouse in Downtown Nashville and look up the records of all the newlyweds who had just gotten married. When they bought their marriage licenses, they had to give all their contact information as well as other statistics. That's where I got all my leads.

Then I mailed each one a postcard with a note that said if they would listen to my pitch on Encyclopedias, they would get three days and two nights in one of several tourist destinations, which they could choose from. From there, we waited for the phone to ring.

At first, Kim didn't want much to do with all this, but she soon realized how hard it was for one person to get all that done. I knew how much she hated talking on the phone, and that was a prerequisite for that portion of this endeavor. Someone had to answer the phone, set the appointment, and get directions on how to get to the person's house (no GPS back then).

Bill, Billy, Jr. & Jimmy Playing in Their Back Yard in Nashville - 1988

Big Dave's message on the postcard was signed by me, but the name they were to ask for when they called was a fictitious name so I wouldn't have to use my real name. The name was Mr. Stone. The postcard said to call and ask for Mr. Stone. So when they called in, Kim would answer and they would ask for Mr. Stone. She would tell them he wasn't in, but she could talk for him. Then she would answer their questions and set up an appointment.

I remember how excited we were when the cards had only been sent a couple of days beforehand, and we started getting calls. I think that first week I sold six sets of encyclopedias. My commission was $500 per sale. With sales like that we were thinking that I could just work one week out of the month to pay our bills, then we'd have the rest of the month for writing.

However, and this was a big "however," since it was an in-home sale, the customer, by law, had three days to cancel. So there we were sweating those three days after I went to all that effort to make the sale. There was the dreaded credit check that had to take place also which was done by the Encyclopedia company. This was done pretty quickly, but you still had a three-day minimum wait.

If it went through, we were good and had money. If it didn't, we were back to square one. We still remember this first time most clearly. Out of the six, two of the sales cancelled and three had bad credit so that left us with one sale. That was quite a comedown from the possible six sales at $500, which would have equaled $3,000. We still made $500 for the week though.

As time went on, we began to see how little time we really had to write and record demos and how much I started to hate just having to go out to all kinds of strange places and situations, some of them actually potentially life threatening on a couple of occasions. I remember telling one really suspicious husband that didn't know I was scheduled for an appointment with his wife that evening to just keep the vacation and call if they wanted to take us up on that offer.

It was kind of scary for me from then on, and Kim became very reluctant to schedule me for appointments. The income from the sales helped for a while, but we both knew it was nowhere near what we had come to town to do, and it was taking up all our time. We still had to figure out what to do next, how to keep us alive in Music City since we just couldn't seem to wrap our minds around the book business any longer.

Bill Playing Football With The Boys

The only positive thing about it was that Kim managed to write songs in earnest while she sat by the phone to set up appointments. Her thinking was, "We gotta write ourselves out of this situation." The song I remember most at this juncture was called, "Listening With Your Heart."

I had that melody in mind for almost two years, but could

never think of a word to write down that went with the tune. I kept playing it around the house all the time. I just loved that melody. Finally, one night Kim and I had a "loud discussion" over a song we were working on (we rarely disagreed about anything except about a line in a song or where the melody should go).

The next morning, she showed me some words she had written overnight. When I applied my tune to her words, lo and behold, they fit like a hand in a glove. It was amazing. We call it our apology song, and I say she wrote it to apologize to me for the loud discussion the night before, and she says she wrote it for me to sing to her to make me apologize for being wrong. We never really settled that one, but we had the song.

OUR FIRST PUBLISHING DEAL

As the days went by, I would call different friends to see what was happening, and one of those calls was to Jim Malloy. He was so very glad to hear from me and told me about a new music publishing company he was putting together.

After we talked for a few minutes, he invited me to come to his home in the hills of Tennessee and play him some of our new songs we had recently written. He really liked the songs and said he would submit us to his new partner and see what might come about.

Sure enough, the partner liked us, and Jim signed us to our first publishing deal in Nashville (he also signed our buddy, Gary Smith, which was a hoot). The song that really got us our deal was, "Listening With Your Heart." We were elated!

Bill & Kim with Jim Malloy

I'll never forget Jim slapping his palms down on his desk right after we played him the song and declaring loudly, "It's a hit!" What a thrill to have someone like him love a song we wrote.

The money was not great at our first publishing deal, but it never is for neophyte writers. The big deal was having a way to pay for our demos and then having someone to actually take our songs to the powers that be to get them recorded by major artists.

We wrote for Jim's All Nations Music Publishing Company for five years. Kim called it her college years. We were so excited about that, and then, thanks to being a writer there, we started being invited to different music events and after-parties where we met some interesting celebrities. Now we were in full writing mode, and we had enough of a "draw" (an advance on publishing royalties) to almost pay the rent of our new place in town.

OK, that's great, but now we had to make the rest of our living. Jim urged us to do a showcase for reps from different record labels, etc., to show them what we could do on stage and what we sounded like live and in person. We got a greatly encouraging review in CashBox Magazine for that showcase, and we still have it hanging in my office.

LOSING MY FATHER

I'm so glad my parents got to stay with us so much in Branson, and also again for many months in Nashville when Kim and I would have to be gone for writing appointments on Music Row. Billy was already in school, but Jimmy was still just 3 or 4. I didn't know that those would be my last years with my father, and now, that just makes them all the more precious.

He spent a lot of time with both my boys, but since Jimmy wasn't in school, he spent all day every day with him, and they became very close. He used to take Jimmy to Wal-Mart just about every day and let him play with all the toys before buying him a hot dog and a cherry coke "Icee" (even if it was only two hours 'til dinner and Kim asked him not to). He did pretty much anything Jimmy wanted to do, and the three of them (Mom, Dad, and Jimmy) seemed to have their own little world.

Dad had been diagnosed with prostate cancer during that most tumultuous time in our lives in 1984 when Keith Sr. had also just been diagnosed with Parkinson's and just before Billy was diagnosed with Leukemia in 1985. He had never been much for going to the doctor; that just wasn't in his thinking. Had he gone for a checkup even every few years, the doctors say they could have caught it in time, but that's just not the way it happened. They said he would only last for 2 years, but he more than doubled that expectation. One day, though, in late 1989, he knew it was almost his time. Dad and mom went back to Houston, and when he was checked into the hospital, I came in with Kim and the boys to be with him. I slept there in the room by his bed as many nights as I could (in those most uncomfortable chairs ever made that the hospitals provide), and we were finally going to head home, but I'll never forget Dad looking at me and saying, "Could you just stay one more night?" So I did, but the next day he looked at me and said, "OK, you need to go back to Nashville and take care of your family now." I didn't want to leave his side,

but I knew he was right. We got back to Nashville, and about a week later, I got the call, and his battle was over.

For those of you who have ever lost a parent, I don't have to tell you how that feels. He was only 73, which is shocking to me now, because as of the writing of this book, I'm 75, and I feel like I still have so much more life ahead of me. I still miss him all the time almost 30 *Bill with His Father, Leslie Nash - 1970* years later. He was one of the kindest, gentlest, most generous men I ever knew, and I was so proud to call him Dad. He was never a wealthy man, but he worked hard to make sure that before he passed, there was enough coming in for my mother to live between his social security and savings. He also made sure she had a house that was 100% paid for where she lived almost the remainder of her life.

His brother, my Uncle Joe, looked just like him, and he lived on an extra 20 years past my father despite having a very similar chart to him, just because he went to the doctor regularly. I was always happy to see my Uncle Joe because he reminded me so much of daddy. It was a gift to have him that much longer. It was also a great reminder to me to have myself checked out regularly, so I can be on this Earth in good health as long as possible for my kids and my grandkids.

The last thing I'd like to say about my father is possibly too unbelievable for some to believe, but I can only tell it as it happened to me. It was six months after the funeral, and I was in my bedroom in Nashville. I was not quite fully asleep, and suddenly I saw him by my bedside. I saw him just as real as could be, standing right beside me. He wasn't old and gray though, like the last time I saw him. He looked like I knew him as a kid, in his prime, strong, standing tall, with his auburn hair and a glow about him that I can't quite describe. He looked at me, and he said exactly this, "I'm in heaven, it's better than I ever told you, and I've got to go, because I'm still saying hello." That was it! He came to me in whatever spiritual form you want to call it just to tell me that one thing. I honestly don't know how it all works, if he asked God if he could appear to me, or what, because if it were that simple, then it seems like everyone would want to be popping in to appear to their kids. All I know is it happened, and I think he just wanted to let me know it was all okay, and he would never have to suffer ever again.

What a dad that is! Even when he's gone, he wanted to do everything he could to make me feel better. I don't think I ever stopped believing in Heaven, even when I was my furthest away from God, but if I had, I certainly would have believed again after that event. When I hear people say that there's no Heaven, and there's only this life, and nothing beyond that, I feel particularly blessed to be able to say, I know without a doubt there is a Heaven. Why? Because my Heavenly Father, AND my earthly father told me (and showed me) so.

CELEBRITY BOOKING AGENCY

As I was around Music Row, just seeing who I could see and talking with different friends and acquaintances, I let it be known that I wanted to come up with something that was show business-related that would be a way to subsidize our income while Kim and I continued to write.

We met several new songwriters thanks to Jim Malloy. Someone in those days mentioned an old friend of theirs who was looking to put a booking agency together. His name was Bob Taylor and he had been a vice-president at the Jim Halsey Management Company out of Tulsa who managed Roy Clark, the Oak Ridge Boys, and many other big stars. I got Bob's telephone number and as we talked, we both got a bit excited about the possibilities of such a venture.

Bob's knowledge and experience in the booking and management business made me think that this was a real opportunity for Kim and me. Not only would we be part owners of a booking agency, but that company could book us to play certain dates as well; it would be our own, built-in booking agency. Bob laid out a plan, and we came up with some figures, and then Kim and I started praying, asking God what to do next. We both felt good about it all.

On a trip back to Houston to sing for Lakewood Church, we met up once again with our good friends, Dr. Ken and Debra Tyer. I was telling them about our plan and the fact that we needed to find someone who might be interested in being in with us on this new business venture. They reminded us about their friend, Ruth, and her friend Dick who had come with them to see us in Branson. They thought Ruth might possibly have some interest. I'm not sure exactly why they thought that, but with that in mind we met with Ruth, and she said she would be interested.

We also remembered our friend, Frank, who we met at Judy Bunch's house on one of those famous Sundays. He said he was also interested. The next thing I knew we had a "yes" from Frank and Ruth, and they flew into Nashville to meet Bob and assess the situation. We had a great meeting, and before Ruth left town, she handed me a check. We asked our close friends, Guinn and Linda Rasbury, to be the accountants on this venture to make sure all monies were accounted for and properly recorded. Guinn was like a dad to me and, in fact, when my dad passed on, I told Guinn that he now had to be my dad. He was a proud Marine who had served in WWII. He came close to death on many occasions in that war, but he survived. His calm nature and business savvy saved me many times over in my lifetime. I thank God every day that Guinn and Linda came into our lives.

Bob and I rented a small office on Music Row and set it up for business. Bob knew a producer who had hits in the pop world with a group called Dr. Hook & the Medicine Show. This producer, Ron Haffkine, now had a new artist he was working with named Davis Daniel. Using Ron's connections in New York, he had signed Davis to a Mercury Records recording contract and was currently producing an album on him.

We successfully signed that artist to our new booking agency called Celebrity International. Bob headed up the company, and I was his partner along with Ruth and Frank.

We were pretty pumped about signing Davis since several other companies were out to sign him, and I mean some real heavyweights. But since Ron had lots of experience in show business, he said he preferred a smaller booking agency where his artist, Davis Daniel, wouldn't get lost in the shuffle.

He didn't have to vie for top spot with us. We guaranteed him that Davis Daniel would be our number one priority and would get all of our attention.

OUR CELEBRITY ROSTER GROWS

We then signed my old friend, Johnny Lee, and one other tremendously successful country singer/songwriter, Eddy Raven. Within the next several months, we also got wind that the great Charlie Rich (the Silver Fox) might be interested in coming back out of retirement.

Charlie had huge hits like "Behind Closed Doors" and "Most Beautiful Girl." If we could just snag this guy, we would have a name that everyone knew, and it would open doors for our new acts.

As it turned out, we did sign Charlie Rich, and we even did an album on him called, "The Very Best Of Charlie Rich." One of our other close friends from Houston, Dr. Sam McManus, invested in that project, and we were off and running. I became the Executive Project Coordinator.

My pal, Gary Smith, worked with me on that project, as well. I can't tell you how exciting it was for Kim and me as we got to attend those recording sessions where Charlie would play those old hit songs and re-record them. We went to Fireside Studios where Porter Wagoner and Dolly Parton, along with many other stars, used to record. I just sat in the control room and listened as the songs went down.

I remember meeting up with Charlie over at our office, and he and his bodyguard/ friend, whom we called Big Al, rode over to the studio

Nash Note 🎵

Gary Smith and I were always like family, but in the late 90's it became official. His son, John, married my niece, Robin, and they had two beautiful kids together, Cason and Keeley. So Gary's grandkids are my great niece and nephew. We both sit back and laugh, and talk about how they got all their good looks from us.

with me. Big Al was from Memphis and was at one time Elvis's bodyguard. When we walked into the studio to Charlie's first recording session, the musicians that were there to play on the session stood up at their instruments and applauded for several minutes, showing their respect for Charlie's talent and years in the business.

What a moment! I kept thinking to myself, man, this is where it's at! I get to be around all the things I love to do, and even though it's not me recording at the moment, I'm enjoying the success of all the things that had fallen in place for me to be there at that particular time doing what we were doing. I was also proud to have put together all the funding for the project.

After the album was completed, Bob started getting Charlie booked on things like *The Ralph Emery Show*, which emanated out of the Grand Ole Opry complex in Nashville. I stayed until

the show was over, and since I was part of Charlie's team, I had backstage privileges. I went up to Ralph after the show and handed him my business card and shook his hand and thanked him for having Charlie on his show.

As I was thanking him, Ralph looked at my card and read my name back to me. He said, "Bill Nash, 1967, 'For The Good Times,' it should have been a hit." I was

Kim Dancing with Charlie Rich - 1991

floored and actually speechless. I stammered and stuttered and thanked him over and over for remembering something that had happened quite a while ago in my past. Ralph was one of the most famous disc jockeys ever to come out of Nashville. He was around when the Nash Family Trio was recording in Nashville, and his "handle" was "the old coffee slurper." That was the extent of our conversation, one that told me what a sharp mind he had to have the power of recall like that. It was unbelievable.

One day, Charlie got an offer to go to England. The offer was for three nights, one in Albert Hall, and the other two in music venues within a hundred-mile radius. I especially remember the $100,000 deposit they sent along with the contract. However, Charlie had a hesitancy about playing overseas. Elvis had the same attitude, and from what I understand, Elvis never did play overseas.

Charlie kept us waiting day after day for his answer. We would call Big Al, and he would go and ask Charlie, and we would get the same answer: give me another couple of days. As fate would have it, the deadline for his answer came and went. We had to send back the $100,000. It made us sick. We were right there on the verge of starting something we could parlay into more dates and television appearances, and we just knew the bookings would have poured in. Oh well, what could we do?

Still, we were honored to do a couple of gigs with Charlie in Texas. One was for the Exchange Club's Great Escape fundraiser. Charlie was the star, and we had a motor home for his dressing room out back of the stage of this huge open, but covered arena. Buzzy Smith was the orchestra leader, and he had the band all rehearsed with Charlie's hits. Kim and I were thrilled to sing back-up vocals along with Sharon, Buzzy's wife.

When it came time for Charlie to come on stage, I announced him, but he didn't show. I stalled again, and somebody went to check on him. We were told he would be out in about five minutes and to stretch the show as much as possible until then. So, I stretched the show. I would sing a song, and then we'd send someone back to the motor home again. This went on for fifteen to twenty minutes. Big Al sent me word that Charlie was throwing up. What!!! Throwing up? This great star who had been on stage most of his life? Yes, throwing up.

Ruth, Kim, & Bill In Las Vegas for Booking Agency Convention - 1990

The great Charlie Rich always had trouble going on stage and had to conquer that fear all over again each time he performed. After years of hearing of other stars going through this same process, I realized that it was not uncommon. Some folks called these moments a panic attack. Donny Osmond suffered this kind of mental anguish also, but was able to overcome it.

Finally, I turned around to look at the motor home, and I could see Charlie and Big Al walking toward the stage. When I announced him again and he finally did step on stage, the crowd greeted him wildly.

Bill Promo Photo

They still loved him and wanted to hear him play his songs. He truly is one of the greatest talents I've ever had the privilege of working with. He played a great show and got a long, standing ovation. Great show for a great cause.

The second booking was for the Austin Rodeo committee's pre-rodeo show. Charlie had asked that Kim and I be his background singers on that night. When he came out to perform, the crowd did the same thing as in Houston.

Charlie played all his hits and then started playing "Spanish Eyes" for some reason. He looked up over the piano at me and said, "Do you know it?" I said yes *Kim Promo Photo* and then he nodded for me to sing it, so I did. How cool was that! Kim and I loved singing back up for the Silver Fox.

GEORGE JONES

Along with Celebrity, I had the opportunity at this time to work on the George Jones Life Story project for Hallway Productions out of Canada. I found a few investors who wanted to sign on with us, so I was introduced to Patsy Cline's Husband, Charlie Dick, who was also involved in this project. Because of Charlie's longtime friendship with the "Possum," the Hall Brothers were able to sign George to a video deal.

I was now included as one of the executive producers of this project. One of my favorite all-time perks was that I got to stand on stage just about five feet from George when he performed at Billy Bob's in Fort Worth. Charlie had introduced me to George and his wife, Nancy, at his hotel room the day before. Nancy was heading up George's contractual arrangements and was great at looking out for his business interests. George was also showing up to all of his gigs thanks to her (he was famously known as "No Show Jones")

The next night, George's bus driver pulled that big old custom bus right up to the backstage door, and George stepped out. He walked into the club just about in time for them to introduce him to the crowd. When he stepped out on that big stage and started the show with a song somebody had written just for him, appropriately called, "No Show Jones," the crowd went literally crazy, I mean crazy. The Hall Brothers used some of the footage they shot that night in the video. I was just honored to be a part of something with such an icon of Country music.

CARL PERKINS

In the meantime, at Celebrity International, Bob Taylor was also able to sign the great singer and songwriter, Carl Perkins, who wrote many hits such as "Blue Suede Shoes." Everyone at the agency was really pumped that we had managed to sign him. He was a legend. Even the Beatles had recorded some of his songs, and he was revered in Europe.

Kim and I went down to his hometown of Jackson, Tennessee and did a TV show with him to raise money for a children's charity. He was big on being a part of his hometown, and he was wonderful to us. We hit it off and had a good time. He loved our story about Billy's healing when we told it on the TV show. Carl was a hugely talented guy who played that old-style rock and roll, and we loved it.

The Nashes with Carl Perkins - 1991

Carl and I went to Los Angeles together for him to perform on the NBC summer show, *Hot Country Nights*. B.J. Thomas and Marie Osmond were also on that same show. I caught up with B.J. and his brother, who I met in times past in Houston. Marie was so personable, and she and her manager and I talked for the longest time. She was so down-to-earth and interesting. I always enjoy visiting with celebs that haven't forgotten that it's the people, their fans, that put them where they are; she definitely loved her fans.

THE END OF CELEBRITY

So here's a play-by-play of how to take down a new booking agency.

First, Davis Daniel's manager, Ron, fell out with his record label, Mercury, and the label gave Davis the ultimatum of choosing them or his manager. He chose the label and, after a few months, was dropped from the label, and he wasn't really bookable for us anymore. Strike #1!

Then the second major blow: Charlie Rich fell and broke his leg. He was in a cast and not in the mood to play. He wasn't going to be ready to work for several months. Strike #2!

Aside from his music career, Charlie was wealthy from investing early in a chain of Wendy's franchises and selling out his part, so he didn't "have" to work another day in his life. That happened before he got involved with us, and partly why he didn't care too much about being heavily booked.

We just had Carl Perkins left and a few other artists we booked just from time to time. I know this is going to sound really wild, but imagine how it sounded to us when we got the awful news that Carl had throat Cancer. Oh no, third major blow in a row! Strike #3!!

Our first thought was for his life of course, but secondly for the life of Celebrity. It took a couple of days for the news to sink in. We were so disheartened. Well, the good news was that Carl did come through it, but his treatment had caused some lasting effects. He did his best, but it was very tiring for him.

So there was that question again reverberating in my head, what's next?

Carl didn't feel like taking on any live concerts or shows for another year or so at least. My friend, Bob Taylor, was really dejected and discouraged. Just when things looked like they were about to explode in a great, upward direction, all this bad news came rolling in.

I wish I could explain my own feelings better, and I wish I could tell you how hard it was for me to call Ruth and tell her the news. She had been the greatest partner and friend anyone could ever hope to have and to know and be in business with. She didn't deserve this downward spiral of events after three years of funding this company.

I reached out to my friend, Roger McDuff, in Houston, who was one of my mentors in Gospel music and a family friend since I was 12 years old. He knew a guy in New York that he put me in contact with who flew in to see if he had any interest in becoming a partner in Celebrity International.

He did fly in and looked it all over. Ruth flew in to meet him, and the guy from New York initially said yes to Celebrity International, but later changed his mind. He said he would rather key on the music than on the booking. It seems as though he had written some songs in the past that got played on the radio up East.

Then Bob Taylor lost heart and resigned from the company. He was the one we had leaned on, the one with all the knowledge of the booking business. There was really no one to take his place who would have that same knowledge and that same desire to build a booking agency. Ruth single-handedly had kept the business from going down when our friend Frank had to bail out due to some stock market reversals with his investments.

Now here she was with a decision to make. She was really gracious to the people Bob had brought on board, but they couldn't keep it going. It was finally over for Celebrity International. We came so close, but no one could have ever foreseen that turn of events. We all gave our all, but sometimes that's just not enough. What's next?

Chapter Sixteen

Finding The Dream At The End Of A Storm

THE GUY FROM NEW YORK, WHO we will call S.C., let me know that he was interested in doing something where he could write songs like he used to do as a younger man and have other writers on board also so we could pitch those songs to artists for cuts.

I called one of our favorite co-writers and close friends that Jim Malloy had introduced us to and asked him if he would be interested in a new publishing company venture. We will call him A.R. He said yes, and soon we formed a new publishing company called Hot House Music.

For the next few months, we moved right along pursuing this venture. Kim and I found a three-story house on Music Row, and S.C. put up the rent. It was not furnished, so the plan was for us to do the leg work and find some suitable furniture to place in the house. S.C. told us to just put it on our credit card, and he would write us a check for it later.

We trusted him due to our friend Roger McDuff's endorsement who told us S.C. was a good Christian man. The furnishings came to over $10,000. When it came time to pay, S.C. only wanted to pay the minimum the first month due to some extra heavy expenses at his company in NYC. This was the first red flag, or at least it should have been.

We had grown to care a great deal about A.R., especially since he had sought us out himself to write with him. He even produced a single on us as artists. We recorded a re-make of "Up Where We Belong" that went #1 on the Independent charts and won us a nomination for duo of the year in the Independent category.

My boyhood friend, James Williams, has a record promotion company in Nashville, and he single-handedly promoted our song week after week until he got it to #1. Thank you James. You've been a great friend all my life.

We were on a good path, and I thought A.R. and Kim and I would be friends for life and that we could start to record more and get James to promote our music to all his radio contacts. We even had a recording studio set-up on the ground floor.

A.R. started signing writers to our new music publishing company. Neither he nor we had negotiated our own writer's contracts with S.C., which would turn out to be a blessing later on.

The big red flag that I continued to ignore was the fact that the money for the couple of writers we brought on was always late, and I had to call S.C. every month and work on getting in those funds as well as the rent. All monies came through S.C.'s accountant, who came down from New Jersey to set up the books. Jimmie Lee (Kim's mom), who we hired as our administrative assistant, sat with him to make sure everything was in compliance.

S.C. used to pray with me on the phone for God to bless this venture and bless the songs. In retrospect, this was a good life lesson that just because someone prays with you, it doesn't mean they're necessarily that spiritual (or trustworthy). We took a trip in the summertime to New York and visited his family and had dinner in his home, and our kids became friends. The final paperwork was in the mill, and we all worked in good faith that this would be worked out even though the first draft of the deal between A.R., S.C., and myself was not totally defined.

Shortly after our visit to New York, A.R. decided that he and his family would go to New York to visit S.C. and his family, as well. That's when the air started to change. That was obviously more than a vacation trip with the family. When A.R. returned to Nashville, he told me he wanted to bring a new guy fresh out of college to run the company and do the day-to-day stuff that I had been doing as interim manager.

It struck me funny at first since we were a fledgling company, and our budget for maintenance of the office was marginal. This young man had a couple of meetings with A.R., and he was hired without any input from me. Then, A.R. called me and told me, not asked me, to "fire" Jimmie Lee immediately. It was a difficult task since she was my mother-in-law, but I finally had to. She told me that I would be next; she said she had a woman's intuition about it, and that certain things that had gone on around the office told her so anyway. But I couldn't believe it. I just thought there would be a face-to-face meeting between the three of us, S.C., A.R., and me, and we would get all the loose ends tied up and straighten everything out. Man, was I in for a rude awakening!

Not long after Jimmie Lee was released, here's what happened. I was on the road to Houston when I got a call from Kim. She said the new kid, Greg, had called her and said there would be no more money, which meant no money for my pay for managing the office.

She said she had been driving when she got the call (on the car phone - no cell phone yet). It blindsided her, and she had to pull over and get her bearings. She had the boys with her in the car and was trying not to let them see how upset she was. She called me, and I didn't know what to think. Her voice was very shaky, and I could tell she was on the verge of tears. We both were stunned!

I got back to town shortly after that and went down to the

office and stuck my key in the door; the locks had already been changed. I banged on the back door until A.R. appeared and opened the door. I told him my key wouldn't work, and he looked at me so strangely and said, "Now, now, come in and let's talk."

By this time my heart was racing. We sat in the front office and he said things had changed. Greg was now running the company, and they didn't need me anymore. I was nauseous, and my mind was on stun. I got a little loud and reminded A.R. that I was the one who had put this company together, but he simply escorted me out the door and closed it behind me.

"Goodbye Bill, thanks for all your hard work, but we'll take it from here!" he said.

Really? I walked away slowly in disbelief. I was so confused after being so betrayed by people I thought were my friends. I felt like I had been stabbed in the back and punched in the gut all at the same time.

S.C. in New York wouldn't even take my phone calls and, as I was told later, labeled my messages as "Trash from Nash." We thought we were on the road to success, but it was more like the road to nowhere. How many more times can we do this?

Kim and I were out, and they were in. Just like that. What really hurt too is that he had been lying to my friend, Roger McDuff, who had introduced us, and told him that we had been stealing money, and that WE were the ones to blame for everything. And lastly to add insult to injury they wouldn't release any of the furniture that was on our credit cards! Ouch! They kept it all.

Kim was sick over it for many days, as was I. We were both in shock and beyond hurt.

Oh God, what's next?

HOW BETRAYAL BECOMES A BLESSING

Only God could have foreseen and made preparations for what came next. Perhaps we were a bit naive, well, more than perhaps. We were. Still, though, this is a great example of one of those times in our lives where God protected us from our own mistakes and from those who wanted to do us harm.

In the midst of all this, we had written a song with Mr. Freddy Weller that we thought would fit Reba McEntire perfectly for her upcoming, soon-to-be-released, greatest hits album. Freddy was a great singer/songwriter and had also been part of the band, Paul Revere and The Raiders.

This would have been in early 1993. Reba was only going to record two new songs for this album, and the rest were a compilation of her previous million seller hits she had had for MCA Records. That kind of album always sold big, and it was every songwriter's aim to get a song on that record.

I remember the day I took the song over to her office, and there was no one around. There was just this basket on a table at the entry of her outer office and a sign that read "drop tapes here" (yes, good old cassette tapes, not even CD's yet). I remember thinking that the odds of this happening were so slim that I couldn't even dream of it coming about.

I didn't know Reba; Kim and I had only met her at a Capitol Records party at the Sheraton Music City where she and Garth Brooks were being honored for their recent hit records. Garth was just coming on the scene and had had a couple of hits, but none yet to the magnitude of "Friends In Low Places." In fact, when it came time to get our picture with Garth, I told Kim to go ahead and get in the picture because I wanted to go grab an avocado (yes, a whole avocado to put in my coat pocket to take home, don't judge me) from the buffet before they took the food away.

Kim with Garth Brooks (Bill Not Pictured Due To His Desire for Avocados)

Garth was wearing a blue tux, patent leather shoes, and a white, Stetson cowboy hat. I had previously been standing in the background listening to the different people as they talked with him, and he was so unbelievably polite, saying "yes ma'am" and "no ma'am" and thanking them for being his fan. He was just a really nice, well-mannered guy from Oklahoma. Kim proceeded to get her picture with Garth, and I was across the room. Whoops! Guess I should have stuck around and got to know HIM better--probably more important in retrospect than getting an avocado. It just shows that you never know who someone is, or who they WILL be.

ONE CALL CHANGES EVERYTHING

A couple months after I dropped off the tape at Reba's office, to my surprise, I received a call from her assistant! She asked if I could drop a copy of our demo off with Reba's producer, Tony Brown, at his office. His office was about 20 minutes away, but I probably was there in 10 to drop off our tape. Kim and I were tentatively excited that we made it through enough of the process now to be heard by her producer, but still knew it was a long shot for us to be one of only two songs chosen.

Then a couple months later, one morning around 11:00 a.m., I got a call from someone named Cliff Williamson, and I wasn't all the way awake yet. Kim and I were still night owls from having night club hours for so many years, and we usually went to bed about 2:00 a.m. or so and slept until noon with the exception now of my taking Billy to school at 7:00 a.m. and returning home to go back to bed for a while before a writing appointment.

So I had just gotten up and was having my first cup of coffee, and Kim was still sound asleep. Cliff asked if I was Bill Nash and was I one of the writers of a song called, "They Asked About You." I told him I was. His next few words sent me to the moon.

He asked in what felt like much too casual a tone for such life-changing news, "Would you like to come hear how Reba cut your song?"

Reba McEntire had cut our song? I stood for a minute, stunned, and then ran from the living room back to the bedroom and hollered to Kim, "Reba cut our song!" She sat straight up in bed and out of a deep sleep she said, "What?" I repeated, "Reba cut our song."

The exhilaration just ran through me like ten cups of double-caffeine coffee. I was jumping up and down and thanking God and trying to calm down enough to set up the appointment with Cliff to go to Reba's office and listen to the song. I never asked

Cliff what he thought about my loud reaction. I figured it wasn't his first time to hear that response.

We set it up for the next day, and we kept the boys out of school to take them with us. When we got to Reba's office, Cliff came out and met us, and we shook hands and went into the listening room. We did a few minutes of small talk, and then he played her version of our song. It was stunning. She had kept our same arrangement of the song and only changed the intro from piano to guitar (Freddy had cleverly put a key change right at the top of the song, and I always thought that helped get Reba's attention). She rang the note on the word "all" just like we had dreamed she would in the chorus.

Cliff asked us right there and then if we would be interested in becoming writers for Reba's publishing company, Starstruck Publishing, and we obviously said yes and subsequently worked out a deal (how could we say no?). It was just the most incredible moment in our music world life, and the prior months of hurt

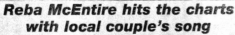

Reba McEntire hits the charts with local couple's song

By DOUG ADOLPH
Reporter

A LOCAL SONGWRITING DUO is putting the Nash into Nashville as their recent small hit, "They Asked About You," is soaring straight to the top of country-western charts.

Former southwest Houston residents Bill and Kim Nash are basking in the success their breakthrough single is receiving. Now in the top 20s, the single, which appears on country superstar Reba McEntire's Greatest Hits 2 album, continues to gain steam as it ascends skyward.

In fact, Robert Oreman, a top Nashville music critic who Bill admits has crushed many of their friends with lethal reviews, says the tune is a "well crafted song writer's gem."

The couple packed their bags for the mecca of country music seven years ago to make a serious run at songwriting glory, and their roll of the dice has paid dividends beyond what they could've expected.

"We believed we had something," he explains. "We're preachers' kids and knew God sent us here."

Indeed, it was a twist of fate that led to the couple's discovery of the tune. The two were at a popular downtown Nashville hangout, the Stoneyard restaurant, for an evening out. Bill left the table to talk with some friends of his onstage entertaining. When he returned, he told Kim, "they asked about you."

At that moment, he says they both knew those were the words that would lead to something special, but neither realized the enormity of their discovery.

"On the way home in the car we wrote the chorus verse on a napkin," Bill recalls.

They co-wrote the tune with Freddy Weller, better known with Paul Revere and the Raiders, cut a demo in the studio and dropped off a copy at McEntire's front desk. Bill says McEntire happened to pick up their cut from a bin of others.

The song made its way onto the superstar's album, which has eclipsed the $2 million mark in less than three months.

Throughout the whirlwind experience, Bill says the most rewarding experience has been getting to know McEntire and her husband, Narvel Blackstop.

whom he describes as the most down-to-earth, good people he knows.

"In a town where people look at music as a product, they are more," Bill says.

Reba McEntire, center, with Bill and Kim Nash

Houston Article About Bill & Kim's Success with Reba

and desperation seemed to disappear. Reba didn't know us and couldn't have known our situation or the timing of such a deal and what it meant to us. We were just trying to start over again, not knowing how or even where to start, and then all at once we were on top of the world.

We've always felt that God had a hand in her liking our song since she told us later that she had gone through about 5000 songs just to pick two for her greatest hits volume two album. The other new song turned out to be "Does He Love You," a duet with Linda Davis, which went straight up the charts to number one, and she later won a Grammy for it.

Our song made the top five in Billboard; it even went number one in select markets around the country. However, the album went number one in six weeks, and went on to sell 11 million copies worldwide, which meant we had mailbox money coming our way! She even included it on another compilation called, "Forever Reba," that sold an additional 1 million plus copies.

Nash Note 🎵

Linda Davis was such a wonderfully kind individual, and we became great friends with her and her husband, Lang Scott, as part of the Starstruck family. Years later, their daughter, Hillary, and our son, Jimmy, ended up going to the same school, where they would perform together for their school's weekly chapel. Hillary then went on to become part of the immensely successful group, Lady Antebellum.

Reba will always be in the very top of our blessings list, and we will always appreciate her choosing our song. It actually saved our lives and confirmed that God really had meant for us to be in Nashville at that time. That album was released in September 1993, but our single came out in 1994. She even took us on a holiday trip in early December of '94 to the Ritz Carlton in Naples, Florida. She brought all her office staff and all of her employees, from the guys who drove the 18-wheelers that hauled her gear for her live shows to her executives who ran all her business for her and her husband at that time, Narvel Blackstock.

We got to know them as best you can with 200 plus other folks around that were involved in her day-to-day operation. But we

Reba, Bill, & Kim in Naples - 1994

sat around the pool at the Jacuzzi in Naples and talked with her and Narvel. They were both down to earth and always fun to be around. The first thing on the agenda after checking in to the hotel was to meet everyone on the beach for a volleyball tournament. There were probably about 5 different spaces with nets with refs at each one dressed accordingly.

By the process of elimination, our team advanced and finally

faced Narvel and Reba's team. It was a hard-fought match but our team won! Reba didn't play, but actually stayed out there with all of us crazy people having the time of our lives. My feeling: God sent Kim and I to Naples, Florida with Reba to have some much-needed R&R.

Bill & Kim at the Ritz Carlton Naples

Later that year, we were honored to be invited, along with our boys, to Reba and Narvel's home for the release of her new book, *My Story*. It was a book signing party. She even mentioned us in her book in a list of Starstruck Publishing songwriters and other people on staff in her organization.

Narvel always loved to have a little fun with me, so when we pulled up to the sprawling estate, the largest in the area, and the only one that had a specifically black fence (because his last name is Blackstock), I rang the buzzer to enter the gate, and he told me we

The Nash Family with Reba at Her Birthday Party - 1994

had the wrong house. I said, "Are you sure?", and he kept it up for about 5 minutes back and forth telling me how I need to go down the block and look there. Finally, of course, he let us in, and we had the best time.

Our boys were already friends with Reba and Narvel's son, Shelby, who was only about 4 at the time. At the company softball games each week during the summer, they would play with/

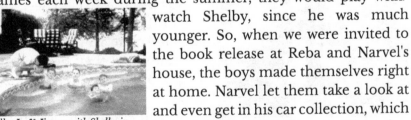

watch Shelby, since he was much younger. So, when we were invited to the book release at Reba and Narvel's house, the boys made themselves right at home. Narvel let them take a look at and even get in his car collection, which

Billy, Jr. & Jimmy with Shelby in Reba & Narvel's Pool - 1994

they loved. One funny thing that happened is when Shelby couldn't wait any longer to go swimming. He stripped down and jumped in the pool completely naked! Reba sprang into action quickly and grabbed him out of the pool and got him into a proper bathing suit. It was pretty funny, and everyone got a good laugh. We have such good memories from that day and that whole time in our lives. She just made us all feel like family.

THE LEUKEMIA SOCIETY

During this time, in 1994, Kim and I were presented with the opportunity to run in the Marine Corps Marathon in Washington D.C. (the same one Oprah ran that year), to benefit the Leukemia Society. I was on the board of the local chapter in Nashville and they had heard about Billy's story and approached us about him being their poster child that year.

At first, we didn't want to say yes because we didn't want Billy (now 12) to re-live any of his past experiences, in the event that it would be too difficult for him. But we sat him down one day and presented their proposal to him. He actually liked the idea, so we said yes. That's when we signed up

Billy at Leukemia Society Event

to run the 26.2-mile marathon which would take place in Washington, D.C. Part of our commitment was to send a letter to all of our friends and ask them to make a donation for each mile we would run.

Reba and Narvel's check was one of the first we received. We gathered quite a bit of money for the cause and they flew us and all the other volunteer runners to D.C. on the same plane, (Kim's mom came along to watch the boys). We had all trained and

Jimmy, Kim, Jimmie Lee, Billy, Jr. and Bill After The Marine Corps Marathon - 1994

trained and had racked up tons of miles and were ready to tackle that incredibly long run.

If you want to know how far that is, here's how I always describe it: run until you can't run one more step and are about to drop from exhaustion and dehydration and then run two tenths of a mile further. That is how far a marathon is. We were so happy to raise over $20,000 for the Leukemia Society of Nashville, Tennessee. Looking back now, this was a precursor to us learning how to raise money for our own cause, Champions Kids Camp.

OLD FRIENDS RESURFACE

Kim eventually learned from our PRO (Performing Rights Organization), BMI, when she was turning in the paperwork to register "They Asked About You" and to inform them of a release date, that A.R. and S.C. (Hot House) had claimed that they owned the song. They already had them listed as the publishers. Apparently, Greg at Hot House had been instructed to give BMI this piece of information even though it was misinformation. Kim let BMI know that this was not accurate and submitted the form with the correct information. BMI accepted our side of the story when our old friends failed to produce any assignment of our copyright. Funny thing is, if they had given us proper contracts, and hadn't kicked us out, they would have had part of the publishing since we would have still been writers at Hot House. Thank God they kicked us out when they did!

I don't know how many days went by, but one evening about 8:00 p.m., we got this loud knock on our back door. When I opened it there was a stranger handing me some papers. He didn't skip a beat. He took one look at me and said, "Sign here, you are being sued."

I stood and just gaped at him a moment. I had never been sued before, and I didn't know how to handle it. It's like your first time at anything. My heart started racing and the fear of a terrible lawsuit welled up in my imagination. We had been kicked out, locked out, and told to go away, which was hard enough to deal with; now they also wanted to steal our intellectual property and keep it for themselves. Later, I heard Dolly Parton in an interview say that you weren't really in the music business if you haven't been sued.

The only attorney I knew at that time in Nashville was an old friend from Houston, Lee Ofman, who was a criminal attorney. So the next day, I called him up. I'll always appreciate his response. He told me to calm down and asked for Kim and me to come see him the next day. He lived in Franklin, just a few miles outside of Nashville. We went to lunch and told him our story. He told us he didn't do contract law, but he knew who to send us to.

Looking back, it's easy to see that God protected us from being in business with those two characters, A.R. and S.C. Thank God we didn't sign anything. We could not have seen the future, but God always can.

Lee set us up with an attorney he knew of in Franklin named Mr. Jordan. We set an appointment with Mr. Jordan and went to a meeting the next day. He listened and took notes and was so kind. He had that deep Southern drawl and wore the kind of suit Matlock wore on TV.

He reminded us both of that character Andy Griffith played for so long. He had this calming effect on the two of us. He quickly took the lead and set up appointments with A.R. and S.C.'s attorneys. He would come back to us from time to time and tell us the results of their meetings. The other attorneys' offices were on Music Row, and one of the partners was kind of a large guy with a big, loud voice, and he proceeded to tell Mr. Jordan that we were nobodies, and that they were going to run us out of town because we didn't have any money and wouldn't last.

Mr. Jordan's nature was more of a quiet kind of guy who just took notes and did his research. As he researched "The Laaawwwh (law)," as he said it, he told us that there was a law put into effect in the 1970s that specifically spelled out that, in order to claim copyright ownership of a song, it had to be in writing from the songwriter and notarized. This had come about from so many writers being ripped off in the past by publishing companies claiming they had the rights to a song and even producing someone who said they had heard the writer confirm this. That had been accepted in court in the past, but was no longer valid. Thank God for that law.

One morning, after weeks of back and forth and on and on, we got a phone call from Mr. Jordan. He asked me in his soothing Southern drawl, "Mr. Nash, are you sitting down?" So I sat down on the edge of the bed in our bedroom and told him I was. He said, "The other side has quit." What? Why? What happened? He said it looked to him like they had run out of money or simply realized that they were going to lose.

Kim and I were so relieved. This all had been going on while the song and Reba's album were climbing the Billboard charts. The album had gone number one in a matter of weeks, and they were playing the stuffing out of our song on the radio. Every time it would start playing on the radio in the car the boys would say in unison, "Daddy, turn up our song!" That made us so proud to know that they felt a part of our success.

A few months later, the phone rang, and it was A.R. He and his wife were on the phone, and A.R. said, "I'm sorry, I apologize." I didn't know what to say for a minute and was silent. He said it again, "I'm sorry and I apologize." S.C. had by that time done A.R. wrong and left him holding the bag with significant debts to pay off because A.R. didn't heed my warnings about the finances when I got kicked out.

I know The Lord's Prayer well enough to remember the part that says, "Forgive us our debts as we forgive our debtors." I was taught that I had to forgive in order to be forgiven. But let me tell you, in case there's someone living in a vacuum somewhere that's never been betrayed, it can be very difficult after you have been violated by someone you thought loved you like a brother who then turned around and stabbed you in the back.

It wasn't the fact that A.R. had decided he didn't need me anymore and could by-pass me entirely, it was the underhanded way he had gone about it. All of this ran through my mind in quick succession as he was talking on the phone, but I finally said okay and that I accepted his apology. It would take Kim a little longer to forgive. As we talked a bit, Kim did ask about the new refrigerator we were still paying Sears for, and what about the other furniture we still owed several thousand dollars on. He said he'd have to get back to us on all that. Well, it's been 25 years, and we're still waiting to hear back on that. Apologies are good, but giving back stolen furniture would be better.

Nash Note 🎵

Shortly after the lawsuit, around 1995/1996, our great friend and co-writer, Lewis Anderson, had pitched a song we co-wrote with him to Faith Hill's producer, Scott Hendricks, and Faith cut the song. It was called "The Silence You Heard." We just knew it would be another financial success like our Reba song. However, that just wasn't to be. Faith and her producer decided to sever their relationship and they scrapped all the songs that had been produced for that new album, our song included. Well, that's the music business!

We paid for the furniture using our Reba royalties. We also used the royalties to fix some much-needed things around our house which by now we had purchased since we finally had a down payment! Nearby, there was a small but nice little country club called

Ravenwood that was offering a new member special where we could sign up as members for $250 a month, with no initiation fee. Well with that fee waived, and by the fact that we actually had income coming in now regularly, we could afford that! That membership allowed us to play golf every weekend with our boys. That was our big splurge, and we've never regretted it. Then we saved as much as we could for their education.

Bill, Billy, Jr., and Jimmy Playing Golf

CASTING A LIGHT

There's a scripture in the Bible that Reverend John Hagee references when he tells the story of the time a man came into his church with a gun and fired at him from point blank range about 5 or 6 times and missed him every time. That scripture says, "Touch not mine anointed," Psalm 105:15 KJV.

They had tried to ruin us, but God had a different plan for us, because we had the truth on our side. "You shall know the truth and the truth will set you free." As I am writing these memoirs and I stop to remember those days, I can tell you that I found out when you put into practice those things you've heard about forgiveness, they really work. It took me a long time, and it was one of the hardest things I ever had to do, but I finally did give all that hurt and anger to God. He healed my heart and reminded me that He loves us all, even those who had done me wrong. So I completely forgave them and moved on.

One day Kim and I were at Reba's office in a writing session. We had been with her company, Starstruck, for a year and were up there that morning. Narvel caught me out in the hall. He had a check in his hand. He told me that Cliff had informed him that we had had to spend about $10,000 on the legal fees of the lawsuit.

The check was in the amount of $5,000, half of what it had cost us. I couldn't believe it. Life was finally good again and God had given us a breather for a while to catch up with the more positive side of life. Thank you so very much, Cliff Williamson, Reba and Narvel. God bless you always.

Chapter Seventeen

Success Brings More Opportunities

WHEN YOU'RE A SONGWRITER, EVEN ONCE you're signed to a publisher, and even once you've had a hit, you're still always looking for other opportunities to earn more income from music. We were fortunate throughout the '90s to have various projects come our way that greatly supplemented our writer's draw, which was usually more or less just enough for us to live on.

The first thing that happens when you have a hit is that you start receiving all kinds of mail from all kinds of people from around the world. Our names were listed in the liner notes of Reba's album, and people would look us up and find our address to contact us. This is before email (or at least just on the verge of it).

The mail we would receive would go one of two ways (and

I paraphrase): One, "Hi, I'm (insert name), here's a demo of my song. Would you pitch my song to Reba instead of you pitching your own music to her that you've worked really hard on for years?" or two, "Hi, I'm (insert name), and I'd like to hire you to write a song(s) for my son/daughter/grandchild/company."

Well, we really liked to receive that second kind of mail much more than the first. Those "custom projects," as they're usually called, became a great source of income, and since we'd just had a hit, we were able to ask for a little better fee. On average, once or twice a year, we'd end up writing anywhere from 3 songs to an entire album for a new young artist (almost always a young girl, paid for by her father/grandfather). I was very honest with them about what we could do for them, namely being able to write/produce a quality session on the artist, and I promised I would play for any contacts I had for their feedback and to gauge their interest, if any, in the artist. Anyone who was okay with those terms, we'd move forward, and we always delivered on our promises. In fact, it was really great all around because we ended up with more songs in our catalog fully recorded, and not just as a demo, but more like a finished "radio-ready" release, so we always sent those around to everyone we could to hear our latest.

On a more humorous note than that, there was one project we had to turn down that still gives us a good laugh from time to time. We received a package in the mail probably a year after the song with Reba came out, and it had a cassette tape in it with Brooks & Dunn on the cover. At that time, they were at the height of their career, but I didn't know why someone I'd never met would send me one of their cassettes. Well, there was a note inside that clarified. This person had written a song that he was so sure would be a hit for Brooks & Dunn that he made a demo and put their picture on the front cover (note to all aspiring writers, don't do this!). The offer followed: if I promised them I could get Brooks & Dunn to cut it, this person was willing to pay me $40,000! Well, Lord knows I would have loved to have had an extra 40 grand (who wouldn't?), but there's no way I could have slept at night. I think of the verse that says, "ill-gotten gain takes away the lives of those who get it." Maybe if the song had been incredible, I could have considered talking to him further about it, but when I popped it in the cassette player, the first minute and a half was just ambient nature sounds. I don't like to overly criticize inexperienced writers, but clearly, he was not in touch at all with what was happening in music at the time. Some people just don't know that they don't know.

HAVE SONGS, WILL TRAVEL

Aside from individuals, it was great fun to write theme songs for companies. The secondary benefit of writing theme songs is that the companies would usually fly us in to sing for their conventions, which meant booking fees and CD sales. We always asked for two extra tickets for our boys to come with us, which made it more fun for us and for the boys. They learned about room service and fluffy hotel robes very quickly. They also loved selling CDs at our table and keeping all that cash in their pockets (at least until we got it from them each night).

Billy & Jimmy Happily Selling at the Merch Table

A few companies stand out to me from that time. Life Trends was a vitamin company, and we wrote a slew of songs about their dieting products. One was a "healthy cookie" that you ate as part of a half-day diet daily. So we wrote, "Just half a day can make a

Billy, Jr., Bill, & Jimmy Enjoying Room Service

whole lot of difference" for that product, and also wrote many general motivational type songs like we'd written in our Amway days. Almost immediately after that, we wrote a whole album for Life Plus Vitamins. For a while there, it seemed like we were only writing and performing for vitamin companies, but hey, as they say, "it's nice work if you can get it."

The last company that was truly the best to us all-around

(and didn't sell vitamins) was Pre-Paid Legal, which offered legal insurance services. Its founder, Harland Stonecipher, and his wife, Shirley, were such amazingly kind and generous people to Kim and me and our boys. We wrote Harland's life-story in a song, and they would play it before he took the stage at conventions. I even got involved in selling PPL because I so believed in it as a service, and I still receive residuals to this day. They saved me thousands of dollars over the years in attorney fees too. They've changed their name now to Legalshield, and I would highly recommend their services. That has been the one project that has kept on giving.

The Nash Family at a PPL Convention

NEW WRITING DEAL

A couple years later after we had fulfilled our contract at Starstruck and had taken a little time off, we started searching for other avenues for our writing – that is to say another publisher who would pay us and get us cuts.

Bill & Kim Playing The Bluebird - 1996

Our old friend, Jerry Taylor, who was Jim Malloy's chief writer when we signed with Jim in '88, now had a publishing arrangement with Sony Music in Nashville. We had written many songs with him in the past, and I brought him a tape of some of the new music we had written. He loved the songs, and the next thing we knew we were both writing for Sony Publishing, the largest music publisher in the world.

Jerry had always seemed to be an entrepreneurial kind of guy that could go out and make something happen when nothing else was going on. He loved our singing, and at one time, we had

Nash Note ♫

In 1997, the group Highway 101 cut a song we wrote, "If I'm Over You." They had big hits in the '80s, and were doing a reunion album. Oddly enough, in '88, they asked Kim to fill in for lead singer, Paulette Carlson, when she took time off to raise her child. Kim couldn't bear the thought of leaving the boys and me for nearly 300 days a year though. It was tough to turn down the money, but we had, after all, decided to move to Nashville, so we could stay in one place and be with our boys. Guess we were meant to work with them in one way or another though!

even tried to be a trio, recording some songs together with Jerry's old friend, Larry Butler, Kenny Rogers' producer. So many configurations get tried in Nashville because you never know what's going to work. You try this, you do that, and you hope that something catches on.

Brooks and Dunn are a perfect example of a producer seeing the talent they both had and feeling like they would make a great match for a duo; he was so right. It seemed like the harmony Kim and I had was very unique, though, and we sounded best as a duo.

So Jerry took us in to Sony studios on 17th Avenue and cut seven sides to present to Elektra/Asylum Records who had expressed interest in signing us as artists. Wouldn't that be something for us to land a new recording deal on the heels of our publishing deal with Sony?

The talks were serious enough with Elektra over the course of several months, and word gets around Nashville quickly, so Sony ended up signing us for a second year on the possibility that we would end up on a major label with them owning a piece of every cut on our album. However, in the late 90s, the Elektra/Asylum label that

Bill & Kim Sony Promo Photo - 1997

was interested in us saw a big slump in sales, so they cleaned house, downsized. All the new artists that had just been signed, or were in talks to be signed, were all cleared out.

Since we were not going to be on a major label, and we had mainly been writing towards our own album, which meant no songs of ours were being pitched to other artists (therefore no cuts or hits), at the end of our second year with Sony, we became part of the 100 writers that were released in a single day from their contracts. So many writers with a long list of hit songs were now scuffling for a publishing deal. Kim and I were in the same boat, and it seemed everybody's boats were taking on water.

Bill & Kim After Working with Bill Anderson & Sen. Fred Thompson - 1998

We no longer had a Sony deal, and the Elektra deal was shot. We thought about what to do from there. Pray! Pray hard. Publishing companies had really pared down to the bone and lots of writers that had big hits were struggling to put something together. We would have to think long and hard about where to go now. What's next?

CASTING A LIGHT

Dr. Harry Yates and his wife, Joanne Cash Yates, who is the youngest sister of Johnny Cash, became very special friends to Kim and me right at a time when we needed spiritual mentors. Joanne and Dr. Harry care so deeply about people and are ministers pastoring Nashville Cowboy Church. I found them on a Sunday morning at the Holiday Inn when I saw their sign in the lobby announcing church at 11:00 a.m. in the bar. I said to myself, "The bar, really?" I still sometimes was not comfortable going to a "regular" church, because of my past. Even though I always felt welcomed in Houston at Lakewood, a part of me was still more comfortable in a bar than in a pew.

I was taking someone to the airport for an early flight that Sunday, so I just decided to drop back by on my way home and check out Cowboy Church. When I returned from the airport to the Holiday Inn, I slid into the back row of the bar and waited to see what kind of service they might be having.

They kicked it off with a live six or seven-piece band, and they started playing great, up-tempo country gospel music. As the service proceeded and Dr. Harry welcomed everyone, he then introduced his wife as the sister of Johnny Cash, and she came on stage and began to sing. She talked about Jesus and let us all know that He was first in her life. The tears started to well up in my eyes as she then sang a Gospel song she had written. I was deeply moved by her sincerity and love for the people. It was an amazing service, and I felt so at home.

When I got home, I told Kim all about it, and the next Sunday she and I and our two boys attended service. We got to know Pastor Harry and Joanne, and they became great friends of ours. As time went by, they asked us to sing, and that started a wonderful relationship with them. We even travelled a bit together and wrote a song with Joanne. I got to sing a duet with her on one of her albums. It's still one of my favorite memories, and I was so honored to be singing with her. They prayed us through many everyday situations and rejoiced with us over our Reba McEntire cut.

We treasure their friendship greatly and still go back from time to time to sing for them. When we know we are going to Nashville, I call Billy Anderson, who I call Bubba, and he books us for a service. Billy produces their world-wide, weekly radio broadcast, as well. It now emanates from the Ernest Tubb Record Shop near Opryland every Sunday morning. *Kim with Joanne Cash Yates - 1995*
I'm very thankful for everyone there at Nashville Cowboy Church and know they were put in our path to help us through the ups and downs of our time in Nashville. Thank God for Dr. Harry and Joanne!

Chapter Eighteen

A Fish Out Of Water

WELL THERE COMES A TIME IN every musician/entertainer's life when they have to consider whether or not to get a "real job." Aside from my time working at the record distributing company in college, I had never been in what anyone would consider a "traditional" work situation. I had always made my living from music. Even in our Amway days, it was my music that had spurred on the growth of our down-line in Houston through all my friends and fans. Now, at 55 years old, I'm facing a career change? But I thought, what else could I do? There are so many incredible writers from Sony all looking for deals now. Kim and I were burned out on writing any new songs, and we lost what was likely our last shot at a major label deal as artists ourselves. I saw no other choice to provide for my family.

At the time, my friend Brian Collins was selling phone service for Intermedia Communications. Brian and I were both from Texas, and he had performed in a lot of the same circuits as me. He also wrote the song, "Hello Texas," which was performed by Jimmy Buffett for the movie, *Urban Cowboy*, and nominated for a Grammy. He felt like he could get me hired there, and sure enough, he did! Even though it was not what I wanted to do, I was grateful for the chance to earn money and keep us afloat while I figured out what's next...again.

So they flew me down to Tampa, Florida for training. Naturally, I brought my guitar. The training was every bit as exciting as you would think (a 0 out of 10), but we had frequent breaks where we could get coffee and a little snack. At these break times, I'd get out my guitar and start making up songs about everything that was going on. Well, as has been the case ever since I started playing at the Melody Lounge back in Pharr, people started gathering around to hear what I was gonna play. They even started suggesting things for me to sing about, and we all made a great time of it (at least until we had to go back in for more training). So it's no surprise at the end of the week when it was time to vote for who would win the "Spirit Award," I won it unanimously.

After those goings on, I flew back to Nashville to begin my work as a full-fledged Telecomm Salesman. This new title came complete with something I'd never had to do: sitting in an office cubicle for 8 hours a day. I know that a 9:00-5:00 isn't easy for anyone, but for someone who is used to being creative and having a flexible schedule to fly here and sing there, that cubicle might as well be a cage. Still, it was work, and I was proud to bring home a paycheck.

For anyone born before the digital age, you'll know what I mean when I talk about the learning curve with computers. My kids had taught me at home how to send and receive emails, but that was it. Now, all of a sudden, I have a company-assigned laptop. What do I do with this black brick that I'm required to use to fill out my weekly reports? I must have asked for help from all the kids in the office (that is to say, anyone under 30) about 500 times a day. Brian and I would take long lunches at the Longhorn Steakhouse on Music Row and dread heading back to the office to keep selling that phone service. Having a friend there was definitely a big help to show me the ropes, and I'll always be grateful to Brian for getting me that job.

It didn't help matters that we were instructed to tell businesses that if they bought our service, they would have phone systems installed within 90 days at the most, when our bosses told us that in reality, they were on a 6-month backlog. I've never been very good at stretching the truth (in other words, lying), and I wasn't aiming to start.

As it happens, my time there would be short-lived. A couple years before I started there, Intermedia had been acquired by MCI Worldcom, and they were still merging departments, down-sizing, etc. I had been there about nine months when my boss called me into his office. I remember it so distinctly, him sitting there at his desk with his miniature rock garden that he tended to throughout the day, and he told me some of the best news I'd heard in years, "Bill, I'm going to have to let you go." Wow! I was thrilled! I shouted for joy, and thanked him from the bottom of my heart. Needless to say, he was a little confused. I didn't know what I was going to do next, but all I knew was I was out of that prison.

A NEW WRITING DEAL...AGAIN

Well, however tired I was of searching for the next publishing deal, it was nothing compared to the dread of taking on another "real job," so that pushed me onwards, back to "hitting the streets" so to speak on Music Row.

I wasn't having any luck with the major publishers, but I had made friends over at Johnny Morris' office on 16th Avenue South, known as Evergreen Studios/On The Wall Music, and I would happen in there frequently. It's hard to describe Johnny. He was quite a "character." All I'll say is that for decades he managed to stay afloat on the row with his publishing company, and that in and of itself is quite a feat. Johnny would let me come in and write in one of his empty offices, and we'd sit and palaver. I wasn't signed with him, but still, it was better to be out on the row where there's a possibility of something happening than to be sitting at home doing nothing. This is where I met Don Goodman, one of the greatest lyricists I've ever met (next to Kim of course), with a list a mile long of all the hits he's had by major artists. "Ole Red" stands out in my mind, which was originally cut by George Jones, then by Kenny Rogers, and later made a big hit by Blake Shelton many years later. Blake even has an "Ole Red" bar now. I also was introduced to a new writer/producer named Sammy Mizell who had a lot of pop influence in his music and was an extremely talented multi-instrumentalist.

This would have been sometime in 2000. The precise month eludes me, but I know it was after we all survived the would be "Y2K Apocalypse."

At this point, Kim was still just too burned out to write. I didn't blame her, and I knew she needed time to recuperate. So did I, I suppose, but I just had to make something happen. It's a pretty exhausting cycle to write for months and months for a publisher, give them your best work, demo those songs, try to get the attention of their pitch person just hoping they'll get you a cut, and then, when your contract is up, you've got to create another batch of amazing songs just to try to catch the attention of a new publisher. When we were at Sony, they had 4 pitch people for several hundred writers, so even once you were in the door, it was still an uphill climb to get heard.

It had been years since I had written a song without Kim. To be honest, I wasn't sure if I could still write without her. She always did the heavy lifting on the lyrics and knew how to nail a song down to the ground. I knew, though, that God had put music down inside me, and everywhere I went, I was always writing down titles and recording snippets of melodies into my tape recorder (we had cell phones at this point, but they did not come with the "voice memo" feature...or any features really).

So I finally decided I had to try to write in a new situation without Kim, if only to prove to myself that I could, and if only for a short while. I called Don and Sammy and set up a writing appointment for the three of us. We decided to show up to the appointment with a "blank page," both literally and mentally, and be open to whatever we might be inspired to write that day.

One of them threw out the challenge to write a song without the word "love" in it. We all said, "OK, let's give it a try."

I don't know how long we sat there trying to make a song that didn't talk about love, but whatever we were coming up with wasn't very good. Finally, one of them (Don or Sammy) said, "But Paul McCartney said you can't say love enough!" Well, I think he was meaning to say, "all you need is love," but whatever brought that statement to his mind, that brought us all alive. We finished the song that day, and then Sammy made the demo right in front of us. He played all the parts and added such a beautiful chord arrangement around multiple harmonies. It sounded less like Country and more like the big boy band songs of the early 2000s. When we played it for Johnny Morris, that was the first time I ever saw him jump out of his chair in excitement, and say, "That's a hit!"

That song was like when you're playing golf and you've had a terrible round all day (or for a couple years in my case), and then suddenly you get a hole in one, and that's all that matters now. It was more than just the song itself or whether or not it would be cut or be a hit. It just meant so much to me at that time that I could keep creating music, and do it effectively, no matter who I was writing with.

With that song, I felt like I was back in action, and it helped me to get Kim back on board to write too. We both ended up signing with Johnny that year and writing more with Don, Sammy, and several other fantastic writers. "You Can't Say Love Enough" was getting pitched around the row, and it got put "on hold" multiple times. That just means that someone was interested in the song and asked us to temporarily stop pitching the song until they decide if they will cut it. One of the groups that had it on hold was Diamond Rio. They ultimately did not record it, but that's just a fun tidbit that becomes an interesting tie-in down the road. We had a lot of songs on hold over the years. "You Can't Say Love Enough" ended up having a slightly different path later, which I'll share with you chronologically, or else this story will veer way off course.

We wrote for Johnny for about a year, but then, as fate would have it, we signed on with his son, Craig, for another year. We didn't receive a major cut out of either deal at that time, but I'd like to say something here about Craig Morris. Craig stands out as a man of incredible integrity, one of the most honest and trustworthy people we ever worked with in music. Lots of publishers were having difficulty keeping their doors open during the early 2000s with the advent of Napster and other music "piracy" sites that were affecting the profitability of music. Craig had made a commitment, though, to us for a year, and even when he had to shutter his publishing venture, he made sure to keep us paid out of his own pocket, which I know was a hardship to him and his wife, because he wanted us to know his word was his bond. That meant the world to us, and we could sure use more like Craig in this business.

So there we were once again without a writing deal. I kept us afloat in Nashville two years longer than the odds would have suggested were possible after being let go by Sony, but now all my personal connections were tapped out to get us another deal. For the umpteenth time in my life, I was asking God, what's next?

Chapter Nineteen

The Call From An Old Friend

I N THE SUMMER OF 2001, I got a call from our old friend and former direct distributor in our Amway business, Jerry Lewis, from Angleton, Texas. His parents were having an anniversary, and he asked me to make a home video of me singing their favorite song that I had written years earlier, "Hold Me 'Til the Last Waltz Is Over." That's what started us talking again.

As I would bend Jerry's ear for an hour at a time, he and I would discuss what might be a meaningful path for the future for me to pursue until this writing thing opened back up a bit. He and his wife, Natalie, were very successful, and I respected their business acumen and appreciated their thoughts on what might be a good fit for me.

We had no idea what God wanted us to do at this time. We

started praying in earnest. Our only income was coming from producing a couple custom sessions and performing at a few conventions. Other than that, though, we were both once again just "burned out."

Kim and I knew deep down there was more for us to do at that point in our lives. Jerry kept on encouraging me, and then one evening, he says to me over the phone, "Why don't you do something that has to do with kids and their self-image or something like that again?" He was remembering our motivational camps we used to do in California and Colorado with kids from all the Champions Amway families.

We kept talking this over, not being really sure about it all until one evening Kim finally spoke up and said, "If we are going to do a camp, it shouldn't be just another motivational camp like we did before, it should be for 'survivor children,' like Billy."

That really struck a nerve in Jerry and Natalie, and in me too. It was like a lightning bolt, a revelation, a new path laid right in front of us. But how would we do it? The greatest challenge we could see right away was raising the money for such a camp. Then, where would we get volunteers to help us, and most importantly, where would the kids come from, and where would we hold camp? Besides that, what were we going to do at this camp to help them? I said this to Jerry and without hesitation, he offered for him and Natalie to help us for one full year to get it off the ground.

My mom and dad had always told me I had been called by God and was set apart from that time to do something special for Him, ever since my dream with the three angels at 5 years old, but I really never knew what that was or how to go about it. In my nightclub days, I used to ponder that dream and puzzle over what it really meant.

Kim and I started talking more and more with Jerry and Natalie and we all agreed that we would start a camp for survivor children and call it Champions Kids Camp, the same name we used before; however, this camp would have a different mission.

We started out thinking that all our kids would be cancer or leukemia survivors like Billy. However, we started getting questions about kids who had survived many other traumatic situations. Well, we didn't want to leave out any child who had come through any kind of trauma, so we just broadened our parameters.

The criteria for each kid then became that they be a survivor of a traumatic event in their lives: a survivor of an accident or injury, an illness like cancer, or a personal loss like the loss of a parent or sibling or caregiver.

I started commuting from Nashville that first year for weeks at a time, finding anywhere and everywhere I could sing or talk about our vision for the camp. My son, Billy, was already off to college at Middle Tennessee State, but Jimmy still had two years left of high school. It got real lonely without Kim, but I was glad she still had Jimmy at home (and the cats), so she wasn't all alone. When I was in Houston, I would stay with my long-time friends and accountants, Guinn and Linda Rasbury. They were a Godsend. They signed on to be our accountants for CKC, joined our executive board, and helped us file all our paperwork to become a 501(c)(3) nonprofit organization. I knew nothing about that side of things, so I was relieved to have them on board to keep us square with our government forms. The added bonus

Bill with Guinn & Linda Rasbury

was Linda was a great cook, and she would make me all my favorite desserts (I may have put on a little weight during my stays).

Somewhere along the way, I got a call from my old friend, Roger McDuff. His very words were, "I don't know why I'm calling to invite you to come sing at this Gospel Music night, but I feel like I'm supposed to." He then told me he would pay me $500, buy me a plane ticket and put me up and feed me that weekend. How could I turn that down?

It was like it was meant to be, a new start in the church world, back to our roots. I was determined to go to as many churches and civic clubs as I could to tell them of our dream for this camp. At this Gospel Music night is where I met then mayor of Pasadena, John Manlove, and his beautiful wife, Gina. They were so gracious to me as we talked in the back-stage area where I got to share my vision of CKC with them. They not only offered to help CKC through their marketing company, John Manlove Marketing; they also donated 5,000 brochures to the cause for me to distribute to potential donors. They were a great blessing. I actually can't believe how much they believed in our mission. We hadn't even held a camp yet. They had to use stock photos of children in those first brochures until we had pictures of our own. It just shows that God will always put the right people in your path to help you and believe in what you're doing, even if you're not quite sure what you're doing yet!

LET THE FUNDRAISING BEGIN

I remember my first meeting at Jerry's car lot, Car Country, in Angleton. Jerry and Natalie and I talked and started kicking

around ideas, and where to go from there to kick off this camp. Even though they had pledged to put up what we needed for that first year, we all knew we would need to expand our donor base beyond just them. So we set it up in early December of 2001 to have our first fundraiser for

Bill & Kim with Jerry & Natalie Lewis

Champions Kids Camp in the auditorium at the Brazosport Community College in Lake Jackson, Texas.

We invited everyone we knew, and Jerry got some of his employees from his car lot to come out and help. We played music, had some food and a small auction, and thankfully a decent number of people showed up, and we raised a few thousand dollars to go towards our first camp we were planning for July of 2002.

After that, Jerry and Natalie's long-time friend, Lee Brantley, had made connections for me in Angleton at two different Baptist churches. He booked me into the Second Baptist Church on a Sunday morning and into the First Baptist Church across town in Angleton that evening.

Second Baptist received us whole-heartedly and liked our musical presentation and our desire to start a camp for survivor children. However, they were between pastors at the time, so there was really no one to step up and commit to anything concerning a new outreach that morning.

But that evening I sang at the First Baptist Church, and after singing a few songs, I told the parishioners about Billy's healing and his Leukemia and the miracle we had received. I explained CKC to them and our dream for it. When I was done, Pastor Rodney Bowman took the platform and announced to the crowd, "We are going to support this camp." He didn't even wait for the church board to approve it. He took it upon himself, stepping out on a limb to pledge his support for us, as well as the church's support.

I was kind of stunned by his announcement, but it gave me confirmation about the work Kim and I had decided to pursue to honor God for Billy's healing. It sort of felt like if a man of God like Pastor Rodney caught the vision, then we were on the right path, and it made me feel the full impact of it for the first time.

While I was singing that evening, a gal came in late for the service and made her way down to the third row where her family was sitting. As goes my sense of humor, I stopped singing and asked her, "Where ya been?" She was so embarrassed, and she answered sheepishly, "Walmart." Everyone got a big kick out of it, and after the service I was introduced to her and her husband, Billie Faye and Dale Moran.

Little did we all know that that was a divine appointment that only God could have once again orchestrated on this road to the creation of Champions Kids Camp. It turns out that she was the administrative assistant to the head of the Gulf Coast Baptist

Dale & Billie Faye Moran

Association, and in their past, Billie Faye and Dale had worked as administrators at a children's home similar to an orphanage. She told us she had a calling from God to work with kids, and here it was presented to her right in her home church.

I could go on about how important she became and still is to CKC because she was and has been a vital part of the success of CKC. We call her Aunt Bee at camp. She helped to book me into numerous Gulf Coast Baptist Association churches, and she did all the enrollment of our campers and on and on. We leaned on her so heavily to teach us the things we didn't even know we didn't know about having a camp with special kids like ours. She has been a tremendous gift and asset to CKC, and we thank God every day for her and Dale.

On Dale's side, we mashed his credit card so many times in the beginning it had to be more than flat. He never complained, however, and he too has been a tremendous blessing to CKC.

There is another couple, Holly and Earl Pryor, who signed on with us shortly after we were invited to sing at their church. With them, we also got their son, Kenneth, and daughter, Morgan, roped in.

When I was commuting to Houston that first year from Nashville, the Pryors never failed to show up at the church where I was booked to sing to help me sell our CDs. They were and still are a great source of encouragement. I sincerely needed the help since Kim and Jimmy were back in Nashville and Billy was off at college. Holly and Earl are still with us to this day and have been an integral part of the backbone of CKC. Thank God and thank Holly and Earl!

Not long after singing for the Baptist churches in Angleton, I was invited to sing at First Assembly of God in Spring, Texas, where pastors Robert and Brenda Hogan were pastoring. His congregation not only gave generously to CKC, but Pastor Hogan took up a special offering for me that Sunday morning and he put his stamp of approval on our ministry. He didn't know it at the time, but that offering paid our bills for that whole month. It was the only church I was booked at that month since I was just getting started again. I will always be grateful to Robert and Brenda Hogan.

In order to balance our own personal financial needs with our fundraising needs for CKC, we created a music ministry, Building Bridges of Hope. So now, when we sold CDs, people made a donation into our music ministry, which allowed us to live and continue, and then they could make a separate donation to CKC. We were sponsored into the independent ministerial organization called The Fellowship. I was ordained at a special service at my Uncle Charles's church in Conroe where Mama Dodie and Joel and Victoria Osteen were in attendance. Now here I was, the one thing I had vowed I would never become, a minister of the Gospel. It was so very special, a return to my roots. It was quite a moment as I looked into the audience when I was speaking. I brought up how much Brother John and Dodie Osteen meant to us, and we all started to cry happy tears.

CASTING A LIGHT

It's quite interesting to say the least when you're raising money for a charity, and you have nothing to show them about what the charity will do. I mean, we told people we wanted to help these "survivor" children who look fine on the outside, but still need our help, but where are the testimonials? Where are the recommendations for our camp from child psychiatrists? Where are the advanced studies on our methods (yet undeveloped), and where and how we will find the children for our camp? This camp was started totally on faith. We just knew we had to do it, and somehow, on the vision alone, people got behind us.

Sometimes I felt like Moses. He was 80 years old, and all of a sudden God tells him that now is the time for him to do the most important thing he's ever done in his life, and all he has to do is go against the most powerful man in the world. Well, of course things turned out pretty well for Moses, aside from the whole wandering in the wilderness part, and I had a couple things going for me that he didn't. One, I was only 57 at this point, so basically a spring chicken next to Moses, and two, I didn't have to cross the Egyptian desert, just the metro Houston area (which is about 5 degrees cooler), asking for donations. Whenever I would get a little discouraged in my fundraising duties, Billie Faye would just say, "Okay Moses."

BACK TO TEXAS CHILDREN'S HOSPITAL

Since Billy had been treated at Texas Children's Hospital, we naturally thought it would be a good idea to reach out to TCH and let them know we were planning this kind of camp. We knew there would be children going through treatment that would qualify for our camp once they were out of treatment. As we made that connection, we met Dr. ZoAnn Dreyer, who took a great interest in what we were doing. She already helped to organize TCH's own camp for terminally ill children called Camp Periwinkle, but she loved our mission too.

What she told us is that the kids we're looking to serve are the ones who slip through the cracks. They look fine on the outside, but they're suffering from "emotional scarring." She especially loved that we included children who have lost parents or siblings. At Camp Periwinkle, siblings are able to come to camp while their brother or sister is going through treatment, but unfortunately, that child going through treatment does not always make it, and the sibling that is left behind is left traumatized. Dr. Dryer, or "Dr. Zo" as we affectionately call her, was excited that our camp could potentially become a place where those siblings could go. As we got to know her and told her the story of Billy's healing, she looked way back in her immaculately detailed records, and found that she had actually seen Billy exactly one time when she was just a fellow at the hospital.

Isn't that amazing? It made us feel like God had already put the wheels in motion for our camp way back in that darkest time in our lives. To have one of the doctors that saw Billy ready to back

Billy with Dr. ZoAnn Dreyer (right), and Nurse Diane (left), Who Treated Him When He Was Two

our mission now just really brought everything full circle. Dr. Zo told us she couldn't attend all of our events or meetings, but we worked it out for her to be an Honorary Advisory Council Member, and she gave us a quote of support to use alongside her name in our brochures. That gave us a lot of credibility at a time when we really needed it.

So, while we were in our last year in Nashville and I was commuting, Dr. Zo called one day and booked us to sing at Reliant Stadium for the Downtown Houston Rotary Club's Lombardi Awards Banquet. President H.W. Bush, (41 as he is affectionately known), was the keynote speaker, and the University of Houston orchestra and a children's choir were performing with us. We were to sing the national anthem and one other song. After the ceremony and President Bush's speech were over, we went back to our product table that the Rotary Club had so generously allowed us to set up to hand out CKC brochures and make our CDs available.

To our surprise, on his way out of the building, President Bush spied us and turned and started walking briskly toward us exuberantly and was telling us how much he loved our music. He stayed at our table a long time and told us how he loved the family aspect of our music and our group (our son Jimmy was now singing with us). The two secret service men were anxious to get Bush #41 out of the stadium, and Barbara Bush kept saying, "Come on George." Mrs. Bush had taken a picture with us earlier in the evening and we are so proud she did. It was a wonderfully encouraging night.

Now this next story has nothing to do with anything, but hey, it's my book, so here it goes!

The story behind meeting George W. was quite different. In my night club days, I met a real unique kind of guy. He was a boot maker named Rocky Carroll, and he was a character. When I went to his boot shop one time, he showed me a video of the inauguration where Barbara Bush looks down at the crowd after the formalities were completed and says, "George, look, it's Rocky." The President looks at him and waves and goes on speaking.

Quite impressive to have the most powerful man in the

world not only wearing Rocky's boots, but also acknowledging him to the whole world via television. This kind of opened the flood gates from then on for Rocky to make boots for all kinds of heads of state from all over the world.

So Rocky called me one day and asked if I would like to go with him to Ranger Stadium in Arlington, Texas to present Nolan Ryan with a pair of white ostrich boots he had made for him to commemorate one of Nolan's new pitching records. Would I! Yes, of course. So we jumped on a Southwest flight and went to the ball park, and they escorted us up to the private suite set up for these kinds of things.

We sat there before the game just waiting for the arrival of Nolan Ryan, and we waited and waited. After forty-five minutes to an hour, the door opened, and this guy walked in. He was dressed in a suit and tie and I wasn't sure who he was, but he stuck his hand out to Rocky first and then to me and introduced himself as George Bush. Oh, President H.W.'s son who was one of the owners of the Texas Rangers baseball team.

Okay, I'm thinking, nice to meet you, but where's Nolan? I had bought myself an instamatic camera (that's what we amateurs had in those days), and was prepared for Rocky and me to get some shots of Nolan receiving his boots and won't it be great. Instead, all we got was George W. Bush who announced to us that since Nolan was pitching that day, he really preferred not to come up to the suite so as not to lose his concentration; he was "in the zone."

George W. was asked by Nolan to receive the boots for him. I didn't have enough foresight to get a picture with this guy named George, whose dad was a congressman at the time. I was so disappointed, I just tucked my little camera away, and Rocky and I went back out to our seats to watch the game. What a downer. I hate to tell on myself, but after seeing George W.'s sense of humor on TV in later years, I think he too would probably laugh. I've still never had the honor of meeting Nolan Ryan, but Rocky has donated multiple pairs of his custom boots for our auctions over the years to raise money for CKC. Thank you, Rocky! R.I.P.

Chapter Twenty

Our First Camp

WHEN WE FINALLY HELD OUR FIRST camp session in the summer of 2002, Jerry Lewis negotiated a great deal with the resort community of Columbia Lakes just out of West Columbia, Texas, where he and Natalie lived at the time. It had a beautiful swimming pool, tennis courts, stocked lake for fishing, and an excellent golf course.

We had our small crew of Jerry and Natalie, their son, Chris, Guinn and Linda Rasbury, Billie Faye Moran (Aunt Bee) and her son, Roy, Earl and Holly Pryor and their two kids, Kenneth and Morgan, and my two sons, Billy and Jimmy. We also had a few other young folks and volunteers with us, and some of the folks from Pastor Rodney Bowman's church, First Baptist of Angleton.

We were still figuring out how to spread the word to find

children that qualified for our camp, and I'm honestly thankful we weren't any better than we were at finding children that first year, because I don't know what we would have done if hundreds or thousands had applied.

33. That's how many kids were about to show up on this hot, July day in Texas. 33. It doesn't sound like a lot now, but it might as well have been 100,000! I sincerely did not know what I was going to do to help one child over their trauma, much less 33, but I knew God had put them in our path for a reason. This was where the rubber met the road. No more

Jimmy, Chris Lewis, & Billy - Camp 2002

talking about doing a camp, no more painting the vision and raising funds for what can be. This is it right here. Nearly three dozen kids were about to check in, and none of us truly knew what lay ahead.

As the kids came in one by one, our volunteers checked them in, and we made sure they got to the appropriate rooms,

"cottages," as they were called at Columbia Lakes. They were really more like 4 hotel rooms connected by a central living room, and for some of these children, it was the nicest place they had ever gotten to stay. One by one, we got each child checked in, until they were all squared away and ready to start camp.

Even with it being our first year, some things are just common sense.

The Pryor Family at Camp 2002

We knew the kids needed a room to stay, we knew we would need to feed them 3 times per day (at least), and we knew we wanted them to have a fun time. Plus, somewhere in the midst of this week, we knew we had to do something that would actually help them work through their trauma. They had mostly all received some kind of therapy before, so we had to offer something they didn't receive in therapy. What that was was hard to define, but we just took it day-by-day, and child-by-child.

The first thing you probably all know about kids is that they don't have a long attention span. You have to keep them entertained constantly if you want them to listen to anything you have to say. We leaned heavily on the music after each meal at rally time, and we did our best to come up with a program that would rebuild a kid's self-image and self-esteem as well as connect them spiritually to Jesus, the ultimate healer. Our new friend, Pattie Smith-McNeese, brought out her Karaoke machine, which the kids loved, and then we would intersperse with our own music and had a few special guests come out through the week to play for the kids and/or offer a great testimony or word of encouragement. Pastor Rodney came out each morning as well to start off the day with a positive message for the kids.

The next thing you probably all know about kids is that they have boundless energy, and you have to wear them out a bit if you ever hope to get them to sleep at night. So we came up with as many activities as possible during the day. Jerry came out to teach baseball to the kids, my boys taught tennis, all the kids

---

Nash Note 🎵

Jerry Lewis was actually a professional pitcher for the San Diego Padres Organization. After one season of pitching, though, he injured his arm while working out, and he never pitched again professionally. His love for baseball never waned though, and he used that passion not only to teach our kids at camp, but a whole slew of kids at his own "Field of Dreams" that he started. It's another great example of how God can take a tragic event and use it for good.

---

loved the swimming pool on those hot days, of course, and the most popular activity actually became fishing.

One little boy only wanted to fish, and he caught 10 times more than all the other kids (it was catch and release of course). I asked him how he got so good at that, and his story broke my heart. He said that he lived with his mother, brother, and sister in an old camping trailer that was near a river. He learned to fish, because that was the only way they would all be able to eat. It reminded me so much of how broke my family was growing up, but even at our poorest, my family never depended on me at 8 or 9 years old to provide food for them. My dad always made sure we had something to eat and a roof over our heads in one way or another. This little boy had lost his father, though, and had taken on that role to provide for his family at a far younger age than anyone should ever have to.

THE STORY OF NATHAN

My first major, life-changing encounter with a camper was an 8-year-old boy named Nathan. I didn't know it yet, but Nathan was going to help us define the way that we were going to help children for years to come. When Nathan's mother and father brought him to registration, his mom pulled Kim aside to speak to her privately. I knew it must be a deep hurt since I saw her crying profusely as she spoke. She explained to Kim that Nathan had lost his little brother to cancer, and it adversely impacted him to such a great degree that he would no longer speak. He was scared of losing everyone else, so he detached himself emotionally. He wouldn't say "I love you" to his family, and he wouldn't talk. His mom told Kim we just had to help him; the professionals couldn't seem to bring Nathan out.

When I heard the story, I actually just looked up at the sky and asked God if He was sure that I was really supposed to do this kids camp thing. I remember saying to God that I had never studied this kind of behavioral psychology except for one course in basic psychology at U. of H., so how was I supposed to know what to do? Even the experts didn't know what to do.

I didn't even have a clue where to start. As the first day drew to a close, we went around to all of our thirty-three kids that evening to make sure they were okay and didn't need anything. When I got to Nathan's room, I asked him, "Nathan, are you okay?" He didn't speak, he just nodded his head yes. I said, "Do you need anything?" He shook his head no. Since I really didn't know what to do or say, I just left there so perplexed. As a father, I always had some insight with my own boys to know what to do. I knew their personalities and what they responded to, but with Nathan, I was starting with a blank slate. I just finished my other bed checks and went on to our quarters. Kim and I prayed as we closed that day out, and asked God to tell us how to help Nathan. Our whole crew was praying also.

The next day as we went about our activities, things were going pretty smoothly. Since it was our first camp, we weren't really sure what to expect. There were kids there with some real challenges in their lives and families and so forth,

Nash Note 🎵

Columbia Lakes was not exactly set up for a kids camp. It was a great facility for corporate retreats, but we were unaware that each room had a coffee maker. We were also unaware that any of the kids would know how to work the coffee maker, or even be interested in it. Have you ever seen a room full of 8-12 year olds drinking coffee? We have. I wouldn't recommend it. Note to self, remove coffee makers before the kids check in.

Nathan Around 8 Years Old

but it seemed like we were reaching them with just pure and simple love and caring. We smothered them with accolades for their achievements. We were trying to build them back up to a place where they could just be a kid again and have the self-esteem to hold their heads up high.

Wednesday came, and I was at the swimming pool with all the kids, and I waded about halfway out into the pool with water up to my waist. Suddenly I felt a deluge of water sweep over me as one of the boys "cannonballed" me. I made the biggest commotion out of it and that pleased the kids. They all started to line up on the edge of the pool and one at a time they jumped in with one thing on their mind, getting me drenched.

We were all laughing and having such a great time, and that, my friends, is part of the healing that takes place in a setting like that. I spied little Nathan just standing there to the side and looking on at all the fun that was going on. His momma had sent with him his matching red pool shoes and bathing suit to wear, so he was dressed for the occasion, but not participating.

So I said, "Nathan, come on and cannonball me." He didn't say a word, but he jumped into the water close to me as if to splash me real good. When he came up, I told him to go back up on the edge of the pool and try again, only this time to pull one leg up and hold it with his hands and jump in at an angle close to me.

Surprisingly, he did just what I told him to do; he got out, stood on the edge of the pool, pulled one leg up with his hands and jumped in at an angle like the other kids. He didn't really execute the move that well, but when he went under the water I went under also and made sure to come up before he did. When he emerged from the water, I was soaked from going under and I told him, "Man, you really got me!"

As I was wiping the water out of my eyes, I heard him say, "I did it!" He actually shouted it.

Those were the first words we heard him speak. He spoke! The unspeakable joy that overtook me at that moment was almost insurmountable. I thought I was going to cry. I couldn't let him know my feelings of emotion, so I quickly said, "Yes, you really got me."

He was overjoyed with the whole situation and proceeded to climb the ladder back out of the pool over and over and SPLASSSH, he cannonballed me again and again and again and again.

I was in that pool for over an hour and a half while the kids, and especially Nathan, continued to cannonball me. It was a tremendous breakthrough. All I did was spend some time like a dad would do with his kids and not give up.

Nathan had responded to all the love that was displayed for all the kids, and finally at that particular moment in the pool, he took a chance and acted on his feelings. He needed to put the death of his little brother aside just for a moment so he could once again be a kid and have some fun. That's what did it, all the love and attention from all of us.

Jerry Lewis then taught him to swim, and later we played some catch and continued in general to do our best to help him have a fun time. He finally let go of the past and moved on into the future thanks to that cannonball experience.

If there's some kind of clinical psychological term for that, I don't know what it is. I just know that kids respond to love and attention. We were all elated at Nathan's breakthrough, and we were just so thankful that we had been allowed to be the ones through which it came. To me, it was a confirmation from God that we were supposed to do this work and that it truly was God's camp. He would provide everything we needed if we would just learn to trust Him.

IT'S ALL ABOUT LOVE

The last day of camp arrived and along with it came the parents, caregivers, uncles and aunts to pick up the kids after the final rally celebration. We had planned to sing the song, "You Can't Say Love Enough," which I had written with Don Goodman and Sammy Mizell at Johnny Morris' office in Nashville. We had subsequently recorded it ourselves (Kim, Jimmy, and I) and had it on a CD to give to the kids along with a few other positive songs to send home with them.

Before we sang it to close the program, I told all the kids that if there was someone in their lives that they really loved, they needed to tell them every day that they loved them. So we sang the song and ended the first Champions Kids Camp.

I put my guitar on its stand and stepped off the stage onto the dining hall floor to speak to the various campers, parents, and caregivers, and the next thing I knew there was this tug on my shirt tail. I looked down to see who was tugging on me, and there stood little Nathan. When he saw he had my attention, he proceeded to say, "Uncle Bill, I love you."

Are there words to describe what that meant to me right at that time? Absolutely not! I have never had such a feeling as that in my life. I don't know how to couch it in words. Here was a little boy who had been brought to our camp with grief so deep that he wouldn't, maybe even couldn't, speak. Now here he was telling me that he loved me with this big grin on his face.

One thing we have found out about young kids is that they are truly honest. If they don't like you, they will certainly tell you if asked. I picked him up and hugged him and told him that I loved him, too.

Then I spied Kim (Aunt Kim to the kids) across the room talking with some folks. I told Nathan, "Go tell Aunt Kim too." I put him down and he made his way through the small crowd, and I watched as he tugged on her shirt like he did mine, and then proceeded to tell her he loved her just as he had told me. She got these big alligator tears in her eyes, and picked him up and hugged him so tight. It was a defining moment in time for her, too, that day. It was like a "come back tomorrow shot" in golf.

Little did we realize that we had reached a turning point in our lives which meant that music was not going to be our main focus anymore; we had lots of kids to help.

Nathan came back to camp each summer for the next several years, and then his time was finished when he turned 13. The last time I saw him, he was over six feet tall, had the most beautiful curly blonde hair you've ever seen, and couldn't wait to show us his new baby sister. He had come through a terribly difficult time in his life, and Champions Kids Camp helped him get past what he will never get over. We later adopted those words to help describe what we do at Champions Kids Camp.

Nathan Grown Up - 2020

MOVING FORWARD

It wasn't until we had completed our first camp that we even thought about having a second, third, or fourth camp, etc.

We were amazed at the impact the camp had, not only on the kids who attended, but on ourselves and our small group of volunteers, also.

We all wanted to continue because the kids totally captured our hearts, and we knew we had only touched the tip of the iceberg of kids who had been impacted by trauma. This presented a much larger challenge for Kim and me since our partners, Jerry and Natalie, had told us from the beginning that they could only commit one year of time, effort and backing to this project; it was all now fully on our own shoulders.

It took all the belief we had in ourselves and in God to step out

The Nash Family with Two Campers The Last Night of The First Camp in 2002

totally in faith and take on this responsibility. We knew we had all the support of our new friends, our small but dedicated CKC team of wonderful people who were very passionate about moving forward with us. As the leaders, though, our first thought was, "Where's the money going to come from?"

Chapter Twenty-One

CKC First, Music Second

FOR THE SECOND TIME IN MY life, I put something else ahead of my music; the first time being with Kim (and subsequently our boys).

What it came down to was the realization that no booking agency could/would take us on to get us where we needed to go to promote and promulgate Champions Kids Camp. We felt like the churches, civic clubs and company conventions were our best bet. In order to make this happen, I had to get out of my comfort zone and get on the phone to talk to people I didn't know. I had to learn to let my passion show through the phone to get someone to say yes. That was the most difficult part for me personally of what I had to do in order for us to succeed. I got a lot of, "No thank you, but we'll be praying for you," but little by little, I finally started getting some bookings.

I had wise counseling when it felt like I was hitting a wall. Billie Faye quoted me Galatians 6:9 that said, "And let us not grow weary in doing good, for in due season we will reap a harvest, if we do not give up" (that's a combination of a couple of our favorite translations). Then Judy Bunch told me one day when I was having a hard time moving forward, "Just make one call." She said just to do one thing, and it will get you going even if it's not a business call. In other words, stop your whining and start calling.

As I prayed for God to help me, my mind would immediately go back to the Nathan story, that first confirmation that we were destined to help these kids.

Everything we have now is because we were obedient to God in starting Champions Kids Camp. It became a "God Thing" to continue because we had very little money to pay for camp initially. Our faith had to grow exponentially, and grow it did as we told the story of Billy's miraculous healing everywhere we went and asked everyone to back our mission at CKC.

AN INTERESTING EVENT

At the Lombardi Awards, where Dr. Zo had us sing, I met a guy who they called "governor" since he had the same name as former Texas Governor, Bill Clements. He was chairperson of a function for the Chiropractic College in Pasadena, and he invited me to the dinner.

I got there, and all of a sudden, the "governor" rushed up to me and asked, "Do you have your guitar in the car?" I wondered why he asked since I hadn't been booked to sing, but I answered, "Yes, of course."

He explained that he had booked some belly dancers for the evening entertainment, and they had called at the last minute and cancelled. I told him I would be glad to sing if he didn't mind if I said a word or two about CKC. I think he would have agreed to about anything at that point, so the deal was on.

After I played that evening, I met Dr. Todd Goodale and his wife, Bernice, who were in attendance. Their daughter, Jenny, was a survivor of Leukemia, so they knew exactly what Kim and

I had experienced, and my story hit home with them that night. To this day, they have not missed one month of supporting CKC, and at the writing of this book that translates to 17+ years.

When they discovered that I didn't take a salary from CKC but relied on our music ministry, Building Bridges of Hope, for my living, they became supporters of both entities and have been a great blessing. They also got their whole family involved in supporting CKC, and the Goodale table is a staple at our fundraisers.

Dr. Todd's brother and sister-in-law, Brad and Linda Goodale, his sister and brother-in-law, Pam and Bill Huddleston, and his mom, Lois, and Dad, Doyle, who we call Coach, all adopted us and our cause.

The Goodales have been a God-sent blessing to CKC and us. We even wrote Dr. Todd a little song. I know the words are kind of corny, but here they are anyway: "Dr. Todd, Dr. Todd, he cracks my back and it helps my bod. He takes the pain, all away, helps me through, another day, Dr. Todd, Dr. Todd Goodale!" I know, why would I put such corny lines out there in this book?... lol. It's all in fun with great friends.

The Goodale Family

I'm so thankful we met them, and I guess I really should also thank the belly dancers who cancelled that night. The Bible says, "The steps of a righteous man are ordered of the Lord." It was meant to be that we met up with that great family for the sake of BBOH and CKC. It was also another reminder that CKC is God's camp, and we just run it for Him. Note: "Coach" Doyle Goodale has since gone on to his reward in Heaven. R.I.P. Coach Goodale.

MORE CAMPS, MORE FUNDRAISERS

Well, logically, since we wanted to have more camps, we needed to raise more funds, and more funds means more fundraisers. In times past, Gary Smith and I held the "Smith and

Nash Christmas Bash." Those had always been successful, so we ended up deciding to throw a fundraiser in December, only this time on New Year's Eve. I was still reconnecting with old friends and fans in the Houston area and wanted to get everyone out I could.

I called up Terry Foyt, who I'd become good friends with through the years. She helped me to get her dad, AJ Foyt, to be our official celebrity spokesperson for CKC! That was huge for us, and he even agreed to donate multiple one-of-a-kind items to our auction that year, including pieces of his cars in which he had won multiple Indy 500s.

So with a little "star power" now behind the event and our organization, I felt more emboldened to invite more and more people. We rented a hotel ballroom and prepared for our first CKC NYE fundraiser on December 31, 2002. I even had Gary Smith and Brian Collins come in as special guests.

Long story short, the music was great, we all had a good time, but we barely broke even. We owe a huge debt of gratitude to our auctioneer that night, Mike Van Norman (Mikey). Before Mikey took the stage to start the auction, he asked me how much we needed to get out of the red. I told him $5k, and he said, "done deal." Sure enough, he got us into the black. We didn't make the huge profit we hoped for, but at least we got the first one under our belt and weren't in debt.

The best thing that came about though from that first NYE was that our friend, Judy Bunch, was in attendance, and she came up to me at the end of the night and said, "I think you need my help." She was right, and shortly after, she joined our board, and has been an integral member of our Champions team ever since.

After that, donated auction items at our events continued to be one of our greatest income sources for CKC. One of the best auction items we ever received was through our good friend, Mr. Ray Pillow, a fifty-year+ member of the Grand Ole Opry.

I called Ray one day and asked if he would help me get a guitar signed by as many Opry members as possible. Ray said he would be happy to get that done, and that Friday, he personally carried a guitar around backstage at the Opry and collected over 26 signatures that night!

Another fundraising idea we had was to run a marathon again like we had done for the Leukemia Society. We trained and trained and ran the Houston Marathon in January of 2003. Running a marathon at 50 was hard enough, so why not run another one at 59? Kim, Jimmy, and I all three ran, along with Morgan Pryor. She actually raised more than all three of us combined, and brought in several thousand dollars to go towards our second camp that year. Subsequently, Jimmy ran one more

marathon, and so did Morgan, but ultimately, we all decided we could raise a lot more money putting on other fundraisers that were also much kinder to our knees.

Not long after this, my sister, Ellen, decided she wanted to help raise funds for Champions, and she thought it would be

Bill, Kim, & Jimmy Nash with Morgan Pryor at the 2003 Houston Marathon

great to organize a BBQ Cook-off in Spring, Texas where she lived, just north of Houston. She went to a local business owner, affectionately known as "Papa," and he agreed to host our event at his place, appropriately named, "Papa's Ice House." She got a group of volunteers together, and in late April of 2003, she held the first Annual CKC BBQ Cook-Off.

She had somewhere close to 20 teams sign up that first year, and this was the perfect place for our Opry guitar to be auctioned off. As it came up for bid, out of nowhere a guy stepped up and bid $7,000 for the guitar. Everyone was stunned! $7,000! I couldn't wait to call Ray Pillow and tell him the good news. He had specifically asked me to let him know what the resulting bid for the guitar would turn out to be. He was elated and pledged more help in the future. With the proceeds from the guitar, my sister's first cookoff raised over $22,000 for Champions Kids Camp.

That 22k saved our bacon, especially after our first New Year's Eve fundraiser didn't raise as much as we'd hoped (or anything for that matter). That, along with a few more donations through the summer, made it possible for us to have our second camp in July of 2003, but first, there was one more thing we needed to do.

Chapter Twenty-Two

Moving Back To Houston

KIM AND I LOVED LIVING IN Nashville. It was where we had raised our boys, had the success as songwriters we'd always dreamed of, and had built a wonderful life together. However, with CKC growing and me commuting more and more, we knew it was time to move to Houston.

We had scouted out some homes to rent when we flew in for the cook-off a month before and put our home in Nashville on the market. Everything thankfully converged very smoothly so that we were able to close on the sale of our home very quickly, and put the security deposit down on the rental in Houston. Jimmy graduated high school the third week of May in 2003, and then it was time to say our goodbyes to Nashville and head back to Houston.

Our home in Nashville had one of the largest basements I've

ever seen. It was just about as big as all our bedrooms, bathrooms, living room, and office combined. We got spoiled over the years to just storing anything we didn't know what to do with in the basement. Combine that with 15 years of living in one spot, the longest amount of time we'd ever stayed put somewhere, and we ended up with unspeakable quantities of "junk." It was probably a very accurate visual representation of what a songwriter's mind looks like with all the various pieces of song ideas just floating around. Since I was mostly in Houston fundraising, it fell to Kim and Jimmy to sort through everything we wanted to keep, sell, or just throw away. It took them six weeks and two garage sales, but they got it sorted in time to move. Note to self: it's okay to get rid of some things along the way. Probably a good life lesson in many ways.

Once we started planning to move, Jimmy had applied to the University of Houston, my alma mater. He not only was accepted but received a full scholarship! Well, given the precariousness of our finances, you can imagine how glad we were to know his tuition was taken care of.

That next week after Jimmy's graduation, we loaded up a 26' U-Haul with a trailer attached, plus our van (on loan from Jerry) with a trailer attached, and Jimmy's Mercury Cougar, and headed to Houston.

We stayed the night on our way at a hotel in Atlanta, Texas. As I pulled into the hotel at 2:00 in the morning in the U-Haul truck, I heard a scraping sound up above. I backed up a few feet to make sure I wasn't hitting something, and down came a mix of brick and wood, and a load of dust. The manager of the hotel came out frantically yelling in a language I couldn't quite recognize as he surveyed the damage to his previously intact overhang, and I can only imagine what Kim and Jimmy were thinking as they watched from their own cars. Our move was off to a smooth start for sure!

Luckily, the insurance from U-Haul covered the damage. The next day, small shards of wood from the overhang continued to fly off the truck as we drove. Looking back, this was probably a clear sign of what was to come over the next few years; a few scrapes, but everything would work out in the end, and we'd have a lot of fun along the way.

THE LINCOLN THAT COULD...ALMOST

Jerry Lewis was still helping me by way of his car lot. He had sold us a car for Billy to take to college for just about his cost, and he had also lent us vehicles over the past couple years at no cost, and we'd swap them out when he needed to sell them. When I told Judy Bunch we were moving back to Houston, she offered a more "permanent" solution. She said she had an '89 Lincoln Town Car in excellent condition that just sits at her house because she always drives her new truck. She would happily donate the car to CKC, and then I'd be able to drive it everywhere for all my meetings as the "company car" so to speak.

Well, this was very generous of her, and even though it was an older model, the car was in great shape, and I had always loved Lincolns with their plush seats and smooth rides. I especially appreciate that smooth ride the older I get.

Right about this same time, almost immediately after moving back to Houston in June of 2003, I got a call from my friend, Alan Bullock, who I met in Houston during my commutes from Nashville. He had gotten a new job at Daystar Television at their national headquarters in Dallas. He invited Kim, Jimmy, and I to come be the featured musical guests on one of their national broadcasts, and we were elated. This would be our first national TV appearance as a family group and give us a chance to talk about Champions.

It's only about a four-hour drive from Houston to Dallas (three and a half depending who's driving), so we decided to take the Lincoln. Everything was going fine at the start. We were on I-45 North and had already gone through the Buc-ee's in Madisonville, which was our first stop. We passed Centerville shortly after that, which meant we were halfway there, and we were rolling along nice and smooth. As we were approaching Buffalo, Texas, though, we heard a few loud sounds coming from the car...then a few more sounds...and then just black smoke. Well, I'm no mechanic, but I knew from experience that we had blown the transmission. Luckily, we were at the top of a hill when this happened, and we were able to coast all the way down to the exit at the bottom of the hill and roll right into a gas station.

Once we got situated there, we popped the hood, and the mechanic there confirmed we had blown the seals on the transmission. It turns out the car had just sat for too long in Judy's yard, and the seals had all become hard and brittle. So there we were now, halfway between Houston and Dallas, in the 105-degree summer heat. We were just within the 100 mile-radius that our insurance covered towing the car back to Houston, but that didn't help us get to Dallas before an early call time the next morning. The gas station attendant told us that there was a car rental center in Palestine, Texas, about 40 minutes away. He couldn't take off work, but he could call his friend who would take us there for $20, and then we could rent a car and drive up to Dallas from Palestine.

This all sounded less than ideal, but we didn't have much choice, so I agreed. Jimmy had that 18-year-old, "everything's an adventure" attitude and had gotten a snack and was playing in the station's arcade happily. Kim responded slightly differently. She was still re-adjusting to the Texas heat, and was just trying to stay cool inside the station while I worked it all out. About 20 minutes later, this friend pulled up in an Oldsmobile that, aside from the fact that it was running, looked like it was in worse shape than our Lincoln. I can't quite describe this man's accent, but it was somewhere between a Louisiana creole and some form of English yet to be identified. He said to us with a big smile, "I hope ya'll don't mind I got no ehhhrrr-conditionin.'" I couldn't even look at Kim when he said that, but I could feel her looking at me. Jimmy just laughed.

So, on the word of a gas station attendant I'd never met before, we trusted this friend of his to get us to Palestine, Texas.

Nash Note 🎵

Eventually, the Lincoln got fixed up, and it was Jerry's idea to raffle it off at our next cookoff. Believe it or not, we actually made a few thousand dollars for CKC from it!

I can't say the ride was pleasant, but we did arrive safely, and what else could we have done? I wasn't about to cancel our first national TV appearance on account of car trouble. Finally, we drove the rental car from Palestine up to Dallas, and made it to our hotel. I'm so thankful Daystar had reserved us a very nice place to stay, and after a good meal, and some time relaxing in the pool/hot tub, we were ready to go for the next day.

Everything went very well the next morning. We sang 3 songs, and Joni Lamb did a wonderful interview with us. When the show aired, that became a great tool for me to reach out and book us, and it also led to more TV appearances along the way. So that was our big welcome back to Houston! A little rocky, but we made it. What's next?

THE SECOND CAMP

In July 2003, less than two months after moving back to Houston, it was time for our second camp. This year, we only had 30 kids apply, down from 33. On one hand, it was disappointing having a smaller camp the second year, but on the other hand, we really had just enough money to pay for that many kids, so I suppose it was all in God's plan.

We held it once again at Columbia Lakes. Just like the year

Billy with Repeat Camper, Garrett - 2003

before, about the second or third day, the kids really all started to bond with us and the other children, as well. We were all nervous if we could recreate the magic from the first year, but sure enough, those kids started to open up to us, started coming out of their shells, and just grew so much in one week.

One story that stands out to me from that year was a young boy who lost his brother to cancer. He was one of our oldest campers, barely qualifying under the 12-year-old age limit, so he was quite a bit taller than the other kids. The first couple days, we couldn't figure out what to do with him, because he always seemed to be stirring up trouble with some of the other campers. As we looked deeper into his file, we found out that he had been the bone marrow donor for his brother, but his brother died anyway. He blamed himself and thought that he was not good enough, not strong enough to save his brother. This caused him to have a whole mix of feelings from sadness to anger, and he took it out on everyone around him.

On about the third day, though, he started to bond with Jimmy over the simplest thing, just a little bit of Spanish. This boy was fluently bilingual, on account of his mother's first language being Spanish, and Jimmy had just finished two years of Spanish in high school. So when it would come time to go from one activity to another, Jimmy would say to him, "Ven conmigo" (come with me), or tell him to listen up, "Escucha." I don't know what it is, perhaps just the familiarity of the Spanish, but he took a real liking to Jimmy. They would sit and talk about how to say this or that in Spanish, the formal way to say something versus how you would say it to friends, or how to use other colloquial terms you don't really learn in school. It wasn't rocket science or advanced psychiatry, but it worked! He started to open up and have fun and stopped picking fights with other campers. He still needed time to let those wounds of losing his brother heal, but the boy who left camp at the end of the week was a different boy than the one who showed up at the beginning of the week.

In those early days, we truly were not qualified in "psychiatric" terms to address the needs of these children, but it was the love that broke through the barriers. There is something that happens when you get a kid away from their normal environment, even if it's a great loving home, and put them in a place that's just built for fun and to be with other kids just like them. They know they're not alone and there's not something wrong with them because they've experienced tragedy. There's something so healing in that.

H FOR HOUSTON, H FOR HOPE

Now that we were back in Houston (Pearland to be exact),

there was no option to go for another writing deal, no running around Music Row, networking, pitching to try to get another star to cut our songs...or so I thought. My clearest goal was to get us booked at as many churches, civic clubs, conventions, and anywhere else that would have us in order to raise enough money for CKC, as well as to earn enough from our bookings and cd sales to pay our own bills.

Through my friend, Roger McDuff, I received an invitation to sing at Channel 14 in Houston, which was the local TBN affiliate. They were doing their annual telethon, and I was thrilled to sing there, not only to reach a larger audience through television, but also to meet all the local pastors and singers and see who might take an interest in CKC. I was supposed to sing for just one day, but they invited me back for the whole week. Later that year, Kim and Jimmy would join me there for other events, but the invite had come before we moved, and they had not been cleared yet. It felt really good to be singing Gospel music again on a more regular basis. It felt like coming home, really, since those were my roots. That was an unexpected turn, but a good one.

I became friends with several of the crew there at the station, and as the week came to a close, one of them mentioned to me that her father was an animator working on a children's project right there in Houston, and they needed someone to create all their music. She suggested we all meet. It sounded like an interesting endeavor. I'd never written for an animated project before, but Kim and I had written some songs geared towards children in years past, so I thought, why not?

We met with Rob, the owner of the company that was producing what was to be the first of a series of animated Christian children's videos. He loved our background of writing for Reba and Sony, etc., and after a couple conversations, we all agreed to work together to bring this project to fruition.

Now keep in mind, we had just moved back to Houston and had just had our second camp with no certain path yet of how we would continue raising funds for CKC and support ourselves. With the sale of our home in Nashville, we had about $12,000 in the bank, only $2,000 more than when we moved TO Nashville (a whole 20% increase after 15 years!). I wish it could have been more, but with the ups and downs in the music business, the great royalties from Reba, and the years with no royalties at all, in the end, it was what it was. We only had a handful of bookings coming up, but we just knew in our spirits we were supposed to move back to Houston and build Champions Kids Camp, and somehow God would provide. Now within the first three months of being back in Houston, here comes a project out of the blue. God is good.

Kim and I were ecstatic to be writing for a new project. Jimmy was not yet writing with us, but we knew right away, there were several songs he should sing as the younger voice in our new Nash trio (Jimmy subsequently renamed us "Nash3"). We not only needed songs for this first video, but Rob wanted to plan ahead for the next 2 at least. We drew from important lessons in the Bible, and tried to write them in a way for kids to understand. We came up with songs like "70 times 7" about forgiveness, and "Too Blessed To Be Stressed." "We're All Different" and "It's Great To Be Alive" both stand out in my mind as songs we still sing at camp to give a positive message to the kids.

In the midst of this, we were talking about filling out the soundtrack with songs that wouldn't necessarily be in the videos themselves, but would help to create a full album alongside the video. Rob said he would really love to include a new, original patriotic song. Kim and I agreed that would be great. We kicked around several different ideas for titles based on national mottos and sayings, including "In God We Trust." Kim said, yes, but it should be "'In God We STILL Trust!' Now I can write that song." Man, what a difference a word makes in the impact of a song. We didn't know it yet, but that song was going to take on a life of its own.

It took us about two months to write enough songs to set up a session to record. When Rob asked us where we wanted to record, without a doubt, we said Nashville. Through our 15 years there, we'd met all the best players around and had become friends with them. They would play on the major label sessions for triple master scale, but as long as we were flexible with them on our dates, they'd play on our songs for the much lower "limited pressing" scale (all scales were set by the Musician's Union in

Nashville). So I called up our friend, Jimmy Nichols, to see if he would be interested in producing the session with us. Jimmy had been leading Reba's band for years, as well as Faith Hill's, and played on countless hit records. He said he was on board and even got us booked in David Malloy's private home studio to record (it's funny how many times we've crossed paths with Jim & David Malloy). So by November of 2003, less than six months after moving away from Nashville, we were back recording a new project. Who but God could have seen that coming?

Everything went very well in the studio, and as we finished up the recording, I called up Ray Pillow again to see if he wanted to get together and catch up. We met for lunch, and I told him what we were doing in town and gave him a CD of our latest session. As we drove off, I guess he had put the CD in his player right away, because by the time we were side-by-side at the first light, he was motioning to me wildly in his car, trying to get my attention. I didn't know what was going on, but a few minutes later he called me, and went on and on about "In God We Still Trust." He said he really thought he could get it cut by a major artist and asked if I would be open to sharing publishing with him if he could do so. It only took two seconds for us to give an emphatic "yes!" Ray also worked frequently with a very famous producer in Nashville, Jerry Crutchfield, who produced Tanya Tucker, among many others. He told me he would strategize with Jerry for our song. Strangely enough, Ray and Jerry were the team that discovered Lee Greenwood, and they had co-published "God Bless The USA," undoubtedly one of the greatest patriotic songs of all time.

BREAKFAST OF CHAMPIONS

Now if you have visions of grandeur of how songs get pitched in Nashville, I'm about to ruin them right now. As the story was told to me later by Ray, he called up Marty Roe, lead singer of the group, Diamond Rio, and asked to meet him at the Waffle House (see how prestigious it all is). After breakfast, he insisted that Marty listen to "In God We Still Trust" right there in his car. Marty loved it and took it the rest of the band. They all loved it, too, and after a few months of waiting on pins and needles (around Summer of 2004), Ray called us to let us know it would not only be included on their new album, but it would be the second single. A single! Even more than we could have hoped for. I can't tell you how many times over the years we had written a song that almost made the album (number eleven on a ten-song album as they say). We not only made the album, but made it as a single, and with an established group, it gave the song a great chance to be successful. Here's an interesting coincidence: this album was entitled "Greatest Hits II," almost the same as our Reba cut being on her "Greatest Hits Volume 2." What are the odds? It's also interesting, like I mentioned before, that they had "You Can't Say Love Enough" on hold just 3 or 4 years earlier.

What's really funny, too, is that a few years before that, the drummer for Diamond Rio accidentally drove into our yard one night in Nashville. We lived at the end of a dead end road, and there were no street lights to see, and we saw his headlights swerve right onto our lawn. Thankfully, he was alright. Perhaps him driving in our yard was foreshadowing for them cutting our song? That would be amazing, or perhaps our street was just really dark. You decide!

CASTING A LIGHT

The ebb and flow is always interesting to look back on, because in the midst of all this excitement, our deal with Rob had come to an end. The first children's animated video was released, and the sales were just not enough to cover the production costs, and no further videos were going to be created. However, two great things came of this: firstly, it caused us to write a song that got us our first major cut in years, and secondly, it provided us a source of income and almost a whole year of networking to increase our bookings to a financially sustainable level.

I've often thought about if Kim and I had had a long string of big cuts like we had wanted to and had made all the money we wanted to in the 90s, I don't think we would have ever left Nashville or done anything other than write. We certainly wouldn't have thought of starting a charity like CKC, or moving back to Houston, and would have never written "IGWST." It's just like to me in the Bible when Elijah's brook dried up. God wasn't trying to make Elijah die of thirst, He just needed him to go somewhere else now. That's how it felt for us; we had a new place to be, and a new dream to achieve.

Chapter Twenty-Three

The Yearly Cycle - NYE, Cookoff, Camp, Repeat

I N MY EFFORT NOT TO CONFUSE anyone, I'm doing my best to tell each story in its entirety while still keeping the timeline straight. There is of course inevitably some overlap in the stories, going back and forth between exciting things happening in music and everything with our growing CKC organization. So right now, let's roll it back to July 2003, just after our second camp, and before yet embarking on the new children's video project. So here we go!

We were once again hooked on doing another year after all the breakthroughs we had at our second camp. Pretty soon, we started realizing what the never-ending cycle would be of raising funds, spending it at camp, resting for a week, then starting all over. Despite our first New Year's Eve Fundraiser being less than we'd hoped for, we decided it was still a good idea if we could just execute it a little better. After speaking with our board and advisory council, we all decided to host it at the Westin Galleria. It was more expensive, but also felt like a more elegant place to hold a black-tie (optional) event than the previous hotel.

Our faith was really put to the test when we signed that contract with the Westin Galleria. It called for a minimum charge of $10,000, and we only had $200 in CKC's bank account. What faith that took for us to sign on the dotted line and for our executive board to give us the go ahead.

With a better location though, and a lot better planning, it really paid off, and we made a much better profit for CKC that

second NYE party, now known as the "Nash New Year's Eve Bash." We've held it now at various locations around town, and it's always a lot of fun. We play all our favorites with a live band and keep singing 'til the last person quits dancing.

After NYE was over, the attention turned fully to the cook-off. With the success of the first BBQ cook-off, my sister was once again on board to organize the second annual event, and Papa once again

Judy B. & Gerald Franklin at The Nash NYE Bash

donated the use of his facilities. In fact, he and his son, Rich, have lent us their property every year since. Recently, they even took up donations themselves in the months leading up to the cook-off and presented us with a check for over $12k! We could use more people like that. They not only let you use their place for free, but they pay you to be there!

So the second annual cook-off was a success again, raising nearly as much as its first year, we had made a profit at New Year's, and we had more donations come in throughout the year as we, now living in Houston full time, continued to sing everywhere they would have us. Along with getting better at fundraising, we had gotten better at spreading the word to find more children that qualified for our camp. Through Texas Children's Hospital, Children's Protective Services (CPS), churches, civic clubs, and other individuals, we would send them applications to forward to families with children that might benefit from our camp.

We also decided we should seek out a camp facility with more activities designed for kids and that could accommodate bigger numbers as we grew. We ended up renting Victory Camp in Alvin, Texas, which was owned by Living Stones Church across the street. Pastor Al Jandl had invited us to sing there (he knew us from our Lakewood days in the '80s), and that's when we got to

The Annual CKC BBQ Cookoff - Surprise $12,100 Check! Sandy Treon, Dave Dempsey, Ellen Cole, Troy Gibson, Kim & Bill Nash, Rich Loughridge

see the camp. It's a good thing we planned ahead, because that year, we went from 30 children, to 75!

There's a big difference between 30 and 75, especially when it comes to the kids we serve. With only 30 kids, I (and all our volunteers) pretty much had enough time to get to know every child individually and help them have the most successful week possible. At 75 kids, we really had to divide and conquer, so to speak, meaning we needed more qualified volunteers, more great young counselors, or "champs" as we call them, as well as camp leaders so that these kids that "fall through the cracks" in society, as Dr. Zo put it, don't fall through the cracks at our camp. Luckily, as our number of kids has grown, God has sent us more and more amazing volunteers so that we can give enough personal attention to every child who attends.

The reason we don't use the word "counselor" at camp comes from the first two years we did use the term. I remember one child having a meltdown, and we had a professional counselor on site with us who tried to speak to him. That kid took one look at them and said, "You're a counselor, I don't want to talk to you!" This child had been to multiple therapists and was tired of having to sit in a room and talk to an adult about stuff he didn't want to talk about in the first place. That settled it for us, our counselors were now "champs." That's such a new, positive word, and the kids are much more receptive to it. Who doesn't love a champ?

I'm going to skip around here a bit into the future, but one of the biggest blessings for CKC is that some of our campers that don't want to leave us when they turn 13 end up entering our intern program. Then once they're in that for three years, if they still don't want to leave us (which we just love), they can become junior champs. Then at 18, they can become senior champs. Looking out at our champs this last year, we realized that well over half of our champs now are former campers. We actually call them "champers." We had inadvertently developed a system of "growing" our own volunteers. The best part about this is that pretty much any trauma that a camper has experienced has also

Our Champers in 2015

been experienced by one of our champs. It touches my heart so much to think of one little girl who showed up just months after losing her father, and the first thing that happened when she signed in at camp was she was taken to her champ who had lost her father at the exact same age. Nothing is quite so encouraging when you've experienced tragedy as seeing someone else who had the same thing happen, and is years down the road, and has not only made it through, but is thriving. The change that happens in a child like that at camp is remarkable.

With the new facility, we found an amazing new way to reach our kids. They had a large, 4-person zip line 40 feet in the air. Some kids were excited to try everything, but a lot of kids were afraid to go off

The Zip Line

of that. We would encourage them through the week, though. I even promised several kids I'd go off the zip line with them if they went (and trust me, after the 4th or 5th time, I really didn't want to go off again). This became an effective way for a lot of our champs to convince their campers to overcome their fears, and it works for so many children. It amazes me every year when they finally go up that 40-foot spiral staircase and get hooked in and take off flying down the zip line, that something changes in them. It's like now that they've faced that fear, they realize they can face and overcome other fears in their lives. Kids are so resilient, much more I find than adults, and if you can just help them get past one fear, a lot of times their newfound self-esteem will do the rest.

There were so many great stories from that year, but suffice to say, we made it through camp 2004 with flying colors with 75 kids, exactly two and a half times the kids from 2003. It seems like, at this point, it was the first time all of us not only wanted to do camp again, but we had to do it now, and had to do it for more and more kids. How could we

"Aunt Bee" At Camp 2004

experience all these breakthroughs and not help as many kids as

possible? This was God's camp, and we wanted to take it as far as we could.

So there began the cycle again. We rested for a week or two, and then in August 2004, we started back up raising funds at NYE, the cook-off, and everywhere we could possibly sing until it was time for our next, ever-growing camp.

ONE OF A KIND FRIEND

There's another character that I am compelled to mention

because without his financial support starting in our second year, CKC would not have been able to continue.

Harold Reese is his name, and his wife is Tammy. When I first met him, he was the jeweler to all kinds of country music stars like Johnny Lee, Mickey Gilley and Eddy Raven. He came to a club where I was performing years ago, and he brought me a piece of jewelry. It was a necklace with a round, gold disc that looked like a record with my name engraved on it.

That's the first time I remember meeting him, probably because of the generous gift. He and Tammy became regulars in my audience, and I'd see him in the crowd quite often. He and I became pals, going out to eat and hanging out a bit.

After Jerry and Natalie finally had to get back to running their car business, I wasn't sure which way to turn to get support for CKC, but I thought Harold might be interested. Thankfully, he was! He couldn't put time in it on a daily basis like Jerry and Natalie had, but he pledged his financial support.

Come to find out he is one of the most tender-hearted people in the world. For the next five years, he conducted our auction at our New Year's Eve event and then headed to his church for the midnight service. He was amazing when it came to getting money out of a crowd of folks, often outbidding them himself, and then donating the item back to CKC for the last bidder to actually take the item home.

Bill & Kim Presenting Harold & Tammy with a "Thank You" Plaque from CKC

Harold and Tammy have been with us since then, and they still support us in our on-going efforts for CKC. Even after coming through a quadruple by-pass, he keeps hanging out with us. I can't help but remember that day when he was in the hospital with all kinds of tubes running in and out of him. We sat by Tammy at the edge of his bed and thanked Jesus that he was still with us. It had been a close call, and he would have to stop smoking, which he formerly said he couldn't do, but when it came to life or death, his strong will kicked in and he beat nicotine. Way to go Harold, and thank you and Tammy forever. We love you guys!

Chapter Twenty-Four

Our Song Takes On A Life Of Its Own

I N THE MIDST OF EVERYTHING WITH CKC, we were so anxious and excited waiting for Diamond Rio to come out with our song. You know that feeling when you're a kid and can't wait to go to Disneyworld? It's like that times 1,000, except you still have to focus along the way because you're an adult with responsibilities. All we wanted to do was live in that excitement, though, and we did live on it for months, and even years.

Finally, in the spring of 2005, just 15 months after recording "IGWST," and playing it for Ray, he called me to let me know Diamond Rio would be playing the Grand Ole Opry that weekend, and they would for sure be playing our song! I'm not sure how many people I called to let them know to watch, but let's just say I increased GAC's (Great American Country's) ratings that week for the Opry in the Houston market by a significant margin. I'll never forget tuning in that night and watching them sing our song. At the end, the audience gave them a standing ovation for several minutes. As I recall, I think the show finally just went to commercial. A couple months later, we were back through Nashville at the same time as they were playing the Opry again, and Ray got us backstage to watch them live. What an experience. The whole band even signed a guitar for us, along with the other stars that night, so we could have another one to auction for CKC. What a great group of guys.

The Nashes Backstage at the Opry with Marty Roe of Diamond Rio

Now this next bit was unexpected (you may be noticing a theme to my life by now). When Arista (their label), started promoting "IGWST" to radio, I guess there was a bit of pushback. A lot of people felt this song was politically polarizing. That was not our intention. We just wrote it to be a patriotic song, a song for God and country, but not everyone agreed with the message. A few stations added it across the country, but many left it off their playlists.

Some say that "In God We Still Trust" was never even released to radio as a single, and that's why it didn't receive more airplay. Well, we know that's not true, because we had friends at different Country stations that told us when they had received the single from the label to add into rotation. The most likely scenario is that there were some complaints about the song being played at a few key stations, and the label just didn't feel like committing the resources to keep pushing it forward through the pushback. The truth lies somewhere in between all that, but it definitely caused a stir.

Then, suddenly, I started getting emails from multiple friends with this video on YouTube. Apparently, someone made up their own music video to the song, stating that the song had been "banned" from Country radio. Now I don't know the full story, or if it was ever actually "banned," but I guess something about that video struck a chord with people, and it started gaining steam online. Pretty soon, as people kept sharing it, it had millions of views. It wasn't long before we started receiving a slew of "compulsory license" requests from across the country. That's just legal terminology for someone else who wants to record their own version of our song. I don't know what the current figure is, but in the first two years, we counted over 55 individuals or groups had recorded "In God We Still Trust," and that number has continued to grow. Along the way, the song started to become popular with many churches, and we noticed a big surge in sheet music sales, especially in the lead up to Independence Day and other patriotic holidays.

Diamond Rio is still the biggest group to have recorded "IGWST," and we'll forever be grateful for that. They even did a new version of it when they switched labels to Word, Curb's Christian Label, and released it again on that album. Even though the song did not go #1 on Billboard, it spurred on countless bookings for us to sing the song ourselves, as well as numerous appearances on the Christian networks and at patriotic celebrations year-round.

THE GAITHERS...ALMOST

Not long after Diamond Rio released "IGWST," Ray and Jerry Crutchfield asked what we thought about them pitching us around to some labels as a family group. Given their track record, of course we were interested. Jerry happened to be old friends with Bill Carter, who is one of the more interesting people we've ever come across given the fact that he was not only a former secret service agent, but the attorney for the Rolling Stones at their height, and there's a load more facts I don't even have time to list. At this time though, he was managing Bill Gaither.

Bill Carter really loved our sound and had recommended we be signed to the Gaither label, which would ultimately mean us going on the various Gaither tours, which have been a huge force in Gospel music for years. This represented a tremendous amount of exposure for us, and sales and so on. We even came back to Nashville to meet with Bill Carter and Bill Gaither's son-in-law, Barry Jennings.

The whole deal didn't work out in the end (only God knows why), but I mention it because it was incredibly close to being a done deal, and I think of the dramatic turn that could have made in our lives. We were only three or four years into CKC and were still growing slowly. Would we have had time to continue if we were on the road that much and had so many other obligations? It's hard to say how we would have been able to do both.

If I'm being honest (which is my goal in this book), the singer in me would have loved to have toured with all those great Gospel acts and be on a label again, especially this time around with Kim and Jimmy, but I have no doubt I would still be searching for that deeper meaning that I found in working with our kids at CKC. God truly does know best for us sometimes, and the more I trust in His will, the happier I am. Kim told me once, "You know that God doesn't care if you're a star." Nobody had ever put it quite so succinctly as she did, the vanity of stardom, and how useless it is unless it's in God's plan for you and used for His will. That really helped me in my thinking more than I can express.

THE 700 CLUB

One of the other amazing things "IGWST" brought about came through our friend, Brad Goodale, at CBN. He submitted us to be featured on the 700 Club, along with our own version of "In God We Still Trust." The story was approved, and CBN assigned a wonderful producer, Mindy Pierce, to interview us and put together a five-minute plus segment as well as a new music video to our song. We told our story, in a very similar way as  *The Nash Family "IGWST" Album Cover* I'm telling you now throughout this book, only in a very condensed form, and shared my testimony of coming back to

God and of Billy's healing. We finished up filming at their studios in Nashville in the Summer of 2006 and headed back to Houston, and a couple months later, the segment aired.

Lots of friends called me to tell me what a great segment it was, and of course, it really helped with our visibility to increase our bookings. We got to talk about Champions Kids Camp too, which was fantastic, but here's the part that really gets me. They say hindsight is 20/20, and looking back, I can see now how even when I wasn't living for God, He still had a plan for me, and in a way, I never really left the ministry, try as I might. After they aired our story, I got a call from Brad. He talked about how they had the call-in line with the number on the screen throughout the program, and how people could call in for prayer. He told me that after the first airing, 1,214 people had called in to receive Jesus. 1,214! He said that was the largest response they had received from a single program that year. I don't know what specific words I said in the interview to spur on that kind of response, but I guess something resonated with people that made them want to come to Jesus or come back to Him the way I did. If no other good thing came about from all the mistakes I made in my life, I would know it was all worth it because 1,214 people now knew Jesus that did not before. I'm so thankful to God that He would use me in such a way, even if I couldn't see His plan for so many years.

FRIENDS COME TO THE RESCUE

Right about this same time, while we were so excited about the success of our song and all that was happening for our music, I remember we were just two weeks away from camp and we were coming down to the wire. With more campers than ever (well over 100), we were still $18,000 short on funds to pay for them all. That's right, $18,000 short with only a couple of weeks left before that money would be due to pay for camp. Kim, Jimmy, and I were booked at a 7:00 a.m. breakfast at the Quail Valley Exchange Club (now re-named the Missouri City Exchange Club). Judy Bunch had re-connected us with all the Exchange Clubs across the Houston area, herself being a member for many years. When it was time for me to speak, I stood up and took the mike at the podium, but was still not sure what to say. I had never before been in a situation like this with everything depending on my words.

As Kim and I talked it over, it seemed like we needed to be plain honest with this great group of businesspeople and just cut to the chase and tell it like it was. In order to do this, we decided to simply read the children's stories as we saw them written on the applications we received in the mail.

As I read the first story and the lines about the traumatic situation a child had had to endure, I could feel my emotions building up inside of me, and I did my best to continue reading. The second story caused those emotions to escalate, and by the time I got to the third application, I could barely finish reading. I could feel the tears starting to well up in my eyes, and then flow down my cheeks.

As I stopped for a second to wipe my eyes, I noticed that some of the guys from the front and side tables had shifted around and were kind of huddled up around a table or two in the back of the room. When I got through, I headed back to our table to sit down. The president then took over and said to us, "We have raised your money." All three of us stood, stunned, in silence. He repeated himself, "We just raised your $18,000."

All those Exchangeites had donated enough money to cover our entire shortfall for camp that year. There are just no words in any language that could express the shock and then exultation that came rushing over me. One minute, we had the weight of the world on our shoulders, and a few seconds later, his few words lifted the load instantly, and we were beyond ecstatic; we could now take a moment to breathe and look forward to camp once again. This was just one of the ways we have been assured that CKC is God's camp and He is not going to let us fail as long as we continue to have faith and believe, tell the world our story, and never give up.

That's also where we met Don Stoeltje. He was an executive for Blue Bell Ice Cream, and he donated ice cream for camp each year for many years. The kids just love Blue Bell. Thank you, Don, and thank you, Quail Valley (Missouri City) Exchange.

CASTING A LIGHT

They say that success is rarely a straight line, and we learned this the hard way.

I'd love to say that it got easier with each year to raise funds and that our fundraising has only gotten bigger and better each year, but the truth is it all fluctuates. One year we raised nearly $50k at our New Year's Eve event, the next it dropped back to $30k. Some years, we'll get a grant for $10k from a foundation, and the next year, they give us only $2,500, but then it goes back up to $10k two years later.

There's not always a rhyme or reason for it. We've just learned to trust God through the ups and downs and remember that He's always brought us what we need. If I'm being honest, what we NEED is usually not as much as what we WANT. I WANT someone to give a $100 million endowment to CKC, and then we could just sit back all year and only think about how many kids we're gonna help in the summer and for years to come, but what we actually NEED for each year is not nearly that much. I think it's good to always want more and keep searching for the next level that God has for us, but we're always thankful that He's provided for our needs.

So we never stop asking and never stop thanking. I often think about the scripture that says, "Which of you fathers, if your son asks for a fish, will give him a snake instead? Or if he asks for an egg, will give him a scorpion? If you then, though you are evil, know how to give good gifts to your children, how much more will your Father in heaven give the Holy Spirit to those who ask Him!" Luke 11:11-13 NIV.

That's the great thing. God will only give us good gifts, better than we could imagine. We just have to be patient and hold tight to the dreams He's given us.

Chapter Twenty-Five

Simple Gifts With A Big Impact

ONE YEAR IN 2008, WE RECEIVED an offer from the Lions Clubs of Texas to come rent their facility in Kerrville, Texas, aptly named the Texas Lions Camp. Our friends, Barron and Karen Cagle, had been "Lions" for years, and they loved what we did at CKC and were thrilled to make the connection. This was, and still is, a beautiful camp in the hill country of Texas, and they had all kinds of great activities and even special equipment to allow children with disabilities to ride horses, go on the ropes course, etc.

We had a great experience at the Lions Camp. The only hurdle for us was getting the children there. Since it was 5 hours from Houston, we had to rent buses, which became expensive quickly. We rented two big buses, but still had a handful of extra kids and volunteers left to get to Kerrville. We were thrilled when

Lindale Church offered the use of their mid-sized bus for us to use for the week so that we did not have to rent another large bus that would only be half full. On the way back from Kerrville, though, in that mid-sized bus, pretty much the worst thing that could happen during a Texas Summer happened: the AC went out.

If you've ever been in a car with your own children when it's really hot out and there's no AC, just multiply their reaction by 100, and that's about how well that went over with a bus full of kids. We felt so bad about it that we stopped halfway at a gas station and told each child that we would buy each one of them a drink and a snack, whatever they wanted (well, not coffee).

Now that's when something amazing happened that we did not expect. Those kids acted like we just offered them a million dollars apiece. They were so excited, in fact, we could only let six into the station at a time so as not to cause a riot. One little boy had five different drinks and even more snacks all laid out in front of him, joyously making his final decision. As each one finally made their choice, we would put down our card to pay for them, and without even prompting them, every single child gave us the biggest hug, and the most sincere thank you I've ever heard.

Well, here's the thing, we had just spent $500 per child (at least) to take them to camp that week, and yes, we had some amazing breakthroughs, but this was something else entirely. We spent somewhere between $5 and $7 per child, but got an enormous response. Don't they know camp costs so much more, and all the weeks and months we spent fundraising to pay for that, and don't they know that this was such a small gift in comparison? Well no, of course not! They're just kids, and all they knew in that moment is that we cared enough about them to spend our money to give them something to make them happy. Wow, it's really not rocket science, I guess. Show the kids you love them, and they'll respond. It's the same thing we do at camp, but on a microscopic, immediate level.

CONTEMPLATING CHRISTMAS

So in November of 2009, I was sitting at my desk at home in our dining room (turned CKC office) one day, and I started thinking about the upcoming Christmas season. I knew in my heart that so many of our campers weren't going to have the kind of Christmas most of us are used to and even take for granted. Over half of them were living in foster homes with up to six or seven other children, and I know with what their foster parents receive from the state to provide for their needs, there can't be much if anything leftover to buy presents.

I mulled over in my mind those little faces and recounted one occasion when we had to buy shoes for a little boy at camp who had to cut the toes out of his shoes in order to get his feet into them. When he got those beautiful new tennis shoes we had bought him, he put them on immediately and modeled them for Kim and me. As I thought of that boy, I started to cry. I must tell you that kids touch my heart, and I cry easily over them. Kim came through the room and when she saw me, she stopped and asked me what was wrong. I tearfully told her what I had been thinking of, and I said that I didn't want to have Christmas if these kids weren't going to have Christmas. She sat down beside me and we started to discuss the feasibility of being able to do something about it.

We not only wanted to help them have a Christmas, but thought if we could reinforce all the good things we put down in them during camp, and if we could multiply that impact by evoking the same reaction we got at the gas station that day, only with even better gifts than just a drink and a snack, man, we could really bond with them even more, so they know they've got CKC as a family now.

We had no budget after paying for camp that summer. Kim and I decided that instead of buying each other presents that year, we would buy presents for as many kids as we could. We started asking our Advisory Council and other close friends to do what they could to make this Christmas outing possible.

Then Kim and I, along with Billie Faye, picked campers that we knew were in a very difficult time in their lives or those whose parents/caregivers we knew were really struggling just to pay their bills. We set a date to meet those families at Target to let the kids pick out some presents. We had about 15 kids and we let them go shopping with a limit of $50 each.

They set about ranging through the toy section first before looking for clothes and shoes. Kim and I walked around watching as each kid looked up and down the toy aisles. We noticed this one boy who went to the girls' section. He was looking for girls' toys. Kim approached him and asked what he was looking for. He turned to her and told her that his two sisters were in separate foster homes, and he was going to use his $50 allotment to buy each of them a gift instead of spending any money on himself.

Kim's immediate response was, "No, you get them something, and then you get yourself something too." What an incredibly unselfish older brother thinking of his two baby sisters. It's that kind of giving spirit in children that blows me away and inspires me to keep working harder for them.

Christmas was a hit event for these kids who hadn't expected anything, and Kim and I determined that we should do this for the whole camp the next year somehow. The following year, we sent out a letter to our supporters and asked them to help us. We called our great pastors at Lindale Church, Randy and Jana Meeks, whose church is very centrally located off the 610 loop in Houston, and asked about using their gym for the event on a Saturday in December. They said "yes" enthusiastically. We sent out the letter, and within the next couple of weeks, the money started to come in. We just let our need be known as the Bible teaches, and the support started pouring in. We asked for everyone to "Adopt a Camper for Christmas" and send $50 for 1 "want" item (a toy) and 1 "need" item (clothes, shoes, etc.). Some sponsored one, and some sponsored many. It was amazing to see the heart people had for our kids, especially at Christmas time.

Kim Amongst All the Presents

Our Christmas party now goes a little bit like this. First, everyone gets their picture with Santa, portrayed by the conveniently white-bearded Associate Pastor of Lindale, Lyle Countryman (who in his wild and wooly days had played the part of Pontius Pilate in the original Broadway production of "Jesus Christ Superstar"). This picture is so significant because most of the families could never afford a professional photo session.

While everyone gathers and gets their pictures taken, we all have some cookies and punch generously provided by Holly Pryor and other volunteers.

Then, Pastor Lyle, dressed in his Santa suit that he purchased himself just for this occasion, gathers the kids in a circle around him and gives a short testimonial about what Christmas is all about. He tells the kids that Santa learned everything he knows from someone very special, Jesus (his wife, Lisa, now joins him as Mrs. Claus). After his words of love and wisdom, our elves (the Champs) start handing out the gifts. As each one receives his or her gifts they are asked to sit back down in the circle and wait for everyone else to receive their gifts. Then we do the long-awaited countdown, and everyone opens their presents at the same time. What a moment in time when they all tear into those packages at once and wrapping paper goes flying everywhere. The excitement and joy in that moment is overwhelming for those receiving and those of us who have given.

The Annual Christmas Party with CKC Campers Ready To Open Their Presents

We've streamlined it now so that at camp, the champs help their campers fill out wish lists, and then in November, we go shopping and wrap their presents. There's also a grab bag stocked with stuffed animals and small toys for the younger siblings of our campers so each one of them can come out with a present for themselves also. Everyone is happy, the music is going thanks to Pastor Jon Peña, and many games are being played simultaneously, and the kids are all happy to see each other again. What a wonderful time of the year, so fulfilling.

Chapter Twenty-Six

The Grand Ole Opry & Beyond

I MUST SAY I'M PRETTY PROUD OF myself for keeping my story on track so far. My family always accuses me of going on "rabbit trails" that take a story in a completely different direction. Of course, in a book, I have the added benefit of being able to go back and edit, which is something I wish I could do in real time when I'm talking.

Having said that, I need to skip back in time just a bit to right after we went to the Texas Lions Camp in 2008. We were looking for a new event that had larger fundraising potential, and we came up with the idea to hold a concert called "Legends 4 Kids" in Houston featuring Grand Ole Opry members. I called Ray Pillow again, and he loved the idea and got on board immediately.

Ray set it up for us to meet with Pete Fisher, VP and general manager of the Opry. Pete generously allowed us to use the

Opry name as such, "Legends 4 Kids featuring Stars of The Grand Ole Opry." A standard licensing fee for the Opry name would normally be cost-prohibitive, so we greatly appreciated him allowing us to couch it so integrally within our own name.

As we set up our committee for the event, once again, so many amazing friends stepped up to make it all possible. Judy B was first on board, then she helped bring on Kerry & Peggy Mazoch, and Gerald & Evelyn Franklin. Kerry & Gerald were both past national presidents of the Exchange Club, and since the Exchange Club's main outreach was and is the E.S.C.A.P.E. (Exchange Sponsored Child Abuse Prevention Effort) Center, it was decided that the proceeds from the event would be split on a 50/50 basis. Champions Kids Camp would receive 50% and the ESCAPE Center would receive 50%.

Melva Meronek, a longtime friend and one of our CKC Advisory Council members, agreed to be our Chairperson for the event, and she recruited her close friend, Deborah Dunkum, to become her co-chair. We were also amazingly fortunate that Martha Turner, one of the most respected and successful real estate entrepreneurs in Houston's history, agreed to be our Honorary Chairperson, and her company ended up donating all of our printing and postage. The committee also consisted of some of our other CKC advisory council members, Marc and Susan Schwartz, Kirby Lammers, Tony Ackerman, and our son, Jimmy.

Ray was also instrumental in contacting the first year's stars. We decided on Whisperin' Bill Anderson, who was gracious

enough to offer us a great price when we booked him and his band. We also had Lulu Roman of the famed TV Show, *Hee Haw*, and Ray Pillow himself guest starred. We called on my longtime friend, Mr. Dave Ward, anchor for Houston's ABC-Channel

Lulu Roman, Bill Nash, Ray Pillow, Bill Anderson, Martha Turner, Jimmy & Kim Nash at Legends 4 Kids 2009

13, to co-emcee with friends from the other two major network stations, CBS Channel 11's Deborah Duncan (who graciously invited us to appear and promote on her show, *Great Day Houston*), and NBC Channel 2's News Anchor, Lauren Freeman.

The show came off beautifully, and our crowd just loved seeing those Grand Ole Opry Stars. It was amazing to see just how much support we received from all the local news stations, our Houston audience, and even from the Opry itself. We made a nice profit for both charities that year even without major under-writers to cover expenses, and everyone on our committee was excited to look toward the future.

Nash3 Performing at L4K 2009

We held the Legends concert one more year after that, and we were looking for a star to headline our event. My son, Jimmy, saw that Larry Gatlin was coming to Houston to play at a supper club called Dosey Doe near the Woodlands, Texas. I hadn't spoken to Larry in a long time and didn't even have his number anymore, but at the urging of Jimmy, I dialed the number of the club to leave a message for Larry. I hung up the phone and thought, "Who knows if they'll even forward the message to Larry."

Within ten minutes my phone rang, and I hear Larry's voice say "Hey, Billy boy." Honestly, I was quite surprised. He was very glad to hear from me again, and after we reminisced for a good while, I asked if he and his brothers would consider being our stars at the next Legends concert?

He didn't stutter at all; he gave me an immediate "yes," and he even said he would perform for half the normal fee his booking agency, William Morris, was asking. He's never failed to be a great friend to me. He even agreed to do an interview with us in promotion of the event at his home in Austin.

Our good friend and videographer from Lakewood Church, Larry Westfall, traveled with us to Gatlin's home to film it all professionally. Larry Gatlin recalled things I didn't even remember about our families' history and how we had done a concert together in Ft. Worth with Roger McDuff, who was a mentor to Larry and me, and brought the house down.

Then Kim and Jimmy sang some harmony with Larry on a couple of his hit songs. They sounded wonderful together. I sat there and listened and enjoyed the whole thing. Thank you, Larry, God keeps good books.

That year, the Gatlin Brothers helped us pack out the big ballroom at the JW Marriot in Houston. It was certainly the largest event to date we had thrown for CKC. It took all of our resources, as well as all of the resources (and time) of our committee members to pull it together, but we more than doubled our profits for the charity from the first year. We would need to reassess after the event where to go next, but that event gave us lots of visibility in the community and a nice boost to our funds for the 2010 camp.

PHIL EVERLY

In 2009, we (Nash3) were performing at a church near Gulf Shores, Alabama. I was talking to our friend and co-writer, A.J. Masters, one day and mentioned we were headed down that way. He said, "I'm gonna be in Gulf Shores that same week writing with Phil Everly at his house there. Why don't you guys come on by?" Well, we all loved the Everly Brothers, and had always patterned our harmonies after theirs, so of course we jumped at the opportunity to go to Phil's house. I had only met him once before that time when Kristofferson had invited me to sing with him on the *Phil Everly Show* in L.A., but I'd never just been able to sit and talk with him.

So we go to Phil's house with A.J., right on the beach in Gulf Shores. Phil's wife, Patti, prepared an amazing spread for us, and they were both so welcoming. As the day went on, inevitably, we all start playing some music (as songwriters do). We had been singing "Let It Be Me" for years, which was a big hit for the Everly Brothers, and decided to sing our arrangement in 3-part harmony for Phil. As we sang, Phil began to cry. When we finished, he said, "I wish my family could be like yours." He and his brother, Don, had a falling out years before, and I guess hearing us all as a family got those feelings stirred up. He even asked us to sing the song again, which we happily did. Then we decided to play one of the Everly Brothers' hits that we knew Phil had written, "When Will I Be Loved," with Kim on lead, and Jimmy and I put our harmony behind it. Phil just loved it, and asked if we would record that for him. What? Phil Everly wants us to record his song? Not only that, he said he'd pay for a 4-song

session in Nashville, and then we could record three other songs of our choosing, and we could own the masters.

As we talked, we realized that it was actually, almost to the week, the 50th anniversary of the release of "When Will I Be Loved." Phil asked A.J. to produce

Nash3 In Studio with Phil Everly

the session on us, and it was A.J.'s idea to produce it as a ballad. When he suggested this, Phil said, "I originally wrote it as a ballad, but it's never been done that way before." How amazing that we would now get to record Phil's song in the way that he originally intended. We recorded it a couple months later, and we also shot a music video in the studio with Phil playing guitar along with us, which you can see on our YouTube. They say you should never meet your heroes, but I'd say Phil was certainly an exception to that. He was so talented, but so humble. When we talked about how much we loved that Everly Brothers sound, he responded, "Well I was just the backup singer," and he truly thought of himself that way.

One last note to give you an idea of Phil's humor, and what a likeable guy he was: Phil and Patti had one of the most massive dogs I've ever seen, known as an Akita. His head was the size of a bear's head just about. We asked Phil about the dog, and he said "Well, Patti wanted a large dog, and I wanted no dogs, so we compromised and got a large

Jimmy with Phil Everly's Akita

dog." What a great time that was. Thank you Phil and thank you A.J., R.I.P. both of you wonderful people.

AN ODE TO MY MOTHER

My mother and I always had a special relationship since I was a boy. It started with the love of music that she instilled in me from a young age. Then later, once my brother was drafted, we traveled and sang together so much just the two of us. We were always close friends, as well as mother and son, and I was blessed to have her for years after my father passed.

I always feel that I got my "drive" from her. She never quit moving, always starting a new project all the way up until the end. When she was in her late 80s, she told me she was going to start playing for the "old folks" at the retirement home. I don't think it even occurred to her that she was older than any of them. She was still in good health minus a couple knee operations and able to live mostly on her own, except when she would need a ride or some help with certain things around the house. She loved going to play piano and sing for anyone who would listen.

Bill, Clara, and David Nash - 1961

To give you just a little more idea about what kind of woman my mother is, here was her last project she started. She was around 80 when she began thinking about all the kids on the border. Her family had a missionary effort in Reynosa, Mexico for many years and still ministered to the needs of the people just over the Mexican border. Not unlike how we were feeling about our kids at camp, she was thinking how most of those kids down there probably didn't have much of a Christmas, and she wanted to do something about it.

Now, I don't know what gave her the idea to do this, except that she still had that mindset from coming through the great depression of never wasting anything, but her solution was toilet cores! Yes, the little cardboard core that is leftover when you're through with a roll of toilet paper. She decided that she could take those, fill them with hard candy (that wouldn't melt) and then wrap them with Christmas wrapping paper, and then all those kids would have something fun and sweet to open.

The first year she did it all on her own. She started telling people to save all their toilet cores and bring them to her, and naturally they all did. If you knew my mom at all, you know that you don't tell her "no." Sitting there by herself at her table in Spring, Texas at 80 years old, she made up 2,000 "presents" for the children on the border. Her pastor, Bill Hamlin, took them down in a van and dropped them off to be distributed by pastors in Mexico to the children there. She called it her "toilet core ministry," although later altered it to her "candy core ministry," which sounded a little more palatable.

Pretty soon, the word got around, and some of her friends at the church wanted in. Once she got a few friends together, they were able to do several thousand more. Later, she downsized from her home that Daddy left to her to a smaller, more manageable townhome in a retirement community. This was not an assisted-living facility, but everyone became like family there, checking up on each other, going to lunch, and meeting in the community center. Well, this streamlined the whole process. Pretty soon, she had quite the efficient operation. I visited one day, and she had no less than 10 volunteers on an assembly line of sorts in the community center. They even expanded from just toilet cores, to using the cardboard tubes at the end of the rolls of wrapping paper. Why not? They were already using the paper, so you wouldn't want to waste that roll. She had one volunteer who was just in charge of using the "guillotine" to chop that big roll into several smaller rolls to be filled.

Over 16 years, she and her team made and distributed over 1 million "candy cores" to all the children on the border, averaging over 130,000 per year. Mom was truly in the ministry right up to her dying day.

On that note, even as she was on her way out to the next life, she still caused quite a stir. About two months before her 95th birthday (around December of 2009), Mom had been hospitalized and actually did die right then and there. The doctors resuscitated her, even though her chart said DNR (do not resuscitate), which is not unusual for someone to have on their chart at that age when they are likely to pass from natural causes. So after that, all of us in the family came to visit her, and she told us her side of the story.

She said that when she died, she was in Heaven immediately, but she told God He had to send her back because she was having too much fun and wanted to make it to her 95th birthday and have a big party with all her friends! Well, I don't know for sure if that's word-for-word how it went down (she may have embellished a bit), but knowing mother, I certainly wouldn't doubt it either. No matter what, though, we had her for another three months after that. She was in hospice care in her home, but we went on and had her birthday party anyways in the community center, and friends would come in and out of her place a few at a time to give their best wishes. Luckily, her place was the closest unit to the center, and Jimmy was even able to run about 200 feet of speaker cable so she could have a speaker in her house to hear everything that was going on at her party.

So as per her wishes, Mom made it all the way to 95, got to say goodbye to all her friends and family at a big party, and then passed peacefully of natural causes a few weeks later. She certainly knew how to set a goal and attain it, from getting us to New York and ultimately landing us on a major label, to even orchestrating the exact way she wanted to go out. As Daddy used to say, "she sure is a pistol, ain't she?" That she was, and I know she's up there with Daddy now. I sure do miss them both, but so excited that one day I get to go to them.

Bill with Mother, Clara, and Sisters, Alice and Ellen - New Year's 2007

The last few days in hospice care, it was getting harder and harder for Mom to speak. Before she lost the ability to speak altogether, though, she motioned for me to come closer, and then she said the last words she ever spoke to me, "I'm so proud of you." I still tear up just thinking about it. I know not everybody gets that experience with their parents, and that's why I'm so thankful for it. If you're reading this and you're a parent, even if you've had cross-words with your kids over the years, I encourage you to keep trying to make things right. My mother giving me those final, loving words was a gift, and one every parent should try to give their children.

YOU CAN'T SAY LOVE ENOUGH

We happened through Nashville around early 2009, and I stopped by Johnny Morris' office to say hi to a couple friends who I knew were still there. Dennis Money operated the studio downstairs, and when I came in, he said "Hey Bill, I recorded some of your songs the other day." He explained that there were twin sisters named Mollie and Jackie, and they were looking for some material, and they liked several of our songs that were in Johnny's catalog that they ended up recording with Dennis. One of them was "You Can't Say Love Enough." Kim and I were thrilled to have some new life for a few of our songs, and it was

also interesting that they just happened to be Wayne Newton's goddaughters.

So we left and just told him to keep us up-to-date as they plan to release etc., and we were excited to see what happens. It wasn't even a couple months later that Kim, Jimmy, and I were invited to play a couple shows on the different stages at the Houston Livestock Show and Rodeo, and who was the special guest that night who kicked

Nash3 Playing the 2009 HLSR Cookoff

off the opening ceremonies? Well, it was Wayne Newton, of all people.

One of our friends invited us to the suite where Wayne would end up after he kicked things off for the rodeo. As we got to talking to Wayne, I mentioned, "Oh, your goddaughters just recorded a few of our songs." He looked really perplexed, and then shortly after he was pulled away and we didn't get to finish our conversation. The next day, though, I get a call from Dennis Money saying, "Bill, you let the cat out of the bag!" Well, what Dennis didn't mention to me before is they were planning to surprise Wayne with their new recordings. He didn't think to mention it to me because what are the odds that I would just run into Wayne Newton? Furthermore, what are the odds of all those things lining up, that I should just happen into Johnny's office, happen to see Dennis, Wayne's goddaughters just happened to

Nash3 with Wayne Newton at the Houston Livestock Show and Rodeo 2009

be recording our material, and we just happened to be performing at the same place Wayne would be so shortly after? I can't really do the math on that, but those have got to be some pretty slim odds.

Anyway, though, it all turned out fine. Not only that, but Mollie and Jackie ended up making "You Can't Say Love Enough" a song to raise funds for the Juvenile Diabetes Association due to the fact that Mollie was born with Juvenile Diabetes. So they asked their godfather to sing on it along with 16 other celebrities and gave it a "We Are The World" kind of treatment where everyone sings a line or two and then together on the chorus. That list of stars included Wayne himself, along with Lee Greenwood, my old pals Larry Gatlin and Mickey Gilley, and no offense to anyone else on the list, my favorite addition, Dolly Parton. Yes, Dolly Parton! I can't tell you how thrilled I was that she was a part of it. Ever since I met her when I was 23 years old, I dreamed of her singing a song I'd written. Even if it was a few lines of a larger ensemble, it was a huge honor to me for her to sing her part on "You Can't Say Love Enough."

This is also a great example to me of how a song never dies. By this point, the song had been on hold several times, but never cut. We put it on the first album that we did with Jimmy when he was 16, and Jimmy Nichols had helped me out by recording it at his house with us, and we paid him as we could. As we started to sell those CDs at various places we played, we'd even receive several praise reports from people who had bought our album with the song on it, and it helped them work through the issues they had with other family members just by telling them they loved them again and again until they worked everything out. Love's a powerful thing, and it doesn't make sense to our physical minds sometimes how it can overcome huge obstacles, but it really can. That's why we kept (and keep) singing it, because you really "Can't Say Love Enough." I'm so glad that the song ultimately got picked up, and the message got sent out to such a larger audience. Who knows? It may get picked up again in the future by someone else. I think it's one message that should keep on going.

CASTING A LIGHT

We came up with a saying between us that says, "Time's Never Wasted." As I look back, there's very little in my life, from the good times to the bad times, that hasn't in some way prepared me for what's next. I grew up broke on the Mexican border, but that's where I learned to speak Spanish, which has been invaluable to me over the years. We went through incredible trauma with Billy's Leukemia diagnosis, but that also brought about a miracle that inspired us to start our charity. We went through the ringer for years on and off major record labels and publishers, but now my friends from those times--from Larry Gatlin, to Ray Pillow, Johnny Lee, and more--all help me to raise funds for Champions Kids Camp.

No one thing in life is just that one thing. It all leads to something else, so no piece of your life is ever wasted. If we could see all of our life at one time, as God can, I know we would not get so downtrodden from one bad blow. Sometimes, we don't know what the silver lining is for years to come, but I hope you find encouragement from my story, and maybe start to see more of the silver linings in your own life.

Chapter Twenty-Seven

New Adventures and New Names

LOOKING BACK IN THE BIBLE, GOD often changed people's names when they were about to embark on a new phase of their lives. Abram was changed to Abraham, Jacob was changed to Israel, and for Kim and I, our names were about to be changed to Grandma and Grandpa.

Our son, Billy, moved to Houston about a year after we did and ended up going to the University of Houston, my alma mater, where he graduated. In Houston, he met a beautiful girl named Sarah Faber, and on May 17, 2008, they were married. Then, one night in spring of 2010 (right after our second Legends 4 Kids), they showed up at our house unannounced with amazing news! When Kim and I found out we were going to be grandparents, a new kind of joy came alive inside us that only anyone who is a grandparent could understand.

As we were approaching our New Year's Eve event that year, we started getting pretty nervous. Not for any possible complications with the pregnancy, but for the simple fact that if Sarah went into labor on New Year's Eve itself, well, I don't know who would have run the event or performed, because I guarantee you Kim and I would have been out of there. Thankfully, on December 29th, 2010, we welcomed Addison Faith Nash into our world. We were still pretty distracted at

the fundraiser 2 days later, but man, what a great way to ring in the New Year.

Bill & Kim with New Grandbaby, Addison

As Addison got old enough to talk, we were then renamed "Mimi" and "PawPaw." I don't think I've ever enjoyed being called something as much as I love hearing that sweet little voice calling me PawPaw.

Down the road, on Jan 23, 2015, Billy and

Bill & Kim with Mason

Sarah blessed us with our second grandbaby, Mason James Nash. Kim and I were thrilled to have one of each now, a granddaughter and a grandson. Of course, they love their PawPaw the most (Kim might disagree). We spend every second we can with them and treasure every moment, because we know just how fast they grow up. Every

Billy, Mason, Sarah, & Addison Nash

morning and every night, we thank God for Addison and Mason.

HEAVEN IS REAL

One day in 2010, another new project came about (wow, what a busy year!). I was catching up with Chris Piper, who worked for John and Gina Manlove who had donated our Champions Kids

Camp brochures that first year, and they later again donated brochures when we reordered them with pictures of our actual camp the second time around. Chris had also designed our logo for Building Bridges of Hope, as well, and I was just checking in to see how he was doing. He told me that he was leaving the Manloves' company to go on the road with his dad. I said, "Well, who is your dad?"

He proceeded to tell me that his dad was Don Piper, and he had written a book called *90 Minutes In Heaven*. Well, at this time, that book had sold over 6 million copies, so of course I'd heard of it, but I had no idea that Don was Chris' father.

For those of you not familiar with the book, first off, I highly recommend it. Secondly, here's the long and short of it: Don was a pastor, and he was in a terrible car accident with a semi-truck on a bridge. He was killed instantly, and declared dead by 4 different paramedic teams that had all arrived on the scene at the same time. There was another man, also a pastor, several cars back that was now stuck in the traffic jam on the bridge. He ran up to the police and told them that God had told him to pray for this man in the red car. The officers thought he was crazy, because Don was clearly dead, and they'd already covered him with a tarp. This pastor was so insistent, though, so they finally let him through since he couldn't really do any more harm. He pulled the tarp off, and climbed in the back seat, and prayed and prayed. When he ran out of prayer, he started singing. After 90 minutes, the dead man in the car started singing along when he got to "What A Friend We Have In Jesus." He was alive! It was impossible, completely impossible according to all laws of nature. It was thoroughly documented that he was dead for those 90 minutes, and undeniable that he's now alive. It can only be called a miracle.

In the book, Don tells about the 90 minutes he spent in heaven, and the wonders he saw, as well as the struggle coming back to earth, and the rehabilitation with his badly damaged body. It's an amazingly inspiring story, and one that I have read multiple times.

So Chris said his dad was coming out with his next book called *Heaven Is Real*. As we talked, I said something to the effect of, "Hey, that would make a great song title." We talked a little more about it, and Chris was very interested in us writing some music to go along with his dad's story. We all met, Nash3 that is, with Chris and Don, and we agreed to make an album, also entitled "Heaven Is Real," that could be sold alongside the book that would benefit both our ministries. As the project started to take form, we ended up writing Don's story in a song called "I've Been There."

That year, 2010 leading into 2011, we traveled with Don to several bookings. We would kick off the event or service with our music, and then Don would tell his story. They were amazingly powerful events, and I never got tired of hearing Don's testimony about Heaven. Hope, that's what it

Nash3 with Don, Eva, and Chris Piper - 2010

was all about. Don's story gave people hope for this life and the next from a first-person perspective as someone who has been to Heaven and back. We were very proud to be included in his ministry in such a way, and it was an honor to write his story in song.

EVERYTHING COMES FULL CIRCLE OR FROM TRIO TO SOLO TO DUO TO TRIO TO DUO

In my life, I've performed on stage in all kinds of configurations. Starting out as the Nash Family Trio with my mother and brother, then going off as a solo act for many years, then becoming a duo with Kim, which was way more fun, and then becoming a trio again with our son, Jimmy. When Jimmy was very young, starting about 8, he would get up and sing lead on a song or two with us, but as he got older, and especially once we started playing extensively in Houston, we became a full-fledged family harmony group. It was a great thrill to sing with Kim and Jimmy both as we would harmonize on our own original songs as well as classic Country & Gospel songs. One of my greatest memories is of the three of us singing the National Anthem at a Houston Astros game.

Life inevitably has to change, though, and as Jimmy got into his 20s, we knew he couldn't perform with us forever (although his Mama wouldn't have minded). We weren't quite sure what was next for Jimmy, but only God could have orchestrated what was to come.

Nash Note 🎵

Our son, Billy, also briefly played guitar with us when he was about 10. I taught him one solo on "Will The Circle Be Unbroken," and that was his big moment. He quickly became more interested in golf though, and we lost our guitar player.

For a couple of years, we had become involved with the Homes For Our Troops organization. We ended up writing their theme song, and while singing at one of their fundraisers, we met someone named Jeanie who volunteered her time to do press for HFOT. She really liked our music, and she took a few of our CDs and said she had someone she wanted to send them to. As it turns out, the person she sent the music to was Andra Dalto, who had managed Hank III (grandson of Hank Williams, son of Hank Jr.) for six years. Jeanie had done some press for Hank, and that's how she had gotten to know Andra.

Andra was looking to take on a new client, and after a couple calls, we flew her in to meet us and come hear us perform live at a couple venues. It happened to be that time of year for the cook-off, so she was able to hear us play with our live band there Friday night, and then we were booked the next night in Madisonville, Texas (home of the great Buc-ee's almost halfway to Dallas) to play in their high school auditorium.

We all had lunch that Saturday afternoon to get her thoughts on our music and what we could do together. She was very honest and said she wasn't sure what to do with us as a trio, but really thought Jimmy could do something great on his own. Well, we knew that day would have to come eventually, and even though we'd be sad not to perform with him, we were excited for him to have an opportunity to work with an established manager on his solo career.

So we played that Saturday night, and then we all headed back home. The next week, Jimmy flew down to meet her at her home in Hillsboro Beach, Florida, just north of Ft. Lauderdale. She suggested that Jimmy work with her friend, Todd Hannigan, in Ojai, California, who had produced the amazingly successful early Jack Johnson albums. She felt Todd would be a great influence on Jimmy's music. It was something far outside of the Country and Gospel he was raised with, and she knew it could help break open a whole new world of music for him, and that it did. Jimmy was still playing a few gigs with us in Houston over that summer, but after a few trips back and forth to California, he and Andra decided it was time to move out to L.A. to pursue his career.

Then around February of 2012, they let us know things had gone a little past just business, and they were now dating, and you can probably see where this is going. On April 20th of 2013, we welcomed our new daughter-in-law into our family. I even presided over the wedding ceremony as the fully licensed minister that I am. It can be hard in this business to find someone who really "gets" you and understands writing and rehearsals and touring etc. That's how it was for me until I found Kim. As I got to know Andra and got to see the two of them together, I knew that they really "got" each other. We're proud to have Andra in the family now, and proud of all that

Jimmy & Andra - 2018

she and Jimmy have done together since they met. That would take a whole other book to tell you about all that, so you should just go follow Jimmy online, and that will save me 100 pages of typing or so.

So this meant that Kim and I were down from Nash3 to Nash2, or Nash and Nash, or just Bill and Kim Nash, as we usually go by. Even though sometimes we miss that third part on our sound (which is only natural), if you've learned anything from my story, you know that I never stop singing, and we still travel and play extensively.

TEXAS BEST MUSIC FEST

Not long after Jimmy moved to L.A., we started a new endeavor. We had taken a couple years off from doing such a large fundraiser like the Legends 4 Kids concerts. They were successful, but also took a lot of time to create and a lot of money just to rent the venues as well as pay for the acts. We knew we wanted to do something else great with music to raise funds for CKC, but weren't sure what that would be yet.

In 2012, though, I was speaking with a new friend, Jim Hatfield, who managed one of the large car dealerships in town. He mentioned how they had cleared all the cars off the lot one year, and had a big concert, and they would be willing to do that for us at no charge and even put up the money for some of the other costs like security, portable restrooms, printing and advertising. What a deal! Who could turn that down?

So we put together a wonderful committee, and decided to make this new concert all about the great Texas Music we have right in our own backyard. One of our committee members, Bob Boblitt, mentioned that he had a good friend named Jeff Tritter, who had a similar vision, but whose life was taken far too soon by cancer. He said his friend had already coined the name, "Texas Best Music Fest," and he felt like Jeff would be honored for us to use it and continue on with that vision.

Bill & Kim with Troy Nehls, & TBMF Chairperson, Melva Meronek. Photo Credit: Kelley Sweet Jensen

Everyone agreed, and in the spring of 2013, we had the first ever Texas Best Music Fest. My old buddy, Johnny Lee, agreed to headline for us. Johnny had a huge #1 hit with "Lookin' For Love" because of it being in the movie, *Urban Cowboy*, and the fans (especially in Texas) never seem to tire of hearing it. He said he'd only charge me a dollar, but he'd donate it right back. Sure enough, he did. We had quite a few acts and made it an all-day concert, ending with Johnny. We raised around $46,000 that first year, which everyone considered a success, and we started looking toward the next year.

Then, Bob Boblitt told me that for the next fundraising event, he would be willing to underwrite the cost of our entertainment, and he also had an idea for a different venue more conducive to a concert. His idea was to use the next few years to create awareness of CKC by drawing bigger crowds with marquis acts. He also got us into Warehouse Live in Downtown Houston for a fraction of the regular rental costs, and he underwrote most of those costs anyway. It definitely makes it easier having a concert in a music

Cody Bryan, Billy, Bill, Jimmy, & Kim Nash, Kyrstin & Bob Boblitt at TBMF 2016

venue since they have so much of the equipment already set up, and all the permits, etc.

The plan really worked, and we had great acts like Roger Creager, Reckless Kelly, and Turnpike Troubadours at Warehouse Live. The 4th year, through Bob's relationships in the beer industry, we switched venues to Karbach Brewing Company, who generously donated the use of their property, and with Josh Abbott Band as our headliners, we had our first ever 6-figure fundraiser! We raised just over $100,000 that year. Josh himself even donated back $5,000 of his already deeply discounted charity rate that year. What an incredible night that was!

It's amazing how long it can take to build a charity organization up to that point, but I think largely, people just want to make sure you're serious and are here to stay.

TBMF 2016 at Karbach Brewing Co. Photo Credit: L Frederick Hinojosa

Those first few years, they don't know if you're going to stick

around, or if you're even effective at what you're doing. Who can blame them? We didn't even know if we would be effective until we just kept doing it and getting better at it. Now that we have a

Larry Gatlin Bantering with Bill On Stage At TBMF 2018 at Mo's Place

nearly 20-year track record, it's a lot easier to show our impact and give the people a reason to support and get involved. As we've heard it said, "Where there is vision, there is provision." We had the vision for a long time, and the provision has increased as

we have stuck with it. Thank goodness it has, because our number of kids has grown exponentially!

As of the writing of this book, we're now holding the annual Texas Best Music Fest (TBMF) at Mo's Place in Katy, Texas. Mo has become a big supporter of our cause and graciously lets us have the run of the place, and we'll keep coming back as long as he will have us. We even wrote him a theme song (imagine that!).

Mo with Houston Anchor, Dominique Sachse at TBMF 2019 - Photo Credit: Kelley Sweet Jensen

Chapter Twenty-Eight

What's Happening Now

I WAS ABOUT TO CLOSE OUT THIS book, but realized I would be remiss not to give you at least as current as is possible of a status update on my life, and our camp, and so on.

Well, I'm happily retired, not really doing much, and just sitting back eating ice cream in my pajamas.

Okay, if you bought that, as the song says, "I've got some oceanfront property in Arizona."

I'm 75 as of the writing of this book, and I'm just as busy as ever. Much like my mother, I can't really sit still too long, and why should I? There's so much to do in this short life, and I'm just getting started.

Kim and I are still singing and spreading the word about our camp everywhere we can. For a few years, we didn't really have a lot of time to focus on writing as camp grew, but just recently, we wrote several new Country songs with Jimmy that we demo'd, and our friends, Tom & Kristi Harrison, who own Three Hounds Music in Nashville, are pitching right now. So we're very excited about those songs. Always exciting to have new music, because every new song is a new possibility.

As for Champions Kids Camp, we held our 19th annual camp this summer. That means, we'll be looking at our 20th Anniversary in the summer of 2021! Time really flies, and we've developed quite an amazing family, and I do mean family, of dedicated volunteers and former campers and people of all walks of life who have helped us build this into what it is today. For many years now, we've had over 200 children per camp, and thousands of children have come through our program, but that's only the beginning.

As I mentioned before, many former campers have been with us since they were eight to nine years old and we've had the privilege of watching them grow up and become our best leaders at camp. We are growing the camp and expanding what we can offer the children, including scholarships to attend college. In fact, in 2016, our first, full four-year scholarship was donated by Advisory Council members Dr. Sam and Mrs. McManus. This is just one of the examples of what we envision for the future of CKC and the children that participate in our program.

Billy Nash Giving a Bear to a Child in Treatment

Recently, we added our "Bears That Care" campaign to what we do for kids. We ask for a $50-100 donation to Champions Kids Camp for a teddy bear. The twist is, however, the person making the donation gives the bear back to us to be given to a child fighting for his/her life at Texas Children's Hospital.

After making the donation, we have them sign the tag on the bear's ear and hug the bear. We pass that little stuffed animal to a sick child. The idea being that this child is comforted by this soft and cuddly little bear that helps them by reducing stress and thus allowing the medicine to work better. It's a win-win situation and so rewarding to us to meet these kids. They are all then invited to our camp, free of charge, when they are done with their treatment.

If you live in the Houston area, or ever happen through, we'd love to have you come see more of what we do at camp. We also have our annual fundraisers, and we are always looking for volunteers, attendees, sponsors etc. My sister, Ellen, still holds her BBQ cook-off in Spring, Texas either the last

Kirby Lammers, Kim, Sarah, & Bill Nash Delivering Bags of Bears to TCH

weekend of April, or first weekend of May (the same weekend as the Kentucky Derby). Our annual Texas Best Music Fest is in June. We now have a golf tournament in September that's been growing exceedingly well the last three or four years. Lastly, we have our Nash New Year's Eve Bash that's held on...well, New Year's Eve.

I wanted to share more of the amazing stories, testimonies, and successes we've had at Champions Kids Camp, and there were just so many to share from so many years that it became difficult to insert them in a biographical, chronological order. So, instead of putting them all in the body of this book, we decided to group these stories of CKC together at the end of this book. Even though they are in the "postface" so to speak, of my story, I do believe these stories represent my true "life's work" (mine and Kim's to be more accurate), more than any song or major label deal or anything else I've ever done. If you take the time to read through these amazing testimonies, I promise you'll find hope and inspiration from them, the same way we do.

Did I leave anything out? Oh yes, did I mention we still love spending every minute we can with our grandkids?

CONTINUING TO EXPECT THE UNEXPECTED

So for the last time in this book, I'm going to ask, what's next?

Well, for me, I know the Good Book says that a man with no dream shall perish. God has never failed to show me new and bigger dreams to pursue and strive for.

I dream of building our own facility for Champions Kids Camp so we don't have to rent anymore, and we can also have other events for the kids throughout the year and host other organizations with worthy causes as well. This will require more than I've ever raised, along with land, personnel, and who knows what other surprises, but still, God owns the cattle on a thousand hills (not just the cattle, but the hills as well). So surely, I can have enough faith for just a little plot of land for our CKC kids.

I still would like to have a song we've written and/or sung go #1. We came close with Reba with a number 1 album, but we were just a couple slots away for our song. My happiness in life is no longer dependent on being famous or having the biggest hits, and man, am I glad to be free of that mindset, but

Bill & Kim Looking Toward A Bright Future

it certainly wouldn't make me sad to have a song top the charts.

Am I crazy to have these dreams at 75? Well, sure, but that's never stopped me before. Was it crazy to think we'd get a top 10 hit by Reba on a multi-platinum album as newly unsigned writers just by dropping a tape in a basket? Was it crazy that we got another cut after leaving Nashville, because of an old friend at a Waffle House pitch session? Was it crazy to start a children's charity at all, much less without having ever run a charity before?

Faith always looks crazy from the outside, because it tells us to look at something other than the facts, the odds, the "reality" of the situation. I've learned that God has the final say on what is possible, and even if I achieve half of what I set out to do, that's much more than if I just gave up now, plus, it keeps me moving on to the next thing, and you never know what's around each corner.

One thing's for sure, wherever I go, God/Jesus will be there, and as long as I've got breath in my body, I'll keep singing.

Postface

Stories From Champions Kids Camp

OUR AGE RANGE FOR CAMP IS 8 to 12 year olds, all of whom have survived an accident, injury or personal loss (some kind of trauma). We have them for a week in the summertime when school is out, and so many wonderful things go on at camp to help these kids rebuild their lives and become a kid again.

It's an incredible metamorphosis from what our Camp Supervisor and Advisory Council member, Kirby Lammers, calls "chin on chest" to "head held high."

When the kids arrive on Sunday afternoon for check-in, they don't know what to expect, and in light of what's happened in their lives in the past, they are very apprehensive and a bit nervous. Our camp counselors, or "champs" as we call them, become the kids' best friend, and he or she also becomes a mentor in whom these kids can depend on at camp like a big

brother or big sister. It is a heart-warming thing to watch as we all become a big family over that week.

At camp, the kids call me Uncle Bill and they call Kim, Aunt Kim, and we love it. That's what I call a real-life honor, to have an 8 to 12-year-

A Few of Our Fantastic Champs

old who never knew us before now want to become a part of our CKC family. There's no amount of money or fame that can rival the feelings those kids evoke in our hearts. That one week has been a life-changing event for the

Our Valued Volunteer Staff: Bob Linzer, Earl & Holly Pryor, Amy Frankhauser, Bill "Doc" Adams, Lisette & Kirby Lammers, Bill, Kim & Jimmy Nash, Ellen Cole

kids who have attended our camp. One week for many of our kids turns into multiple years in which they are a part of camp each summer, receive birthday cards from CKC, and attend our annual Christmas party.

Here are just a handful of the amazing experiences we've witnessed at camp.

THE STORY OF BILLY

There was an 11-year-old boy named Billy one year at camp who really was not interested in anything. We didn't know a lot about him from his file, except that he had lost his mother. During rally time, he would sit at the back and hold his ears. During go-karts, he would just sit over on a bench. At swim time, he wouldn't even change into his swimming suit.

One day, we were teaching a class on music and how to write a song. He said to one of us with complete sincerity, "I'm sure this would be interesting if I liked music." It was actually very humorous, and well thought out how he put that, but this little boy presented a new challenge to us. He wasn't acting up or causing trouble. We realized he was actually extremely intelligent, likely with a much higher IQ than the average person. He had just lost his desire for anything in life, and children that intelligent often feel more isolated because they don't relate to other children, which was one of the main ways our kids get to heal at camp, relating to other children like them.

Arts & Crafts with Brenda Robinson, a Long-time Supporter and Volunteer

He also said that his dad had told him that if he couldn't do something perfectly, that he shouldn't do it at all. Now, I'm not holding anything bad against his father. For all I know, he may have said it differently, and just meant to encourage his son to do his best. However he meant it, though, Billy took it as a reason to just stop trying to do anything. That mindset, coupled with the trauma he had experienced, made him incredibly difficult to reach. Unlike most of our other children, he didn't have that moment two or three days in where he naturally opened up.

So when nothing's working...well, you have to try something else, anything else. It's up to us to find what works to help these kids, not just the easy cases, but especially the hard ones. In this

Kirby with a Camper at CKC 2017

case, our friend and camp supervisor, Kirby Lammers, made it his personal mission to reach Billy that week. Thankfully, Kirby figured out that Billy really loved playing ping-pong. There was a ping-pong table in the cafeteria, and when Billy would get put off by the loud music during rally time, Kirby would take him right outside the doors into the cafeteria and play a game of ping-pong.

They played for hours that week, but what Billy didn't realize is that while he was playing, he was also talking to Kirby nonstop. While he talked, Kirby got to know more about him and talk to him in easy conversation, instead of sitting him down and trying to get him to open up in a "counselor-style" setting. During this time, Kirby was able to tell him how great he was, how smart he was, how he could do anything, and just filled him full of positive encouragement.

The rest of the week, Billy had a noticeable improvement in his overall response to us, but he still wasn't really participating in a whole lot more than ping-pong with Kirby. Finally though, Friday rolled around, the very last day of camp. We had all stopped even trying to get Billy to do the activities, because we had surmised that he wouldn't do anything unless it was his idea. To our amazement, Billy stepped into line to suit up to go down the zip line. He was in our son, Jimmy's group, so Jimmy notified Kirby, and Kirby got in his golf cart and got all the rest of the camp leaders ready so we could watch and see, just hoping Billy would really go down the zip line.

We didn't dare go anywhere near Billy or try to talk to him before he went up, for fear that he would change his mind. One

by one, though, he made it up each step of that 40 ft spiral staircase. We watched as he got locked on to his line and sat down at the top of that deck, just waiting to go down. It's

"Aunt Bee," Marc Schwartz, Amy Frankhauser, Bill & Kim Nash, Susan Schwartz, Sue Lockwood, Kandi, Kirby & Lisette Lammers, Mike & Jackie Reichek

not a guarantee that a child will go down the zip line just because they climbed up to the top. In fact, about 20% of them get too scared and climb back down the stairs. However, when the zip line operator gave the all clear, Billy was the first one off the line!

We all cheered him on from the ground like we had just won the Super Bowl! When Billy came down off the zip line, Kirby gave him a high five and asked him what he thought, and without hesitation, Billy said, "I wanna go again!" That was the first time we saw him smile all week. It was the very last day, but we did it, we got through to him. Those moments stick with a child like that. They stick with us adults, too.

THE STORY OF JORDAN

Jordan was a little boy who had been in a horrific car accident where his stepfather was killed, and he had extensive injuries including brain damage. He was having to learn to walk, talk, eat, and everything else all over again. He had been in the Texas Institute of Research and Rehabilitation (TIRR), and the physical therapy was exhausting, I'm sure. However, when his mom applied for him to come to camp, she said he was fully functional and would be able to do all the things we had for the kids to enjoy at camp like go-carts, water slide, Olympic swimming pool, zip line, and so on. His mother actually worked for one of our good friends and CKC supporters, Marjorie Evans. Marjorie thought camp would be helpful in Jordan's recovery, and she made a donation to sponsor him to camp that year (all children are accepted free of charge regardless, but donors often sponsor specific children to cover our costs at camp).

That Sunday at check-in when Jordan and his mom arrived, Kim and I saw her exit the car and get the walker out for Jordan to use. He was helped out of the car and entered the check-in building on his walker. Our hearts skipped a beat and we, along with our whole check-in crew, wondered whether he was really ready for a camp like ours that is so physically active. We were only equipped to help children with emotional trauma, not physical trauma, which can be much more entailed and specific to each individual's needs. We were worried that if he couldn't participate in all the activities with the other kids, it would only serve to discourage him further.

We went over and visited with the mom, and she told us that Jordan's doctors gave their approval for him to participate. It seems as though he had reached a place that he really could do more, physically, but just needed a situation to motivate him to do so. Kim and I introduced ourselves and talked with Jordan and noticed that his speech was still a struggle for him. Kim and

I and our whole CKC team all felt that we really needed to pray for this child and ask God to make this a positive experience for him.

Jordan was a sweet kid, but he still had difficulties doing things like holding his fork to eat, brushing his teeth, showering, etc. on his own. Our Champs seemed to rally around him immediately, and they were magnificent in their assistance with all his needs.

After dinner, we all went into the rally room to go over camp rules and regulations. We always enter with lots of music and dancing and fun and games. He was a bit overwhelmed at first, but somehow, he coped with it all. The 8-12-year-old campers could see that Jordan was using a walker, and as they interacted with him a bit, I can't explain the compassion that flowed from each one of those little kids toward Jordan, and how he picked up on the fact that they cared about him even though they didn't know him.

That is the spirit at Champions Kids Camp; as Billie Faye always says, "It's a God Thing." He made it through that first night in the dorms, and the next morning after breakfast we were all back in high energy mode for Monday morning rally time. All the kids kept saying hi to him, and he picked up on all that energy coming his way.

As the day went on, I remember distinctly getting a call from Kirby Lammers on my cell phone while Kim and I were at Walmart. We were making our usual Monday morning run to pick up clothing and tennis shoes and everything and anything else that was needed by our campers as noted by their Champs.

Kirby was exclaiming in a loud and excited voice to me, "Jordan is driving a go-cart." We were on stun because we didn't even think this would be possible. It seems as though Jordan was determined to conquer the go-carts. He saw the other kids doing it, and he made the declaration that he wanted to do it, too. So they cleared the track and put him in a go-cart all by himself

Jordan Giving A Thumbs-Up After Riding a Go-cart

and turned him loose to take a lap or two. The situation was that his mind was sharp, but his body couldn't always obey him. When they explained how the go-cart worked and what to do, he took off and never ran into the wall one time. After a few laps, they let the other campers go on out there with him, and they successfully ran their time around and around the course.

Everyone was cheering him and high fiving him. All the kids in his group had taken him under their wings and were just as excited as if they themselves had overcome a major obstacle. We got back to camp as soon as we could and ran over and congratulated Jordan. He was absolutely beaming.

When it was lunch time, we watched him come in the door and park his walker in the corner. Then he headed across the floor to get in the lunch line. There he went without his walker. Somebody help! Well, as it turns out, he didn't need any help, he just needed a little time. Even though his walk was slower than the other kids', it was still him walking without the aid of that walker.

Jordan Taking on the Diving Board with His Champ's Assistance

It felt miraculous as we watched him take on each challenge and win. By the time the next rally came around, everyone had heard that he had conquered the go-carts, and he announced that the next day he was determined to take on and conquer the zip line.

The rule was that to ride the zip line, someone had to climb the forty-foot-tall spiral staircase unassisted, no help from anyone. That was the rule set by Victory Camp. We told him that, but his spirit was adamant he could, and would do it.

So, the whole camp held their breath the next day when it was Jordan's team's turn to do the zip line. This zip line had four different lines so that multiple campers could go at one time. They got him all suited up with three other campers, put his helmet on him, and then helped him to the bottom of the stairs and turned him loose. If you could just have been there to see this kid who had been so badly injured decide to take this challenge on, your heart would have been up in your throat as it was with ours.

Oh, we prayed, "Dear Jesus, please help Jordan do this. It will mean everything to him to be victorious on this ride on this day. It is more than a ride down the zip line for him; it's his next step into a new beginning, a new horizon."

As he held onto the railing and slowly took each painstaking step up that spiral staircase, we watched the pain on his face coupled with determination like I've never seen. Step by step by step, he ascended those stairs until finally he reached the top.

It's a wide, open campus, and you can see the zip line from all over. The cheers went up from one end of the camp to the other. Everyone clapped and chanted, "Jordan! Jordan!" He still had the next part of the challenge to go now. The instructor at the top of the platform hooked Jordan in and checked his gear. Then the other three campers took their places. All of us were down below with our cameras ready, and we were praying for Jordan.

Would he really take the "plunge" and head straight off that forty-foot platform or not? When the time came, and the instructor said, "Go!", Jordan was the first one to push off and head out into the wild blue yonder. Upon seeing this, the whole camp started jumping up and down, and renewed their chant with more gusto than ever, "Jordan, Jordan, Jordan."

Oh, what a wonderful day. For me it was like watching a baby eagle taking its first flight out of the nest. It lifted everyone's spirits to have someone win when all the odds seemed against him. I have no words, honestly, to describe the exhilaration we all experienced. It was breathtaking!

He became the most popular kid on campus, and he just ate it up. He also loved to flirt with the girl Champs. He had them numbered, in fact, as to who was his number one girlfriend and his number two and so forth. It was all in great fun.

So, on Wednesday, his mom came to see him at lunch. She thought he would be ready to come home after three days because she just knew he would be physically exhausted by then. She sat down at the table beside him in the lunchroom for a moment, and she asked him if he was ready to come home.

He didn't say a word, he just got up from the table in his slow manner and walked away from her...without his walker. She had tears streaming down her face, tears of joy, of thankfulness. What a great day for Jordan's mom and the whole family.

She went on home and returned for him on Friday, the usual

time we wrap up camp. None of us will ever forget Jordan and his story, the story of conquering every challenge that came his way. He ended up riding all the rides and doing everything everybody else did, a little more slowly, but surely, he did it all.

After CKC, Jordan went on to join the Clear Creek Intermediate

Jordan Leading His Football Team

School football team in the 7th grade. He was made an honorary member and participated in all the games by hyping the team up during pre-warm up and standing on the sidelines, giving them support through cheer and, of course, high fives! In High School, Jordan continued his studies and eventually got into a work program where he began doing volunteer work. In 2018 Jordan graduated from High School and walked across the stage.

If you had seen him on his walker on check-in day at camp, you would never have *Jordan Grown Up* pictured this scenario ever happening. We will always love and remember Jordan for the inspiration he brought to all of our lives.

THE STORY OF RICHARD

One year we had a 10-year-old boy who just couldn't keep from causing problems. He didn't want to do what his Champ asked him to do and he had a chip on his shoulder most of the time. Sometimes these kids who have been through some grave, traumatic situations have an attitude about the world, and they have a negative slant on everything.

This sometimes settles down as they start feeling the positive vibes from everyone at camp and all the fun things that there are to do, but that wasn't the case with Richard. When Tuesday morning rolled around, I got a call on my cell phone that he was at the go cart track and was causing trouble again over there.

His Champ had done about all he could do, so as a last resort he called me. I grabbed Kirby Lammers and told him to come on with me. I apprised him of the situation on the way over, and when we got there, we sat down at the picnic table near the go-cart track under the tree in the shade. As Kirby and I sat across the table from this poor kid, Richard, who sat there so resolutely, avoiding

Dodie Osteen & Johnny McGowan at Camp 2019

my gaze, I started a conversation with him. I kept it simple, asked him how it was going and what I could do to help him. He did the usual thing a kid like this does and he blamed his Champ and the other kids that were around him for his negative behavior. After he stopped talking and before I could respond, Kirby said, "It's your teeth, isn't it?"

I about dropped MY teeth. I did recognize that this kid's teeth were not very straight, and they stuck out a bit from his lips. He had not only endured the trauma brought on by growing up with no dad, he was also mercilessly teased at school for his teeth. His first response at school was to fight. So here we are, face to face with this troubled child, and Kirby just comes out and mentions the kid's teeth; it was something I would never have done.

This kid was obviously very sensitive about it. However, Kirby himself at one time in his life had teeth that looked like that, and he knew how it felt to be teased and made fun of. He was able to explain that to Richard, that he knew exactly how he felt. Kirby used to get into fight after fight when he was 10 years old because he was angry about some things in his life, and especially his teeth.

Our CFO, Leon Jordan, with Camper

Richard's attention was totally captured by Kirby's words, and he sat up a bit, and then he started to shed tears. Kirby went on about a camp he had attended when he was 10 years old where a man saw Kirby's situation, and took him aside and told him things that changed his outlook on life, and subsequently his whole life. Kirby went home and, instead of joining the local gang that was pursuing him, he became a model kid with a brand-new attitude just because of a 10-minute conversation with a grown-up who cared.

It turned out to be a breakthrough for Richard to finally find

Nurse Barbara, Nurse Wyliene, & Nurse Kristi Who Generously Donate Their Time for Our Kids

someone who cared enough to spend some time and communicate his feelings with him. He opened up about his terrible home life or lack thereof, and all the problems he had already had to face in life, and how the whole world just stunk. That's how he put it at first, but then he started to lighten up and took on a whole new aura. It seems to me like he became a 10-year-old boy again instead of someone trying to be a big bad bully in a terrible world. The hope came back in his eyes. I was amazed! Kudos to Kirby and his perception, and I'm thankful that we had that great breakthrough that day for Richard!

THE STORY OF THE TWINS

These two little twin girls had lost their dad in an accident just a short time before camp, and were unbearably sad and inconsolable. They didn't even want to stay when their mom dropped them off. That first day, Monday, and until just after

Bill with Dorm Dad, Randy Rogers, Checking in Campers

lunch on Tuesday, they sat with their backs turned toward our speakers during rally time and refused to participate in any group activities. Even at the rides outside they kept to themselves, guardedly interacting with the other kids and having minimal conversation with their champs.

Our son, Jimmy, had met a beautiful young lady from England at the University of Houston where they were both students. She was a professional dance instructor, she loved music, and her personality was magnetic. Jimmy had invited her to come to camp to teach the kids how to line-dance on Tuesday afternoon. All the kids were in the rally room, and Jimmy got up and announced that Nikki was now going to teach line-dancing. The twins turned around to look at Nikki as the music started, and

"Aunt Ellen," Jimmy "Deuce," & "Aunt Kim" at Camp

Nikki invited anyone who wanted to learn to get on up and get out on the floor. The girls then looked at each other questioningly and then took to that invitation and jumped up and got into the spirit of the dance. We all looked on in amazement. What had happened? We still don't know to this day, but that was the breakthrough moment for these two beautiful girls. That's why at camp we try to expose the kids to as many different positive activities as we can because we can't predict what activity will pique a child's interest. It's amazing how one dance brought

Bill & Kim & "Aunt Bee" with the Camper of the Year 2015. He said, "This camp has changed my life."

those girls out. They both were smiling so big, and we knew then that they were going to be okay.

Sure enough, they continued to participate in everything else throughout the week. It just took that one thing to break the ice so they could start opening up. After that, they bonded with their champs and other campers, and we saw amazing emotional progress for the rest of the week.

A LITTLE BOY LIKE OUR SON, BILLY

We received a camper application for camp 2012 in the mail for a little boy named Peyton who had almost completed his treatment for Acute Lymphoblastic Leukemia and was in remission. He was still 7 years old, but on the brink of turning 8. His mother knew that our age range was from 8 to 12 years old, but she took a chance anyway that we would consider accepting him, because his 8th birthday was just a few weeks away. We had never really accepted a kid who was still 7, but his mother talked so persuasively to Kim over the phone about how her son really

needed to come to camp after all he'd been through. Of course, Kim and I knew exactly where this mom was coming from since our son, Billy, who was the inspiration for us even starting a camp like ours, had this same form of Leukemia. Kim went on to tell Peyton's mom that the

Bill & Kim with Peggy & Kerry Mazoch and the Three Campers They Sponsored to CKC

camp we rent (Victory Camp) would not allow anyone under 8 to do a lot of the activities like go-carts, giant waterslide, zip-line and so on. In fact, he could only participate in swim time and basketball and attend Rally Time. However, her immediate response was, "I can explain that to him and he'll be okay with that!" What else could Kim do then but accept him?

So, little 7 yr. old Peyton came to camp. He always had a smile on his face, and it was obvious that he was having a great time! I'm sure he was just thrilled to be having fun being a kid again without anyone in a white coat in sight. That year, he was voted Boy Camper of the Year! He kept coming back, and in 2017 he became an Intern, one of our "Leaders in Training" at CKC. There were no camps like this when Billy was in the same situation as Peyton, so we were thrilled that we could be there for him.

TWO BROTHERS LOSING THEIR SIGHT

Paul & Diego Martinez are brothers. In 2007, when Diego was diagnosed with LHON (Leber's Hereditary Optic Neuropathy), his Aunt Melva Meronek, friend and CKC advisory council member, gave us this news. He was only 9 years old and was too scared to come to camp alone because his new condition so greatly affected his ability to see. Even though his brother, Paul, was 14, and too old to be a camper, we

Diego, Bill, & Paul at Camp 2007

made an exception so he could accompany Diego. Paul was having a difficult time watching his little brother lose his sight.

Paul & Diego with Their Family at the End of Camp 2007

Thanks to Paul, though, Diego was able to manage every challenging activity at camp; from the zipline, to the rock wall, he did it all. They both learned about overcoming challenges at camp, and it helped that they met other kids going through difficult situations. The next year, Diego was so excited to tell us that he was able to play football at his school where he was a lineman. He could see well enough to block that other player in front of him, and he was thrilled to be able to be on the team. He was MVP two years in a row and went on to play football through his high school years.

Little did we know that not long after that first camp they attended, Paul would also be diagnosed with the same terrible disease. He went through some very dark times, where he was self-medicating with substances that led to an unintentional near-death experience. It was this moment when he hit rock bottom and was then able to receive professional help and support from this family. His life was miraculously spared, as his Aunt Melva and Uncle Richard stepped in to help him get back on the path to overcome his obstacles. Paul had expressed interest in learning the guitar, so one day we had lunch with Melva, Richard and Paul where we surprised him with one of my guitars. Kirby Lammers then stepped up and offered free guitar lessons. So every week, Paul was not only getting guitar lessons from Kirby - a life coach – but

Diego & Paul Grown Up

was also interjecting life lessons along the way. A few years after this all took place, Paul had not only graduated from Texas A&M University Corpus Christi, but also went on to earn his master's degree in Counseling, with a concentration in Clinical Mental Health. He now counsels those who have been through trauma, and who better to lead others through their own life trials and tribulations!

"Attending Champions Kids Camp really was a good lesson to learn at a young age to be out of my comfort zone away from my parents being forced to meet new people and new friends. I'll always remember my time there." - Diego Martinez, graduated high school and attended college, is currently working with his father as Assistant Body Technician.

"It was helpful and meaningful because it introduced me to a second family. It made me realize that I wasn't alone and I found love and support at the camp." - Paul Martinez, Addiction Counselor Licensed Chemical Dependency Counselor

FUTURE VISION

As we are looking toward the future and all the many more lives we want to reach, ultimately, we know we need to have our own facility. We are still in early planning stages, but we are looking at land close to Houston that would make a fantastic new camp. I wanted to share our initial drawings and layouts with you here (larger size at very back of book), just to help paint the vision. God says to "let your request be known," so here is our request to God, and to all of you who have a heart for these kids: a beautiful camp facility where we can help thousands more children for years and years to come.

Initial Sketches of the central "HUB," and the residence quarters/dorms:

CKC SUMMER CAMP
THE HUB
MAY 29 2020
A DALTO

CKC SUMMER CAMP
RESIDENCE QUARTERS
MAY 29 2020
A DALTO

Preliminary Layout:

Acknowledgements

There were just too many of you who have helped me along the way to try to work into my story, so I want to make sure I mention all of you here. Praying to do my best not to leave anyone out (if that's even possible!). If I do, please forgive me, and I'll make sure you get in the next printing. You all mean the world to me, and I want to make sure you know it, so I'm putting you in here, forever emblazoned in ink!

1. Doc Bill Adams: Hey Doc, Kim and I love you & Becky bunches, and you can't get away from us now. Love and blessing always.

2. Scott & Cookie Joe Arthur: You two are just the most unique couple and so gracious, so thoughtful and generous with your time and money in support of CKC. We love you and thank you from the bottom of our hearts.

3. Bruce, Terrie, Riley and Hayden Baker: What a great family and blessing for CKC. Love you guys.

4. Rick Baker: Our first "roadie" and now, life-long pal on this CKC journey. Love and blessings Rick.

5. Mike Barber: Mike, thank you so much for gathering up Bum Phillips and bringing him to the CKC dinner where we honored him. God bless your ministry always, love you pal.

6. Bob Boblitt (Mr. B.): Thanks for naming our Texas Best Music Fest and also for making sure it has happened every year. Thank you, Kyrstin, for getting your dad out to camp.

7. Pastors Rodney & Joan Bowman: Thanks for being the first pastor to embrace our vision and dream of a camp for survivor children and bringing First Baptist Angleton in on our side.

8. Renee Branson: You are such a loving, giving person and you have been a huge blessing to us and to our cause for kids, CKC. We sincerely love you and thank God for you.

9. Kendal & Starla Bridges: We count you guys as great friends and blessings to us and to CKC. Always love being around you, it really gives us a lift. Love you bunches.

10. Noel Casares (Tamigo): Hey Tamigo, can't thank you enough for your friendship, "hermano". You are family to us. Love you mucho.

11. Brian Collins: Big B, you will always be a brother to me. Love and blessings.

12. Jerry Crutchfield: Hey Crutch (as Pillow calls you), thanks for the encouragement and help with our music. "In God We Still Trust," still true.

13. Jimmy Disch: Dr. Baseball: what a great blessing you have been to us and CKC. You are a great friend (you've made our golf tourney what it is today), totally grateful.

14. John & Laurie Dollar: Thanks so much for being such a blessing to CKC and for caring so deeply for these precious kids we serve.

15. Deborah Duncan: Deb, we sincerely love you and thank you for having us on your tv show and for being such a blessing as emcee for our TBMF event. Love you!

16. Deborah Dunkum: You are so kind and thoughtful. You and Melva chaired our Legends4Kids event, making it a huge success. You are a part of us and CKC forever.

17. Dianne Duperier: We are still friends after all these years and still doing projects together for kids through Champions Kids Camp. Thank you so much. Love and blessings.

18. Doug Earle: Thank you for introducing golf to our campers. You are a blessing.

19. Marjorie Evans: We just love you. Your belief and encouragement have been a blessing and we thank you and love you so very much.

20. EXCHANGE CLUBS of HOUSTON AREA: Sugar Land Exchange, Ft. Bend County Exchange, Hobby Exchange, Memorial Exchange, Missouri City Exchange, National Exchange: God bless the big heart and mission of Exchange for children who have been abused.

21. Faith Faber: thank you so much for having such a beautiful daughter, Sarah, that joined Billy in his life. The grandkids we share are the light of our lives.

22. Gerald & Evelyn Franklin: Hey Big Pal and Evelyn, your generosity and encouragement have been incredibly meaningful on this journey to help kids. Blessings and love to you both.

23. Bob Gonzales: Can't thank you enough for donating the printing for CKC for so many years and being a blessing by supporting our golf tourney. Thanks always Bobby.

24. Buddy Griffin: you have been a great friend, great pal and wonderful sidekick in this thing we all call "MUSIC." Love you & Sandy "mucho."

25. Pastors Mark and Mary Grimes: Who couldn't love and respect a couple who could start with nothing and build such a significant work for the Lord! Blessings always.

26. Dennis Hamann: You sponsor kids to camp, watch over Mama Dodie at our events, and bring a team to the golf tournament. Thanks with all our hearts.

27. Pastors Bill & Beverly Hamlin: Thanks for being Momma's last pastors and allowing her to continue playing piano for your gatherings. Thanks also for your support for CKC. Priceless!

28. Laura Hanks: Thank you for taking us under your wings at TBN. You were a huge blessing and your faith and belief in our ministry meant & means so much.

29. Tom & Kristi Harrison: Tom & Kristi, we count you family. Thanks for being such a blessing in our music ministry and CKC. Love you guys (and that beautiful Gracie).

30. Roy Head: My boy Roy... Friends for 50 years. Can't believe we just lost you. Thanks for singing for CKC every time we asked. R.I.P. my friend. So proud of Sundance as well.

31. Larry & Sandy Hendrick: Best friends at P.S.J.A. High, still pals after all these years. Thx for helping us get CKC started by having us at your church (never forget that $800 offering!).

32. Linda Herron: Hey Sis, thanks so much for loving us (especially me...lol) and keeping those prayers coming to cover us with God's will and blessings. Love you always.

33. Pastors Robert & Brenda Hogan: Your Spring First Assembly Church, Thanks to you, was the first Houston church to support CKC when it was just a dream. Always thank God for you.

34. Sandy Hulquist: Taking over for Laura, you continued booking us on TBN and supporting CKC personally as well. Always love you and thank God for you.

35. Pat Hunt: Thanks for being a great pal after all these years you greatly talented person!!!

36. Mo Jeloudarzedeh & Family: Mo, you, your sons, Mo, Jr. and Joe along with their beautiful sister, Shireen, have been a monumental blessing for CKC. Thank you, God bless you always.

37. Leon Jordan: you've been a pal since high school and are now the CFO for CKC. Thanks for keeping the books all in line for CKC and being such a blessing to us. Love ya pal.

38. Robert Kern: You will always be the "Judge" to me and a great friend. Always look forward to seeing you at S.L. Exchange Club meetings. God bless you.

39. David Lanagan: Let's see, sponsoring kids to camp, donating pillows and blankets, P.A. system for S.L. Exchange...can't you do more... LOL! Thank you so very much, blessings!!

40. Karen & Danny Leader: Karen & Danny, thanks for believing in and supporting CKC. Your intro to Albemarle has been tremendous. Love and blessings always.

41. Bob Linzer: Thanks so much for your tremendous dedication to

CKC. Your influence as a Godly man has meant so very much. God bless you.

42. Johnny Lee: You've been a pal, a brother, and a blessing to us and CKC. Thanks so much.

43. Bob Livermore: You are just one incredible friend and Pike Brother. Can't thank you enough for your belief and support since we met at UH. Always Pal!

44. Jim and Sue Lockwood: You are both such "giving" people. The world needs more like you two. Thanks so much for your support and belief in us and CKC.

45. Dick, Nancy, and Rich Loughridge: It's the family aspect of you guys that makes it all so special at Papa's Ice House. Great family, great blessing to us and CKC. Thanks so much.

46. Christopher Lowman: A terrific thank you to our incredibly wise attorney who has never charged CKC a dime for the last 20 years. Thank you to your beautiful wife, Sara, for her belief in and support of CKC too. God bless you for lending a vital hand to our charity.

47. Ruth & Clay Lueckemeyer: Thank you for loving us, supporting CKC and keeping us up with Mama Dodie. Sincerely love you guys.

49. John & Gina Manlove: Thank you, Mr. Mayor, and beautiful wife, Gina. Thanks for being such a blessing to us and CKC.

49. Kerry & Peggy Mazoch: Thanks for always being there at the last minute; many kids would not have been able to have camp without you guys. Love and blessings always.

50. JoEllen & Ernest Maxwell: My two talented cousins that I love so very much. Thanks for including us where you've pastored and for blessing CKC.

51. Pastor Johnny McDuff: Thanks so much for inviting us back to Faith A.G. year after year. You and your family have been just a huge blessing to Kim and me.

52. Johnny McGowan: Man, you can pray, as my dad used to say, "Like a house afire." Thanks for bringing Mama Dodie to camp and for being a great blessing to Lakewood.

53. Renee & Mac McGuire: Thanks for supporting BBOH, CKC and everything we do for the ministry. It's been great walking beside you as you light everyone's path with love and generosity.

54. Pastor Mike McMahon: Pastor Mike, you have been an incredible blessing to us and CKC. Thanks for your belief and support over all the years.

55. Dr. Sam & Lee McManus: Forty something years and counting. Love you so very much and those beautiful kids of yours. RIP Lee.

56. Sid Medford & Deb: Hey Sid, I've always admired that you are a Silver Star winner and great patriot. When I needed a friend, and you know what I mean, you stepped up for me. So glad for you and Deb to be together after all the years and ups and downs.

57. Craig Morris: Craiglet, you were great emotional support and great friend. Thanks for signing us to write songs for you. Still means a lot. Blessings Pal.

58. Johnny Morris: That $5k check more than once kept us going. Thanks for helping us keep the dream alive. You know I still pray for you.

59. Randy & Linda Moore: You travel the world to spread the Gospel of Jesus Christ and you still work in ministry at Lakewood. Love and blessings always, now and through eternity.

60. Tommy & Angela Mouser: You and your Angel have been such a blessing sharing your video craft/talents with CKC and us. Thank you guys so very much. Love and blessings to you.

61. Cheeto Musquiz: Thanks for the much-needed signage for our fundraisers. Your company, Bullprints, always comes through. Blessings always pal.

62. Trever & Troy Nehls: Thanks for all your support for CKC. The one thing we do all agree on is helping kids who have been through trauma. You guys sure have done that. Thanks again.

63. Chad Nimri: You are not only a great tire man you are a great guy. Thanks for the discounts and oil changes to keep me on the road. Thanks for sponsoring kids to camp every year.

64. Dodie Osteen (Mama): I have no words for you, our Spiritual Mom, that would adequately, possibly describe the love we have for you; you started it all by praying me out of the night clubs six nights a week. We are going to spend eternity together with you and tons of kids who have come to Jesus because of your efforts. Love and blessings always.

65. Joel & Victoria Osteen: You guys are world famous and yet you still take time to remember Kim and me. You have been so generous and supportive of our music ministry. Thanks for loving us, we love you.

66. Lisa Osteen: Lisa, you are the kindest, sweetest gal we know. Your folks put that sweet spirit of the Holy Spirit down inside you and it shows. Love and blessings to you always.

67. Dr. Paul Osteen: Paul, as you always tell me to call you, thanks for being a great host to us at Lakewood and for being so kind and supportive. We do love you and pray for your ministry.

68. Jerry & Annette Parks: We are so thankful God brought us back together after so many years. You guys have been a huge blessing and we thank you from the bottom of our hearts.

69. John & Lou Piegsa: Words can't describe the dedication you guys have for those less fortunate. You have blessed CKC enormously and we love you two so very much.

70. Ray Pillow: Great co-pub partner and friend. Thanks for getting the Grand Ole Opry sigs on a guitar for CKC fundraiser (more than once). Thanks for securing the name, "Legends 4 Kids". God bless you and JoAnne always.

71. Chris Piper: Thanks for taking the music project to your dad and

encouraging us so very much. You are a great friend and a blessing to have in our lives.

72. Pastor Don Piper: Thanks so much for the honor of collaborating on a music project for your book. Loved hearing about your experience every time we were together. God bless you and Eva and your ministry always.

73. Garry Plotkin: You are quite a "K-racter" but we love you pal. Thanks for being a blessing to us and CKC.

74. Dino Price: Thanks for the encouragement all along the way as I set out on this journey to write my life story in a book. God bless you Dino.

75. Karen Rasso: Dear sweet Karen, you have always been a quiet blessing to us and CKC. Thank you so very much. Love you.

76. Mike & Jackie Reichek: You guys always brighten things up for Kim & me. Thanks for the putting contest and friendship at Exchange Conventions. God bless you two always.

77. Harold & Tammy Reese: There would be no CKC without you in the midst of our beginnings. Whenever the CKC story is told, you will be part of it forever. Love and blessings always.

78. Bob & Brenda Robinson: Brenda, how you headed up our arts & crafts at Kids Camp for that long is a mystery to me. You are just one of those "givers" that the world needs more of. We love and appreciate you and Bob so very much.

79. Randy Rogers: You have been a huge blessing each year at camp. You never run down and are always smiling and "Up", just what our campers and volunteers need. Love you brother.

80. Dominique Sachse: What a fun event at Mo's that you so graciously agreed to emcee for us. Thanks again for being your beautiful self and sharing a Sunday afternoon for CKC.

81. Mark & Martha Sappington: You guys have supported CKC for many years now. Thank you so very much. God bless and keep you and Martha and kids always.

82. Marc & Susan Schwartz: Thanks for your continued support and for being a part of the Advisory Council for CKC. Love and blessings always.

83. Betsy Scofield: You've been a great dorm mom at camp for CKC and a blessing to us personally. Love you, Bets.

84. Bob & Maria Siegrist: Bob, thanks for all the auction items for the Nash Bash fundraiser and thanks to Maria for being CKC's Queen of "Bears That Care." Love and thanks.

85. Buzzy Smith: Thanks for your creativity that has produced two #1 independent records. Love recording with you and re-living our music history from the past. Love you Pal.

86. Jimmy "Deuce" Smith: Aunt Kim and I love you with all our hearts. The incredible light display you put up at New Years is incredible and we love and appreciate you for working so hard to help us with all our fundraisers. Praying for you always. Love and blessings.

87. Pastor Keenan Smith: You've started our camps off every year with your feats of strength, bending rods of steel and tearing phone books in half. Then your story of salvation blesses us all. You are an amazing man of God/Pastor, and we love and thank you.

88. Dan Pastorini: thanks so much for being my pal since 1975 and supporting our mission for kids like you have for the past several years. You are the best.

89. Larry Dierker: Dante suggested I call you 6 years ago and I'm so glad I did. You have been "there" every time we called on you. Thanks so much for caring about those less fortunate.

90. Jillian Ginn Stewart: Jillian, we have missed that incredibly great smile and joyful attitude you exude to everyone around you. Your help with fundraising has been such a blessing and I am thankful you still talk about CKC to your friends. Love and blessings always.

91. Mary Templeton: We think you are the greatest rep BMI has. Thank you so very much for caring about our songwriting and CKC. Love and blessings.

92. Ron & Wyliene Tidwell: With you two CKC got a great, full-time nurse and a big ol' dorm dad who loves and cares about kids. We love you guys and thank you for your support and time.

93. Sandy Treon: You have been such a blessing helping my sister out with the Cook-off, the golf tournament and New Year's Eve. God bless you, we love you, so stay well and kickin'.

94. Mike Van Norman: You are the guy whose auctioneering skills rescued us from total defeat at our first New Year's Eve fundraiser. I am eternally grateful. Love you Pal.

95. Robert Volberding (RoBear): Thanks so much for creating a cd catalog of our songs. The days and weeks you spent are not forgotten. God bless you, we love you pal.

96. Dave Ward: You are one of my "bestest friends." Many times you got me on the air at Channel 13 and even wrote the script for PSA spots. God bless you and keep you as we face the "fourth" quarter of our lives. Let's do it together pal.

97. Del & Cindy Way: What a great couple! Thanks for having us at your beautiful Kerrville church and for being a spiritual pillar in our lives. Love and blessings you two, always!

98. Patrick & Andrea Wehrly: Your belief in BBOH and CKC are incalculable. Looking forward to our future together. You truly have been a great blessing in our lives.

99. George Weimmer: When Kim and I had to come home to Houston and start all over again I remember that first rehearsal where I was worried that Kim's bass playing would not come up to your "metronome" standards, but who knew? She did it and you guided her on you all's first set of music every night just like a big brother would do. We both love you very much

and so appreciate the times we've worked together and had fun together. Blessings always Brother.

100. Freddy Weller: I am so glad that we finally sat down and wrote that little "diddy" that Reba McEntire recorded for us. It was great to write with you, Freddy. God bless you.

101. Steve & Linn Wells: You guys have been a great blessing to us and CKC. Always cherish your friendship and memories of fun times at convention. Love and blessings always.

102. James Williams: We met at Dad's church on the Back Hwy. in Pharr when we were just 10 years old and we're still friends this many years later. Thank you for promoting our records to those #1s. I count you as family and appreciate your sharing your family with me/us at CKC. Of course, that would be Amber & Jay and your precious grandkids. Love you brother.

103. Dr. Irv Wishnow: Hey Doc, what a great friend you have been to us. You and Marcia are salt of the earth folks and we love you. God bless you richly.

104. Bro. Jack & Kathy Womack: Bro. Jack, you are always just you and you are for real. What a blessing for us, BBOH and CKC. Love, blessings and thanks to you and Kathy.

105. Harry & Joanne Yates: You were our spiritual stronghold in Nashville. Still pray for you two and your ministry all the time and will always love you with all our hearts.

To anyone who I may have forgotten to include on this loooonnnnngggg list, please know I appreciate you all. I guarantee you I have forgotten somebody who has played an important part in my life, but please keep in mind, I've lived a long time now, and there's just so much to remember in this old brain of mine. If you have been left out, I promise I'll add you in the next printing.

NOTES FROM FRIENDS

"I'm 68 years old. I have been listening to Bill Nash sing for 58 of those 68 years. I have never heard him sing a bad note. I have never even heard him sing a good note. Bill Nash only sings great notes. He is a great guy and an old and dear friend. He has a big heart full of love for his fellow man. I love my friend Bill Nash. P.S. Almost forgot, he's also a great songwriter. P.P.S. His beautiful wife Kim is even better at all of the above than he is."
- Larry Gatlin
Grammy-Winning Singer/Songwriter

"Two of the most talented people I've ever known. Remember the old saying 'when I first heard that song I almost ran off the road?' Well that is exactly what happened to me when I first heard 'In God We Still Trust.' I have always thought it was a hit song. Still do!!!! Bill and Kim Nash, wonderful writers, singers, and most of all wonderful people. Proud to say we have been friends for many years."
- Ray Pillow
Artist/Publisher/Grand Ole Opry Member

"When I first met the Nash Family I was immediately impressed with their perfect harmony, great songs, and a total

dedication to their work. This coupled with just simply being 'fine folks' is a winning combination that can't miss."
- Jerry Crutchfield
Writer/Publisher/Award-Winning Producer

"Bill Nash.....Absolutely, one of the best singers I ever worked with. He is also a great friend. GOD bless you Bill!"
-Jerry Kennedy
Grammy-Winning Producer

"Kim and Bill Nash have been my dear friends for years. They are amazing singers and wonderful Ministers for the Lord Jesus. Their talent is God given and their love for children is admirable. I salute them for all they do."
- Dodie Osteen
Co-Founder of Lakewood Church

"Bill and Kim Nash have a story everyone needs to hear. I've known them for many years and they have stayed consistent and true. Their talents are world class, and I have been blessed to have shared the stage with them on many occasions. Most important, I'm glad to call them my friends."
- Del Way
Country Gospel Singer/Songwriter/Pastor

"Bill and Kim's music has touched millions around the world through their own recordings and through other popular artists who have recorded their songs. What is even more exciting to us is how Bill and Kim have dedicated their time, effort and resources to enrich the lives of children through their Champions Kids Camp. Their ministry is making a difference in this generation.... and the generation to come!"
- Alvin and Joy Slaughter
Pastor/Singer/Multiple Dove-Award Nominee

"Bill Nash is a longtime friend of mine. He has a heart as big as Texas and the voice of an angel. He has recorded beautiful songs with his family. His kids camp has brought joy to countless

children, and given them values that will last a lifetime. I'm proud to know him and call him my friend."
- Dave Ward
Anchor, KTRK Houston's ABC 13

"I first saw Bill Nash perform on the North side of Houston... blew me away...one of the best entertainers I have ever seen in my life. Over the years Bill and I became good friends. I still am amazed with him, especially by how big his heart is and what a beautiful soul he has. Other than being an amazing artist, he's an amazing human being who genuinely cares about children and he shows that by the camp that he sponsors. Bill, I love you, always have, always will."
-Johnny Lee
Singer/Songwriter - "Lookin' For Love"

"Without question one of the best voices I ever heard, I was jealous back in the day, when I also made records for SMASH/Mercury label. His vocal texture was over the top. Proud to call him my pal!"
- Norro Wilson
Singer/Songwriter/Producer
Nashville Songwriters Hall of Fame

ABOUT THE AUTHORS

Photo Credit: Sebastian Vikkelsoe

Bill Nash is a singer/songwriter whose career spans seven decades and five major record labels.

Along with his wife and songwriting partner, Kim Nash, they have written hit songs for Reba McEntire and Diamond Rio, among others. They reside in Houston, Texas, love to travel and spend every minute possible with their grandkids.

Bill and Kim also founded Champions Kids Camp, a camp for survivors of traumatic events, in honor of their oldest son's healing of Leukemia.

Find out more about CKC at
www.ChampionsKidsCamp.org

Find out more on their music at
www.BKNash.com

FUTURE VISION FOR CHAMPIONS KIDS CAMP

CKC SUMMER CAMP
THE HUB

MAY 29 2020
A DALTO

CKC SUMMER CAMP
RESIDENCE QUARTERS

MAY 29 2020
A DALTO

CKC PRELIMINARY LAYOUT

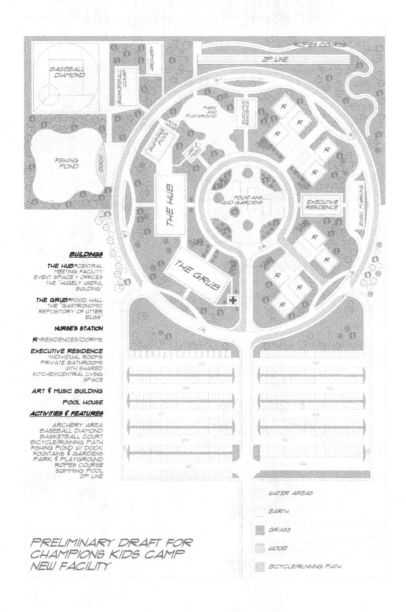

BUILDINGS

THE HUB="CENTRAL MEETING FACILITY" EVENT SPACE + OFFICES THE "HUGELY USEFUL BUILDING"

THE GRUB="FOOD HALL" THE "GASTRONOMIC REPOSITORY" OF UTTER BLISS"

NURSE'S STATION

R=RESIDENCES/DORMS

EXECUTIVE RESIDENCE "INDIVIDUAL ROOMS PRIVATE BATHROOMS WITH SHARED KITCHEN/CENTRAL LIVING SPACE

ART & MUSIC BUILDING

POOL HOUSE

ACTIVITIES & FEATURES

ARCHERY AREA
BASEBALL DIAMOND
BASKETBALL COURT
BICYCLE/RUNNING PATH
FISHING POND W/ DOCK
FOUNTAINS & GARDENS
PARK & PLAYGROUND
ROPES COURSE
SWIMMING POOL
ZIP LINE

PRELIMINARY DRAFT FOR CHAMPIONS KIDS CAMP NEW FACILITY

WATER AREAS

EARTH

GRASS

WOOD

BICYCLE/RUNNING PATH

CPSIA information can be obtained
at www.ICGtesting.com
Printed in the USA
LVHW011220110521
687090LV00004B/508